Mastering the Practice of Expressive Arts Therapy

of related interest

Solution Art
A Textbook of Art and Resource-Oriented Work
Paolo J. Knill and Herbert Eberhart
Translated by Wayne Sutherland
Forewords by Margo Fuchs Knill
ISBN 978 1 83997 760 2
eISBN 978 1 83997 761 9

Principles and Practice of Expressive Arts Therapy
Toward a Therapeutic Aesthetics
Paolo Knill, Ellen G. Levine and Stephen K. Levine
ISBN 978 1 84310 039 3
eISBN 978 1 84642 032 0

Poetry in Expressive Arts
Supporting Resilience Through Poetic Writing
Margo Fuchs Knill and Sally S. Atkins
Foreword by Shaun McNiff
ISBN 978 1 78592 653 2
eISBN 978 1 78592 654 9

MASTERING
the **PRACTICE**
of **EXPRESSIVE**
ARTS THERAPY

A Practitioner's Guide

Judith Greer Essex

Jessica Kingsley Publishers
London and Philadelphia

First published in Great Britain in 2026 by Jessica Kingsley Publishers
An imprint of John Murray Press

2

Copyright © Judith Greer Essex 2026

Cover Illustration Copyright © Carey X Kramer 2026

The right of Judith Greer Essex to be identified as the Author of the Work has been
asserted by them in accordance with the Copyright, Designs and Patents Act 1988.

A CIP catalogue record for this title is available from the
British Library and the Library of Congress

ISBN 978 1 83997 333 8
eISBN 978 1 83997 334 5

Printed and bound in the United States by Integrated Books International

Jessica Kingsley Publishers' policy is to use papers that are natural,
renewable and recyclable products and made from wood grown in
sustainable forests. The logging and manufacturing processes are expected
to conform to the environmental regulations of the country of origin.

Jessica Kingsley Publishers
Carmelite House
50 Victoria Embankment
London EC4Y 0DZ

www.jkp.com

John Murray Press
Part of Hodder & Stoughton Ltd
An Hachette Company

The authorised representative in the EEA is Hachette Ireland, 8 Castlecourt
Centre, Dublin 15, D15 XTP3, Ireland (email: info@hbgi.ie)

Acknowledgments

To Dr. Richard Wainwright, who said, "Yes," he would. How does the climber thank the belayer? I am grateful for all the rescues—you were steadfast while I flailed. Thank you. Learning by doing.

To Heather Dawson, who suggested he might—sharing her wealth. Thank you. Learning in community.

To Elizabeth McKim, my womentor, who said, "Yes, you can do it," and showed me how by bending to her own work and cranking out her seventh book of poetry while I witnessed. Thank you. Learning by example.

To Shara Claire, who said, "Yes." It was important it gets out. She looked carefully at my words. Thank you. Learning with details.

To Donna Otter, who said, "Yes," she would make the time to edit despite great personal changes, to make sure it got done. And who said, "The more personal, the better," when I shuddered at what I had written. Thank you. Learning by exposure.

To Kathrin Keune, who grabbed the seat of my pants with her canine teeth and would not let go. Thank you. Learning by commitment.

To all my students, who said, "Yes, we need this. Do it." Thank you. Learning by doing for others.

To Dr. Margo Fuchs-Knill, who gave me permission, and said, "E.G.—YES!" Thank you. Learning through camaraderie.

To Prof. Dr. Paolo J. Knill: First, you set my heart on fire. I danced to your piano. Then you set my mind on fire. I opened an institute to teach your theories and methods. Then you challenged me to write. Then you swam away. But how lucky was I that the mountains met the sea? Thank you, dear Paolo.

Contents

Preface: How a Life in the Arts Led to a Career in Expressive Arts Therapy

There are questions we carry with us over a lifetime. Mine have been about the body, dance, healing, art, imagination, and the pursuit of a life worth living. These questions have shaped my professional and personal choices. Serendipity, loss, and a happy accident landed me in the lap of expressive arts therapy at the European Graduate School, divisions of Arts, Health, and Society, high in the Swiss Alps. It is from the richness of this experience that I write. I want to share what these years have taught me, and my take on this sophisticated and broadly applicable professional education.

Some background: With a Bachelor of Science degree in dance and theater, I opened a private studio along with others to continue my investigation of improvisational music and dance. Subsequently, I pursued a master's degree from the University of California, Los Angeles, in dance/movement therapy, and became a registered dance/movement therapist. My career in mental health, in both hospital and residential treatment, led to positions of responsibility.

Because of my connection to a small dance and music ensemble, I was invited to Germany for a couple of years to work as the artistic program director of a primal therapy clinic, while at the same time performing. When I returned home, I auditioned for and was accepted into the San Diego Repertory Theater, where I both performed and taught in their conservatory.

I never focused on one thing: While I taught movement for actors and physical imagination at various universities and theaters, I was also working in a variety of mental health settings, creating a dance club, and doing my own performances. I was a busy woman. While I waiting for UCLA to develop a PhD in dance/movement therapy, I completed a second master's degree in counseling psychology and took the California licensing exam for Marriage and Family Therapists. For about 25 years I taught at local universities and privately, performed, worked in mental health, and pursued various educational opportunities. Having been a registered dance therapist, licensed counseling psychologist, and teacher, I considered opening a training program in dance/movement therapy. It seemed time to teach and train others in earnest, to share what I had learned. My brother's death put all these plans on hold.

Danny was my closest sibling, being the only other artist in my conservative religious family. While I was a young single mother, he made a big contribution to my daughter's upbringing, and was central in our lives. He was a gay man who wrote poetry and drew intricate illustrations of fantasy landscapes and creatures. His decorator's flair brightened my life. My home and studio always wore Danny's touch. He was ever there, yet despite towering over me, he was also fragile. Danny suffered all his adult life from brittle diabetes. After one particularly harrowing night, he was hospitalized because of complications. After a week, the crisis was over. He was due to come home the next morning. Instead, I received a 4:00 am call from my mother. Danny was dead; a fatal heart attack. At 42.

The loss of my little brother crushed me. I staggered forward, like a zombie doing what was listed on my calendar. At some point, I felt adrift, and knew I needed to stop working; needed to make room for my grief. It wasn't that I couldn't do my job; work was a welcome refuge from my emotions. Work was the only thing I could do. At my studio, I would teach or see clients, and then come home to utterly collapse. That was no way to live.

While reaching out to my community for support, a close friend told me about the European Graduate School. The university offered a PhD in expressive arts therapy. She knew I had been waiting for UCLA to open a doctoral program in dance therapy, which never happened. So, I was disposed to consider another program, another option.

As a private practitioner in the States, I had never taken more than a long weekend off. The thought of shutting down my business for the requisite month in Switzerland to begin doctoral studies seemed ridiculous and impossible. But it also seemed like a proportional response to my pain, my loss, my disorientation. Examining my bank account, searching my heart, creating art, looking for signs, I decided to apply. From southern California I flew to Zurich, took the train from Zurich to Visp, and then rode the PostBus up to Saas Fee. Coming into Saas Fee, a village without combustion engines, the first thing I saw were the peaks of the Alps, snow-covered and shining.

The tiny, car-less village nestles in a bowl of mountains, whose presence is majestic and fierce. Our Swiss hotelier arranged our lodging and meals.

The family Zurbriggen had run the Hotel Allalin for generations. The following weeks were an introduction to the theories of Paolo Knill and others. It was the perfect mix of intellectual stimulation, philosophical discussion, and theory with the satisfaction of art-making: large community movement pieces accompanied by improvisational music, painting workshops, poetry circles, lectures, and performances. Our daily schedule moved from small cohorts to the whole university moving or listening or watching something, teachers and students together. At night, the Milky Way reminded us of our place at the curving edge of our galaxy, with the imposing Alps looming.

After my second year, I wanted to bring this approach to my hometown: the arts as change agents, and a reinstatement of the philosophy of aesthetics. This orientation invigorated me. There was something here beyond the stale reductionism of psychological theory, something that returned humanity to the relationship between helper and seeker; something that restored dignity and gravitas to the endeavor of art-making, yet preserved the mystery. I wanted to share these ideas. One morning before class, I serendipitously met Paolo in a cow field. It was a short-cut worn by people going across the soggy soil from our residences to the school road. The sky was bright, the air was crisp with notes of green, soil, and faint suggestions of cow. I felt both small and bold as, with a dry mouth and pounding heart, I asked about the possibility of a San Diego institute. He said, "You will be the right person for that territory." So that adventure began. I opened the Institute in San Diego in 1997.

Chapter One

INTRODUCTION

ABOUT THIS BOOK
What Is This Book?

This book offers an overview of both the theoretical foundations and practical applications of expressive arts therapy as taught at the European Graduate School (The EGS); filtered through my experience and understanding, which is considerable, but never complete. It features a collection of examples from my long practice that illuminate the transformative power of expressive arts therapy. I want to share the knowledge and enthusiasm I have cultivated throughout my career with you, dear reader, and to inspire the emerging generation of practitioners who will become leaders in the field.

The book came about as a result of an assignment from Dr. Paolo J. Knill, as I will tell later. The graduate students in my studio or classroom regularly asked me to write about my synthesis of expressive arts therapy. My conversations with field founders and leaders like Paolo, Herbert Eberhart, Elizabeth McKim, and Stephen Levine have brought me a certain clarity in my ability to express the details of the complex and broadly applicable field of intermodal expressive arts. My greatest rewards in teaching have been to see my students become articulate and exceptional leaders in their work, in our community, and across the globe. Teaching brilliant graduate students and responding to their incisive and probing questions has honed my vision of the field and its interlocking components into something I hope is worth sharing. Today's answers are tomorrow's questions.

To understand the purpose of this book, I must tell you a little about the EGS and my relationship with its founding rector, my mentor, teacher, collaborator, and dear friend, Prof. Dr. Paolo J. Knill. He has given shape and definition to this field in a way no one else has. He articulated theories and concepts, often in conversation with his friend Professor Dr. Herbert Eberhart, that make intermodal polyaesthetic expressive arts therapy a field in its own right; more than an additive array of techniques, to be applied without particular direction. As Paolo said, we are not adding the arts to psychotherapy to make a better psychotherapy (Knill *et al.*, 1996). Expressive arts therapy (ExA) is its own field, based on the power and procedures of the arts. In fact, this organized, theory-driven, and differentiated approach was most attractive to me. Many therapeutic schools use the arts as techniques—but they interpret and understand the process by using the psychological premises inherent in their original domain. They pull the art experiences through the knothole of their pre-existing theories. Intermodal polyaesthetic expressive arts therapy stays within the domain of the arts. This gives a clarity and an elegance to this way of working. We stand on the power of arts, aesthetics, and philosophy to understand how the arts are our helpers and healers. This is unique.

As a student at The EGS, I attended Paolo's classes and heard him deliver lectures to the whole university. I read his books, chapters, and articles. An early chance meeting in the studio anchored my personal connection with him.

STORY: From the Mountains to the Ocean

With my career in dance and movement, I was in the habit of going to the studio as early as I could manage to stretch and have a *danse du jour*. In Saas Fee in those early years, that meant the gymnasium of the elementary school where we were meeting. I walked through the village, climbing up the long, broad stone staircase. As I approached the door to the gym, I heard Paolo's piano filling the room with melody. I cracked the door open silently and peeked in. Paolo was bent over the keyboard of the black Bösendorfer grand and, if he noticed me, he did not acknowledge my presence. I slipped in. I moved to a corner in the back of the room, out of his line of sight, with the thought that my simple stretching would leave his concentration intact. It was wonderful to have this beautiful live music to begin my day. What a luxury! As time went on, I grew bolder and allowed myself to move into his range of vision. He played; I danced. After some time, who could say how long, we stopped and spoke about our experience of having the other in the room. We spoke of the synergy of the moment and improvisation as a discipline. We walked up to the hotel to have breakfast together, and continue our conversation, the first of many. I met him there artist to artist, as well as student and teacher.

Paolo was one of the most patient and excellent teachers I ever had. Many people loved and admired him. I was one among many who appreciated his original contributions to the discourse on how and why art was helpful as a change agent. Throughout our relationship, we collaborated many times in community art, symposia, and class work. We were in a continuous dialogue about the work. Our conversations continued across the years and the distance from San Diego to Schaffhausen until our last conversation in August 2020, just weeks before his passing. For three summers, we conversed about a new book, an update to his theories and approach. Because of macular degeneration his eyesight was too deteriorated to write, so he asked me to undertake the task with him. This is not the book Paolo and I would have written together. It is the result of my desire to fulfill my last assignment.

STORY: First Assignment: Travelers and Traces

During the faculty meeting, which happens the day before the classes start, Paolo asked me if I was going to dance during this session. I casually said, "yes," because I always dance during the session. It seemed an odd question, and I felt I had missed something, but I had no question to ask, so I let it go. The next day when the entire university was gathered he asked me in front of the community if I would create a dance with the student body. I said, "yes," I would; easy enough. He said some dancing was private and some was public. "Ok," I thought. "What's going on here? Is there more?" Then he asked if I would create a dance with the student body for the Arts Festival, a public event. I felt hesitant, I hadn't done that at The EGS. It felt like a big assignment but again I said, "yes," thinking I had the three-week session to work on it. Then he told me I had one week to do it. I remember feeling stunned and I know some tears welled up. I felt set up somehow or shocked. But I said, "yes." Later in the faculty lounge as I was expressing my doubts and fears, other members of the faculty encouraged me to say "no," that I didn't have to do it just because Paolo asked me to. It's hard to remember the dread I felt. "Just say 'no,' Greer," they said. Yet, I felt I had to try. I had to try to do it, for Paolo's faith in me, or something like that. I announced that any student who wanted to be in the performance should join me in the plenum during lunch. About 30 students showed up. We needed to build an ensemble feeling with these mostly strangers, so we spent some time sharing where they came from and why they were here and moving together. They named themselves and the work they were to create together Travelers and Traces. They had traveled from all over the globe and felt this dance work would leave traces on them as well as traces on the university.

My creative partner at the time created an original score for the performance with naïve musicians—i.e., players with little or no formal training who bring fresh, un-theorized responses to sound-making—in an ensemble. About 15 languages were spoken in the group, although everyone spoke

English as a second language. Some people had no experience whatsoever in dance, some had a little, and a few were dancers with education and experience. The musicians had a similar spread. We began. For the next week we worked about two hours a day with the students. I created themes and a score, which I gave to the dancers to work with. I coordinated the music and dance themes after the end of the teaching day. As is my habit, I asked everyone to try everything in rehearsal, but they could pick which themes and arrangements they felt comfortable to do for the performance. It was arduous, frustrating, and exhilarating. We had only suggestions of costumes and simple lighting, but we had a show. We improvised with our score. Anything could happen. We've had about ten hours to both create and learn the score; about eight takes, no two the same. On the evening of the festival the audience filled with members of the student body and faculty but also guests from the town. I was nervous. The overall score ran about 90 minutes with no break. The music used both standard and found instruments; lively and lovely. The musicians were exuberant and committed. The dancers were on fire, energetic and totally present. The room was full of life. It flowed like a river, from one exploration to another. At the end, the audience burst into applause and stood up. It felt surprising and triumphant. I was so proud of everyone who had worked on the piece. I also felt a great sense of relief; I had done it, we had done it. The praise and comments people gave to the work and to me made me happy, but the main satisfaction? I successfully completed the assignment Paolo had given me. He could count on me. He would give me other mission impossible assignments over the years. This book was his last.

Who Is This Book for?

This is a book for students, for professional expressive arts practitioners and for those in adjacent fields wishing to better understand our methodologies and underlying theories. It is for helpers who are seeking a way to help beyond, instead of, or in addition to the standard prescriptive medical model or educational paradigm.

If You Are a Student of Expressive Arts

A detailed overview of the work as provided in this book provides a solid foundation. Terms and concepts from classic texts of the field will be illuminated with concrete examples.

If you are a graduate student in any of the creative arts therapies, you may find it valuable. Diverse fields, i.e., social work, psychology, education, coaching, and change agents of all types can find nourishment and inspiration here.

If You Are a Practitioner

You will find the book beneficial for internships and beginning practice, providing insight into the nature of the field based on the experience of a working professional, rather than theoretical discussion. A book is never a substitute for a living teacher, but this might help. For a long-experienced practitioner, this book may help you clarify your thinking about practice, and help give you specific language for your experiences from another perspective. If you are curious about the "how to" and "when to" of intermodal expressive arts therapy: welcome.

The purpose of the book is to make concrete connections across the disparate roles of the practitioner and the applied components of ExA practice, to give one picture of how our philosophies, theories, and methodology come together in an internally consistent "theory of practice" as field founder Paolo would say. The challenge is to do this simply and accessibly, something that is critical to the educational process of change agents, therapists, educators, and coaches. As expressive arts practitioners, we often find ourselves working in teams that are unfamiliar with our philosophy, theory, and methodology. Practitioners need to feel competent and comfortable explaining the field in simple, direct, and comprehensible language. The book is also designed to help working professionals find the language that helps them articulate their experience.

Since the situations and challenges of the people we work with are so diverse, the philosophy and theory need to be simple. It is simple, but not easy. When Paolo said, "You are the tool!" (Knill *et al.*, 1996, p. 127), he was referring to what he calls the existential presence that the practitioner brings into the therapeutic relationship. You have to become the work. The guiding principles need to be in your bones. No time to consult your notes. Multiple decisions need to be made and they are made *in situ* with your client. Every decision both opens a way and closes a way so your spontaneous choices are best if they have been long simmered in the broth of the theories. It is exciting to always be in the emerging moment, working with imagination, art materials, and people. I can think of no more satisfying occupation.

BECOMING AN EXPRESSIVE ARTS THERAPIST

Self-knowledge is the first responsibility of a change agent. You have your own unique story for why you have chosen this path, or maybe it chose you. Take some time to reflect on the journey you have made so far to reach this point. How have the arts operated in your life to enlighten you, support you, expand your horizons, and help you manage changes and challenges? We need to be cognizant of our own development, biases, and imaginings, and understand how our interests impact how we work.

Learning to Do the Work

The next responsibility is education. An expressive arts therapist holds a master's degree at minimum and has specific training in helping through the arts and engaging the imagination. This must include several hundred hours of supervised clinical internship, as well as an ongoing commitment to education and exploration in the arts. It includes self-study in an art discipline and experience in the ExA client role. It includes supervision.

Over time, the student learns to incorporate the accumulated field knowledge and methodology into the session. They develop the muscle of "witnessing," that pristine attitude of the professional helper, observing all the communications of the client. This simple practice is arguably more strenuous in its demands on the practitioner than any other I have encountered, and more rewarding. This book will provide some basis for your continuing development.

The key to being a competent practitioner is learning to reliably help people in your care gain access to their imagination, in a relaxed and embodied way. It requires a cool head, a playful spirit, and a passionate heart. It brings out our best. It sets the foot on a journey to celebrate the inner life, maximize the contribution of the person to the world, develop the life of the mind, participate in the riches of the arts, and the conscious community. It adds to the store of humanity's goodwill. I would say it changes the practitioner as much as it changes the client. This requires a careful guide, and a practitioner humble enough to know the responsibility of being a catalyst, not a carpenter. Under careful stewardship this seems to happen automatically, effortlessly.

THE GROUND WE STAND ON

The path to becoming an ExA practitioner has some fundamental understandings which are a kind of prequel to gaining mastery in the techniques of the studio. This section will address some of the fundamentals that make up the worldview and philosophical basis for the practice of ExA.

ExA Is a Post-Psychological, Aesthetic Way of Helping

STORY: Dr. Know-it-All and Nascent Meanings

In my career at a residential treatment center for children and youth, I attended treatment team meetings. Representatives from the various departments would report on a client's progress. Back in those days, the client did not attend these meetings. First, the psychiatrist would speak, then the psychologist, the mental health professionals, and finally the activities department: the recreation therapist, the art therapist, and the dance therapist. Once, as part of my report, I brought a drawing a resident had done after a movement session. The psychiatrist looked at the drawing and said, "You know, there is the overt and manifest content of the drawing, but there's also the latent content." He then proceeded to reveal what he thought were the secret meanings of all the objects in the drawing—like looking something up in the dictionary of symbols and their meanings, reducing the drawing to a kind of message in a bottle. He believed he had the key to the real meaning, even though the drawing wasn't from his client; he wasn't present when it was drawn, and didn't know or consider what the client had to say about it. I didn't have the confidence or stature at the time to challenge him, nor was my own philosophy clearly articulated in my mind. He swept out the door, and I lingered behind—stunned by what I now see as the assumption of superiority by the medical model and its disregard for the experience of the artist and the witness. It seems to me now this was image abuse at its finest.

The EGS teaches ExA focused on promoting health and managing change in individuals, groups, and communities. Although there is a kinship with other approaches in therapeutic arts, intermodal expressive arts therapy has a distinct theory and methodology unique to arts-based helping professions. Our methodology is rooted in philosophy and the disciplines and practices of the art studios, as well as the theories indigenous to this field. Our work may be rightly referred to as post-psychological. This means our focus is on the aesthetic relationship and the power of images, rather than the modern medical model dichotomies of "illness versus wellness." This is likely the most significant difference between ExA's methods and other methods using art, although it is not the only difference. Ours is a solution-oriented approach that seeks more than problem-solving. Not merely symptom relief, but development of the inner life.

MASTERING THE PRACTICE OF EXPRESSIVE ARTS THERAPY

ExA Is Based in the Arts

A student asked if she could do a talk-only session. ExA practitioners train in the arts as both the catalyst and investigatory method of the constraining situation, but it is not a non-verbal endeavor. Arts-based means no additional counseling education is required since our approach is sufficient to the entire endeavor. However, there are other counseling fields that are compatible with the philosophy and theories of ExA. A key feature of the ExA approach is that the aesthetic impulse and power of the client is activated and directed to art-making activities—whether dance, drama, music, visual arts, or expressive writing. In the beginning, clients might need to express their questioning in story form before going to other art expressions. However, if a person doesn't ever want to go into that aesthetic space, a referral to a talk therapist might be the best course of action.

Taking a single individual as our example, the client explores the art materials and explores their relationship with any emergent artifact. By treating this emergent image as a repository of information, as a resource, a guide, they gain access to new perspectives and ideas. In working with the image in various ways, the art speaks about how the stale or stagnant aspects of their life might also begin to shift and change. People become more closely aligned with their authentic desires. Their actions and thoughts can change. Their values and identity can change. The sense of purpose develops or returns to the life-world of the client. They can see new avenues toward hope. They can recover what was missing, grieve what was lost, or repair what was broken. Over time, the client-artist creates a new vision for themselves, for their future. They can write a new narrative that helps make sense of challenging life experiences. It will not happen in one session, but over time, changes can be cumulative and transformative. I want to help people to let go of unnecessary suffering.

This work of transformation is done through what Paolo called the "rites of restoration"—the expressive arts session (Knill *et al.*, 1996). First, the client seeks help from the practitioner. They share a conversation about the reason for seeking help. Through this interview, the therapist helps to make the nature of the challenge as clear and concrete as possible. Having identified the challenge, the therapist now offers the client an opportunity to move into the imaginal realm through art-making, entering the "already here but in another state of mind" world; the world of "as if" which uses the imagination and the senses. This is the defining feature of an expressive arts therapy session.

Think of it this way: We take action with our art materials, we play. We move as dancers, we put color on paper or canvas as painters, we make sounds as musicians, and these actions call forth the imagination and its contents and inhabitants. Scratching on the paper with your pencil or chalk is like knocking at the door of the imagination. If I want access to the imaginal realm, its contents and inhabitants, I need to make marks and keep doing it. If I am dancing and I want to encounter the wisdom of my inner images, I need to move and keep moving. It needn't be fast or intricate. As with all the art disciplines, I need to be doing something, letting the elements play, while I wait for the emergent image to begin to make itself known. This is the call. I am waiting for something to appear. While I wait, I dance or sing, write or create an installation, which is my supplication. I wait so that something can move me so that I can notice something, and then begin to pull on that thread that will lead to an encounter with an art image. When it emerges, it begins to tell us what to do... "more yellow over here," it might say to the painter. Or "more quickly, on a lower level," to the dancer. When the image emerges, when something seems to be taking shape, we begin to serve the image and let it lead. Not everything I make is a self-portrait (unless it is), yet, it is related to me and knows me intimately: my history, my invisible scars and struggles, and my hidden resources, dreams, and undeveloped strengths. Is it duende, that passion and inspiration that arrives in its own time? Or the Muse? It is my imagination, but I surrender to it, I let it lead with its other-world logic. It activates the non-ordinary aspect of myself.

Scope of Practice

The scope of practice for an expressive arts practitioner is as broad as the human condition. People of any age or situation can benefit from engaging in the resource-generating aspects of art-making as demonstrated in intermodal expressive arts therapy. Interns and practitioners have brought expressive arts to neurodiverse children and adults on the autism spectrum, elders with Alzheimer's, people with brain injuries, veterans facing PTSD or homelessness, and individuals recovering from addictions. They have worked with survivors of sexual trafficking, torture, and domestic violence, as well as those who have caused harm, people in prison, and clients dealing with eating disorders or other mental health concerns, including couples seeking help for their marriages. The same creative approach has also proved valuable for educators, nurses, doctors, executives, business leaders, chambers of commerce, professional artists, and a wide range of groups, families, teams, and communities. Since art is an inherent aspect of the human experience, it makes sense that returning to this basic human activity can help create and manage change in almost any endeavor, as it has been with us since the beginning of time. The arts are an indispensable element. They are a human existential.

Scope of Competency

The scope of competency is as broad or narrow as the practitioner's qualifications. Among the many fields practitioners may have additional education in are social work, education, philosophy, medicine, school counseling, ecology, psychotherapy and psychology, coaching, sports education, and many others. In these settings, the application of expressive arts can enliven and enrich professional relationships with clients/artists, enhance the perceived value of the work done together, and lead to greater cohesiveness among teams and workplaces. Art forms such as opera, open mics, jams and slams, dance teams, musical ensembles, movies, and visual art studios can benefit from the incorporation of our principles and ethos to enhance the creative process and engage the audience in a more meaningful relationship with both the images and the art-makers.

Custom Made for You

An important foundation of ExA is the notion that every individual is unique—there are not 12 types of people, not 16 types, not 5 types. There are roughly eight billions types of people, because that is roughly how many people are in the world. Not only is the combination of DNA in each individual unique, but the time and circumstances of their birth and life are unique. Were they born in 1500 to a poor farmer, or in 2024 to a rich capitalist? In the States, or Latvia? Wartime or peacetime? Rural or urban? Male or female or something else? And have you noticed that even siblings born into the same family, with the same mother and father, in the same era, under the same economic circumstances, are different from each other? One gets mom's red hair, the other gets her allergies. There are just too many variables for any two people to be the same. Of course, we share much but not everything. So our therapy needs to be bespoke. You must create a new approach for each person. ExA allows for that.

This method can help any suffering person. Any individual, regardless of their circumstances, can be supported and assisted to make the changes they desire or need in their lives if they are willing to seek change. We have used ExA to help neurodiverse children and adults, elders with Alzheimer's disease, brain-injured people, veterans with problems of homelessness, people recovering from drug and alcohol addiction, victims of domestic violence, people who commit said violence, people in prison, and people who suffer from eating disorders or mental illness. Also included are executives, nurses, doctors, professional artists, and people whose marriages need help, not to mention the various groups and communities that have benefitted. Schools, both public and private, have benefited. These examples are taken from my personal experience and that of the graduate students I supervise, as well as my 20+ years teaching at the EGS.

Social Contract and Situational Analysis

For ExA to be successful, it is important to understand your social contract with your clients and situational analysis and how they relate to the various forms of practice: individual, classroom, small group, and community. The foundations of the building must be taken care of before the door can be opened. The following foundations and cornerstones are included:

Social Contract

An agreement a practitioner enters into with a person or group is referred to as a social contract. It might also be called an informed consent. It helps define the role the practitioner is entering into when serving a particular population, in a particular setting, and therefore the expectations and limits of their duties. A practitioner's role can change greatly, depending on the expectations of the setting: in a prison, they might be a teaching artist, while in a school, they might be a counseling artist. The skills and responsibilities expected of the practitioner in different settings can vary from speaking to facilitating to coaching. The social contract also depends on how often the practitioner meets the individuals or group members, who pays for their services, whether they are an employee or contractor, and what their legal constraints and ethical considerations are. These things change based on the setting. What does the client expect the limits of the roles to be? When a practitioner is an expressive arts teacher, the limits of confidentiality are different from when they are an art-based psychotherapist. When they are a contractor, the expectations are different still. The role is not changed willy-nilly depending upon mood but rather on the demands of the situation, ethical standards, and best practices of the professional community.

In a formal and legal sense, the social contract defines who the practitioner and the client are to one another. It outlines the ethical boundaries of the relationship as seen from the outside. For example, there are different expectations between a teacher and a student, between a therapist and a client, between a consultant and a professional, or between a supervisor and a supervisee. Each of these roles has a different social contract—each carries varying expectations and responsibilities for both the client and the practitioner. There could be paperwork involved if the practitioner is a therapist, with informed consent and discussion of confidentiality and exceptions thereof. Will insurance pay the fee or will it be fee-for-service and the client pays the practitioner directly? Is the practitioner meeting the client in a community non-governmental organization that pays the practitioner? If the practitioner is a consultant, do they need a Memorandum of Understanding? (A formal document about their role and the expectations of each party, which defines what the practitioner will do and what the client will do, how the practitioner will be paid, and the rate of that compensation.) It helps both parties to know who they are to each other and why they are meeting. It may define the use of electronic communication. There is a different social contract for each of these relationships, and boundaries can change. While it may not be appropriate to go for coffee and have a chat with a therapy client, it may be more acceptable to do so with a graduate student, even though both relationships are professional.

Practitioners must know and carry within them the limits and boundaries, the ethics, and the legal responsibilities of the social contract they enter into. This includes knowing any necessary laws and ethical standards that apply to the practice of using art processes or helping people in any capacity. The state of California, for example, requires practitioners to carry malpractice insurance. Additionally, practitioners are mandated to report abuse against children and elders to county agencies who will investigate their reports. Membership in a peer organization can help establish a practitioner as a bona fide professional. Some states may require practitioners to have a certain kind of business license for their private practice, as well as for any institutions they operate. Practitioners may also be subject to additional rules, laws, and tax codes for city and federal governments. It is important to know what applies to each practitioner. Although no one can safely perform a role outside the scope of their education and competency, roles can change and evolve depending on the situation and the practitioner's continuing education.

Situational Analysis

Situational analysis takes into consideration all the aspects of the encounter that can be known or imagined ahead of time. This includes the social contract as detailed above for the roles you and your client will play, but it includes much more. It includes all of the details of the comprehensive situation. I recommend that you do this in writing for yourself, as I do, so you can be inspired by the formula that emerges. As Paolo said, "We easily assume that we know what is needed [for the encounter], but writing it down... is superior preparation." The act of writing it down helps it become embodied and therefore available for reflection. "This is to make sure that you do not forget that you serve the people, not getting rushed so that you do what you always do, and therefore serve yourself rather than others" (personal communication, 2018).

To prepare for the greatest possibility of success you must know where you are going and for whom you are working. This seems obvious, doesn't it? Yet, a detailed written review of your role, the setting, the situational analysis, and the social contract will help you in numerous ways, and reveal aspects you might not have been aware of when you see it altogether.

Ask yourself:

- WHAT was I hired to do? Who was the contact and what is our relationship? Who are they to me, who am I to them? How does this inform my plan?
- WHY was I hired? Why you? What expectations might there be about your work? Are you expected to present something educational about expressive arts? A training or in-service workshop? Part of a panel? Demonstration?
- WHO am I working with?

Be curious about the life of the group. What binds them together? What have they achieved? Is it a flex point, an important ending or beginning of something? What is their motto, their mission? Has an important member come or gone? Let your offerings be tailor-made for these specific people, considering where they are and what they are doing.

Consider any socio-political factor: Are they LGBTQIA+? Veterans? BIPOC? Are they teens? Younger? Older? Much older? Are they refugees? Are they from a culture different from your own? What does this require of you? Note every influence you can think of: class, culture, defining experiences, demographics, histories together, skill sets. Write the strengths and trouble spots, if known. For example: working with a group such as adults over 65 with limited mobility, in nursing homes, most without close family, but with financial resources, who love music. How does this help you with your plan? Or young adults (19–26), mixed race and genders, who have lived on the street and been trafficked, most did not complete high school, who love rap, graffiti, and fashion.

Review factors such as their formal roles to and with each other, time spent together, and what you can know of their back stories. Are they a creative youth development team, a corporate leadership team, staff of a local school, a group of graduate students, neighborhood mothers concerned about traffic, a chamber of commerce doing their annual review, people with similar health problems like asthma or heart disease, or an age-related group like seniors? For each choice, the facilitator should consider the traditions, history, and life of the group.

Let the facts stimulate your imagination. Write what you know and let it simmer and guide your choice of materials, time frames, and other choices. The sooner you do this, the more it can ripen in your imagination and contribute to your preparation. Let ideas and images of your work bubble and multiply.

Assess the various needs of the people you serve. Even if you are working with the same art materials, you might offer different frames for geriatric Alzheimer patients versus unhoused youth versus adult women survivors of domestic violence. It is your job to be sensitive to the possibilities and differences of your people. Modify your frames and materials to meet the specific situation.

Where:
Where will this work take place? What are the benefits and limitations of the setting?

I need to take my "animal self" to the place, if at all possible. Look for the aesthetic resources or limitations. Will the session take place in a large room so movement is possible? Is there furniture in the room or is the space empty? Is it a conference room with a huge table in the middle, so everyone will need to sit? What is the light source: are there overhead fluorescents, lamps, or large windows? Is there natural light or not? Would a candle be allowed? Evaluate the type of flooring: carpet, wood, concrete, or linoleum, since that will influence what you can do. What is the amount of space in relation to the number of people? Are there other atmospheric elements—e.g., a garden nearby or a kitchen with cooking odors? Acoustics? Better to know so you can make modifications. If the session is outside, will it be on the lawn or under trees? Is there any ambient noise? Look for elements of beauty in the environment.

When:
Consider the timing of the session. Did the school calendar set the date and time? Does it coincide with someone's observed celebration of something? Is it scheduled during an open house or at the end of something, such as school, training, or retirement? Could it be a book launch, an annual meeting, or another event? Consider what is happening locally and nationally. There may be outside events or times of year that can bring inspiration to you and your session. For example, an upcoming holiday or local festival could be relevant. One of my students was working with Iranian

immigrants. When the Persian New Year came, she emphasized the celebration of Nowruz. Her chosen art materials and frames reflected her knowledge of this, including poetry and even some little bites of food in that tradition. This brought a feeling of warmth and home and an acknowledgment of their culture.

Do your homework:
Capture these aspects, either as a list, if you are a list person, or as a mind map with its various limbs and branches, if you are more of a doodler, like me. See if it inspires you to write out the specifics of your clients, and see if you discover resources. Write what you know of the reason you were called. Write what you know about the life of the group.

Take into account the local customs (e.g., Cinco de Mayo in San Diego), weather (e.g., the monsoon in Tucson), the season (e.g., the cows come up to the Alps in spring in Switzerland), a full moon, or solstice, special holidays (e.g., Pride Parade). These might provide a valuable anchor or stepping-off place. Consider the milieu, the culture of the place itself.

It is more difficult to make an accurate assessment if you are an outsider coming in, but not impossible. You must have this anchor. My are not arbitrary—they are based on the group I am facilitating and all the details I can amass, including details of my relationship with the client (am I a new guest or a familiar teacher?). My notebooks are full of my mind maps, lists, diagrams, and scribbles about what resources and themes might best serve any given clientele. I review them every night for the next day based on what occurred.

STORY: A Step Beyond

The leadership team of a nonprofit creative youth development organization, A Step Beyond, invited me to work with them. Institute graduate, Jenn Oliver, was now the artist director there. My situational analysis was as follows: four young women—passionate dancers and dance teachers—working together at this after-school performing arts organization serving predominantly Hispanic youth. These four teachers were meeting in a leadership retreat for the first time. They knew each other well. The last person to join the team came in two years ago, so I concluded that it was a stable team. I was to come in for the first two hours of the three-day retreat. We would be meeting in one of the dance studios with a Marley floor. The studio had floor-to-ceiling windows on one side. I could have whatever art materials I wanted. My situational analysis included the resources of the room, the time of year, the people gathered, and their purpose.

Having done the necessary things associated with the social contract and scribbled out some details of the situational analysis, you can then enter the room, knowing the foundation and walls are firm.

STORY: The Long View

Mercy Hospital, San Diego hired me to introduce expressive arts practice to hospice and palliative care nurses. We met in a conference room on a high floor of the hospital. I wasn't able to visit the room before my in-service, but because I had taken the time to get a clear description of the room, I knew I couldn't do any movement work at all. A large conference table took up the entire center of the room, with barely enough space for people to squeeze sideways into the big executive chairs around the perimeter. I planned carefully to bring a wide variety of props and materials so I could keep interest up and avoid highlighting the room as a problem. It was the reality; I had to deal with it and didn't want to focus on it. There was the additional restraint that the patients we were discussing would be bedridden, so things had to be small, easy to handle and manipulate. We couldn't get messy!

I had prepared various musical experiences, including bringing Amy Andrews, an Institute graduate who would play guitar to provide sonic ambiance. I had to bring things that were ready to use—"readymades." One such choice was laminated scenes from magazines that I typically use for writing prompts, but in this instance used as storytelling prompts. I brought cards of various types, easy poetry ideas, colored paper, small stones to write on, and other things one could do in bed. I was grateful I didn't count on my usual body movement beginning, and although we did some limited stretching and breathing, we could not move out of our chairs once everyone in the room sat down, unless it was one at a time. As I shared the various materials, we discussed the possibility of using these with dying patients. The nurses shared their thoughts and feelings.

As the presentation came to an end, I wanted to bring attention to the value the aesthetic experience can have for all of us, patients and nurses alike. My attention suddenly went to the wide panoramic window that ran the length of the room. The view spanned over the San Diego River and Mission Valley, all the way to the ocean. I saw what it offered. The sun was beginning to set into the Pacific; the sky was lovely with wispy pastel clouds and the long view to the horizon. Tops of eucalyptus were below us. It was a beautiful scene from our vantage point, revealing the great vista of nature and the smallness of human activity. The freeway and shopping mall below were like a mini-town. I asked the nurses to file, one at a time, out of their chairs and line up by the windowsill. We stood shoulder to shoulder and spontaneously linked arms to make room for everyone. We took a breath together. We lingered, wordless.

The group ended here, at the window, with the long view. The moment became solemn, a feeling of pause. These hospice nurses work daily with terminally ill people. The sun was setting. The human activity below, "getting and spending," seemed insignificant and small. The metaphoric moment was not lost on us. As we held each other and breathed together, some tears came. At my prompt, we ended silently, going slowly and softly out of the conference room. It was a good presentation, with a great ending. The view was my partner. Sometimes a difficult setting can yield an aesthetic advantage. Look for it.

Go to the arts to research the unique needs and properties of your specific population. Their playwrights, poets, filmmakers, choreographers, painters will inform you. This is part of your cultural literacy. Be inspired with interdisciplinary excursions into psychology and sociology or other disciplines.

Read memoirs about the lives of people different from your own. Some examples: A Black woman with light skin wanted me to know about the internal prejudice within the Black community against people who could "pass" for white, "high yellow" (her words). This was a source of pain for her in her family, so I appreciated learning about that phenomenon. I also read about the Kibbutz for a client whose childhood involved that style of upbringing. The human experience is vast and varied. Not all my clients bring me books to read. Even so, I learn something about the culture of their family, community, race, religion, education, and their unique narrative of distress as well as their internal and social resources. This is an intersection with many avenues coming together. Inform yourself.

The Safe Container

You are the most important element of the safe container. A person needs to know you and like you before they can trust you. The two qualities or elements you can display to engender the necessary trust are presence and professionalism. No matter where or under what circumstances you meet your client, your complete and total presence is a necessary element (Atkins & Eberhart, 2014). This means that you have taken care of your own needs to completely attend to the other. See them. How they present themselves—the obvious aspects like possible age and manner of dress, but also what spirit inhabits their character. The posture and gestures of the body. The color and quality of expression on the face and where the eyes go. The cadence and rhythm of the voice, its timbre, its volume. I view the person before me with open-hearted curiosity. Within myself I find tenderness for their plight, for the creature-ness of the person. It's a little like birdwatching; observe without judgment, appreciate what is, accept it exactly as it is, be present without interference. They are also birdwatching. Here is an opportunity to encounter my prejudices, let them emerge and vanquish them, or set them aside for further investigation. I work with people I like—I want to find a thread of relatedness as soon as I can. Listening to the voice, the story, the way it is told, the expression of emotion or its lack, the vocabulary, the lilt or drawl—the whole thing, as an instrument, as a song.

Presence is necessary, but is it sufficient? I wish I could say yes, but I cannot. As you explore them, they are also investigating you—what do they see, and hear? There is no single checklist or mold to fit into—yet, consider what your client will encounter.

PROFESSIONALISM AND CONFIDENTIALITY IN PRACTICE

STORY: The Midnight Call

Sometimes neglecting a principle can reveal its importance. A new intern was assigned to work with teens who were living on the street and in some cases involved in prostitution. He was excited about the assignment. In those days, I was checking social media right before bedtime when I saw a photo of this man and one of his clients. It's funny how much one photo can reveal. First, I was horrified to see the face of a client. This was an absolute breach of confidentiality, and then I saw what the intern was wearing. It looked like he was going to a festival—something too tight and revealing—just too much skin. It showcased his muscular physique, but not his professionalism. He was presenting himself as a friend, one of the gang, not a professional helper. The client had said this post would be okay because "it was all for fun." We had that midnight call to take it down immediately. He said he meant nothing untoward by it, a sentiment I absolutely believed. This breach of professionalism led to the inclusion in the student handbook of a description of professional dress and another paragraph about the necessity of confidentiality and the dangers of exposing one's personal information in social media or other public areas. The protection afforded by professionalism goes both ways.

Nothing fine will occur if people do not feel seen, heard, and respected. This is a human encounter of the most delicate and potent type. Here's a story that reveals another angle of the safe space and how to negotiate it.

STORY: The Teenage Blondie

A mother brought her teenage daughter to see me. According to the mother, the daughter had been drinking and climbing out her window at night with unpleasant and possibly dangerous sexual encounters. There was also the matter of her symptoms of severe depression. We sat at the art table. My studio was large, airy, bright, and clean. I greeted the mother and then greeted the daughter, eye to eye. I offered my handshake. I asked the girl for her thoughts about why her mom had brought her to me. She mumbled. We discussed confidentiality and its exceptions, the ethical envelope, as it applied in California. I explained what I would and would not report to her mother, what I would and would not report to authorities. After the perfunctory paperwork, and payment agreement, the mother left. The girl was dressed as a punk-rock star; loud colors and clashing prints. There were rhinestones. She had short red hair, the red of a crayon, and purple-ish lipstick. I asked what her desire was for the session. Her mom had told us what she wanted, but what did the daughter want? Was she having any problems? Was she drinking "too much?" What about her sexual experiences?

I had two clients (the daughter om and daughter) and my treatment plan needed to take both into account (Berg & Steiner, 2003). To address the mother's agenda, I needed the cooperation of the client herself. Were any of those issues a problem for her? We began with what would become our ritual start: sitting in the middle of the studio, on big pillows. As we sat, she talked about her situation. Most of the issues her mom mentioned were true, she said, and in some cases, the situation was even worse than her mom realized. Not all of these issues were equally important to the daughter, though. For instance, the teenage client did not want to stop drinking, but she was willing to think about drinking less. That was a start. As we sat, I asked about her aesthetic history: I commented on her rock inspired outfit and I inquired about music. She really liked to sing. Had she brought any music? Yes, she had. Would she like to sing here, now? Yes, she would. So, with her proficiency in using electronics, she connected her phone to the sound system and she chose classic Blondie, "Call Me." What would she like me to do? I should sit. She sang with the recording as she started to dance, pausing here and there for emphasis. Singing and other musical activities would be a cornerstone of our work. To gain trust with a reluctant teen takes time, and it was a good start. After a while, she became so eager to see me she would run into the room and plop down, saying, "I have so much to tell you."

Did I create a safe container and if so, how? I established personal and direct contact with her, not merely speaking with the mother about her. I followed her lead to sit, noticing her body ornamentation and movement.

I inquired about her aesthetic preferences and supported her choices. In the areas where her perception differed from her mom's, I listened and accepted her description of her situation. I took her seriously. Over our three years together, we would paint, collage, mosaic, dance and sing a lot, work with installations and miniatures, make books, and write poetry and stories. Over time she got control of her drinking, discussed the sexual assaults, their legal implications, and the connection to alcohol. We discussed her depression, its origins, and manifestations. When she graduated from high school she was off to a prestigious university. I saw the empty pillows in the middle of the studio.

Safe Container–Group Work

Establishing a sense of safety with one person is one thing. The challenge is amplified in group work.

STORY: The Boys of East Hill

When I worked with teenagers as a dance therapist at a residential treatment facility, I managed groups of 10–15 adolescents. We discovered, over time, the things that made the group work well for the teens and also for me. It involved, in part, managing expectations and establishing guidelines for success. One tradition, removing shoes before they entered the room, was a signal that we were going to be in a special time/place, the group room, different from the unit where they lived. Another tradition was to sit around the room against the walls, which gave the group an oval shape. Everyone could see everyone. We developed a set of rules for "how it works." These ranged from removing the shoes and sitting, to listening while others spoke without interruptions and disrespectful language, taking turns, "listening to Greer," and having all participants clean up afterward. All groups develop their own mores. It is more powerful to have these emerge than to impose them, but you are also a member of the group, so things have to work for you as well.

As new teens were admitted to the facility, I would ask a more experienced group member to tell them "How it works" in my group. If they left something out, others would be eager to fill in. Over time we built a culture, a therapeutic milieu. It gave shared responsibility to the members for the smooth running of the group. If I ever had to ask one of them to leave, it was clear why. We had agreements with each other, if these were broken, the person who broke them left for the day. It was important to keep this consensus. It created safety which would allow me to take (limited) risks with these rambunctious teens—they knew I required complete cooperation for some of our dance therapy experiences.

The opening of the door and greeting phase is in the same spirit with a group as with an individual. The task remains the same: get to know each other enough to proceed. Often group sessions have more time than individual sessions, and they need additional rituals and traditions to keep the boundaries of the time frame crisp. Over time, you and the group will develop a unique culture and milieu. If the group is a new one, start with some sort of greeting ritual; self-made name tags or name games are useful. As soon as possible, establish the notion that "we" are here together.

Keep in mind, the needs of the human animal: to know their environment and explore it to feel safe. Where am I exactly? What is that thing over there? Who else is here? Is there water? I have to pee. I allocate some time to address these concerns, so they don't interrupt the concentration as the session progresses. I do this with things I call Public Service Announcements and Housekeeping: when we take breaks, where the shoes go, open cups on the floor are prohibited. When a group is new, I use socio-grams and spectrograms to discover their aesthetic histories together.

In closing, there is a need to balance the excitement of the studio work with safety for the individual. As with other aspects of ExA, there can be an equilibrium, an ongoing dialectic between holding and shaping. We want the Dionysian fire as an antidote to the rigidity and boredom of modern life, but need the Apollonian structure to provide the just-right amount of security. This is not a problem to solve, but a dance in the in-between.

Chapter Two

ARCHITECTURE OF A SESSION

STORY: The House That Knill Built

I sat in the plenum at The European Graduate School alongside the rest of the faculty and student body. It is a beautiful room. The back wall is curved, the room is wood-paneled, warm, and rich. The floor-to-ceiling glass doors look out at flowering meadows with the tops of the Alps behind. Paolo gave a lecture on the Architecture of a Session. While he constructed an intricate diagram, the unity of time and space became concrete, palpable, and practical to me. This understanding came to rest in my body in a corporeal way. Space-time was tangible. He drew a blueprint of a kind that helped concretize the amount of time allotted to various aspects of the practice and their sequence. It helped me conceive of the flow of time in terms of where it is spent, and the possible actions taken during that time. The scaffolding was revealed. Now I could make decisions about the portion of that limited and precious resource, time, for the various tasks that must occur during any expressive arts session or activity in the space. Like most important concepts, it was simple but elegant. He gave me the keys. The building was mine.

For our current purposes, let me construct this building in a basic way, following the blueprint that Paolo leaves us, in "big stitches," and in simple terms, as he asked. I will examine how this works as a template for an individual adult client and build a model. As we progress, I will show an alternative plan for groups. Later, I will translate this into a plan for large groups, specifically community art. I will contrast and compare how the space-time changes as the needs of the client change and show how the same tasks are accomplished but in different ways. An individual adult requires one type of building, a group of teenagers demands a different arrangement, and a community of a hundred necessitates yet another setup. This construction of time and space is divided into three main sections—rooms. Various tasks take place in these rooms made of time. It is important to know that the rooms are flexible—they can expand or contract depending on what is done there. Think of a Japanese-style home with movable shoji walls.

Envision this session, custom-made. You are both architect and builder. Thus, you can adapt the blueprint to fit the time and the space you need, moving the "walls" as necessary. The concept of a purpose-built place where this work occurs is a beautiful idea. We construct this special place every time we work—even in the humblest surroundings or circumstances. The walls are constructed in our imagination.

If you're working in a three-day marathon, you'll need a different blueprint arrangement. Similarly, if you're running nine sessions—like I do in Saas Fee—ranging from 90 minutes to three hours over 23 days, another arrangement is required. Whether you are in private practice or in a school, those particulars of time and circumstances need to be considered. This is a built-to-purpose space. Every circumstance deserves its own design.

THE BASIC PLAN

Before delving into the details of the architecture, let me provide you with a quick overview:

- Let's call the first room the Counselor's Chairs, where we welcome the client and discuss the reason for their visit. This is the first conversation. It consists of a filling-in, an examination of the constriction or troubling situation. We are sitting and talking about the issues at hand.

- The second room, the Studio, contains the second conversation. Many tasks take place here, such as activating the imagination through the senses as the client encounters the art materials, called sensitizing or warming up. Then, decentering through play, art-making, or ritual. We conduct an Aesthetic Analysis, a careful examination of the artifact that was created, at the end of studio time.

- The third and final room is a return to the Counselor's Chairs. Again, sitting and talking together. The final conversation. The main task is harvesting—finding the ready resources for the client and an everyday understanding of what occurred in the art-making process, and what changes may already have taken place. This is where the whole session comes together, responding to the question: "How did this help you?" It is about what occurred and how that might be helpful in the life-world of the client. Later, I list many ways that change may have occurred.

All these "rooms" are in one physical place, wherever it is that you are working. The division into the three rooms takes place in your mind/imagination. Nevertheless, the organization and the thresholds leading from one to another are literal. In the next section, we review the rooms and their options and tasks in depth, so keep this basic organizational diagram in mind as I lead you through some examples of how we can use "The House that Knill Built" to make our sessions more organized and effective. Let's take a closer look.

THE HOUSE THAT KNILL BUILT

Architecture of a Session

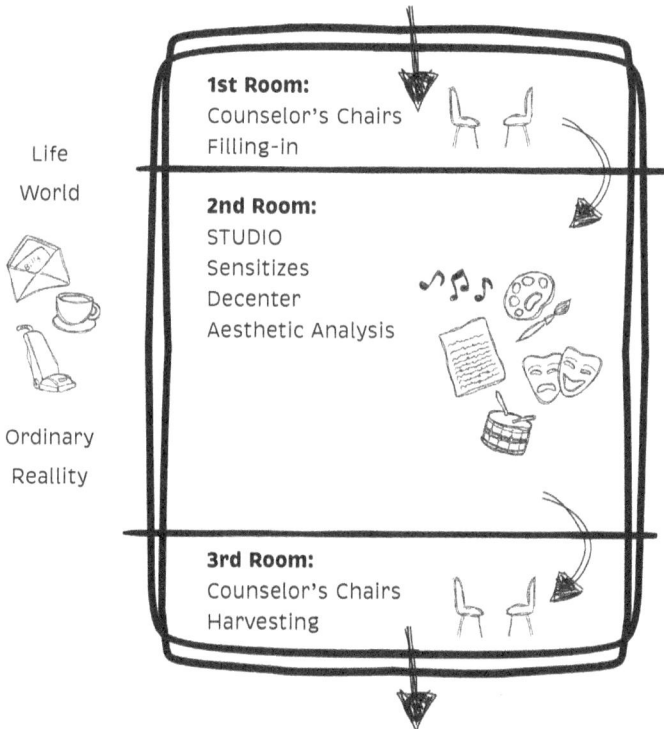

1st Room:
Counselor's Chairs
Filling-in

Life
World

2nd Room:
STUDIO
Sensitizes
Decenter
Aesthetic Analysis

Ordinary
Reallity

3rd Room:
Counselor's Chairs
Harvesting

Image credit: Kitty Cullen, MA, Expressive Arts Educator

ROOM NUMBER ONE: COUNSELOR'S CHAIRS—THE FIRST CONVERSATION
From the Life-World to the Front Door and Over the Threshold
Task: Greeting and Filling-In

Begin any expressive arts session with the actual circumstances of your client. This "current reality" or "life-world," as Heidegger called it, is the scene and the setting they come from. A person coming in from a blizzard enters with a little gust of wind and a bit of snow, or someone coming in from the beach tracks in traces of sand and the smell of the sea—they bring traces of their environment and circumstances into the expressive arts session. They come from the clock-driven circumstances of everyday life, marked by hustle and bustle. They carry the stress of commuting, work, family, health issues like the consequences of the COVID pandemic, and financial concerns. They come from *chronos—clock-time*—the everyday world that drives our lives, the watch, the calendar, the phone, the reminders, and alarms.

At your door, they step into a world designed to allow a different agenda to emerge. You are a companion whose job it is to guide and attend to a journey of their inner life; an alternative world of inner experience. Together we will explore creative images and impulses as they refer to their life-world and the situation that is brought into the room. This alone is a big change, a shift. They come into the kind of time where you look up and the whole hour has passed in the blink of an eye. This is the kind of time where you get absorbed in what you are doing, you "lose track of time." This is *kairos*, time out of time. This flow state or mindset allows the ordinary world to move into the background. This is as it should be, and you are in charge of guiding the process from beginning to end.

This is where people are greeted. We take off our overcoats and muddy boots. We sit and check in with our client: "What's going on? What happened to you?" They have come from a place where troubles seem to be wrecking their lives and wreaking havoc. Warmth and safety are communicated. It is essential that you make real contact with the person as soon as you can.

When they set their foot upon the threshold, hand upon the doorknob, they take a mighty step. This is the dividing line between their ordinary world and the world awaiting them, a world of imagination, the arts, beauty, and surprise. You open the door. They come to you and you welcome them into the space, your space. They come in as guests, as strangers. Do what you can to set a tone of welcome and beauty. Have a centerpiece with flowers or a candle. This is your job now, to create a safe, welcoming, and beautiful space. Offer a glass of water. Circumstances may be humble, and the environment might be rough. It doesn't require a silver candelabra, but rather an acknowledgment that this place is special to you—and, by extension, to them. This threshold marks the possibility of a liminal experience. The word "liminal" comes from the word for "threshold" in old Latin. Now it connotes a transitional or initial stage of some process. It means occupying a position on some kind of a boundary; neither here nor there. I emphasize this because nothing that happens over this border is ordinary. They have entered one layer of the liminal space that you have prepared and created for them.

When you greet your client, it is your job to help them feel welcome. You are the timekeeper, making sure the process is flowing so as to accommodate the important parts of the feast to come: the hors d'oeuvres, the soup, the fish, the salad, and the dessert. Part of developing mastery is to know when to let time run, and when to squeeze it down. A common error for the beginning ExA practitioner is to let the greeting and filling-in take up too much of the precious commodity—time—not shaping the flow of the conversation enough. This is especially true with the individual client, whose only model for what you are doing together might be a typical psychotherapy session, where the client talks for an hour. It is your job to make sure more than that happens. Let me show you how.

The image of this room is the "Counselor's Chairs," regardless of your seating arrangement—be it conventional chairs or floor cushions. This is your opportunity to begin a helping relationship in earnest. Allow the client to come to know you—enough to trust you. Bring yourself fully into the room, be emotionally available, and listen with all your senses.

"Filling-in" brings the practitioner up to speed with the current reality from the client's point of view—what is the issue, what is troubling them, what happened to them, what is constraining them, why have they come? Paolo calls these stories the "narrative of distress." People come into this room because their lives are not working in some way. Be willing to hear where it hurts, what they have suffered, and how distraught they may be.

Determine the main complaint. We need to set reasonable expectations of what can be accomplished in a session. Herbert Eberhart asks, "What would be a good outcome of this meeting?" This lets us both know if we are on track or not. It allows the client/artist to have direct input and does not assume that the practitioner is making all the decisions and choices.

Listening, summarizing, and helping the client feel understood are what need to be accomplished here. For example: "I think I have it. You are concerned about your drinking and the consequences of drinking, but you are unable to stop. Is this right?"

The Template—With an Individual

Depending upon the social contract, you might be the expressive arts therapist, or another title. They may have chosen to come to you independently or might be mandated in some way to attend. If these beginning tasks are reminiscent of a typical therapy session, it turns a corner swiftly—and I recommend the *aesthetic history* as one way to do this. This aspect of the client's life may have never been explored or honored, and it will be the root of your work together, so don't neglect it. I prefer to use papers minimally, so I do this freehand, although you could have a form or a checklist. Over time, build on their experiences in dance, drama, music, visual arts (including photography, pottery, book making, basket weaving, etc.), and expressive writing, such as poetry, memoir, and journaling. One of my clients was doing advanced lace knitting; this ability turned out to be a resource for her. Another created her own beads and doll heads. One fellow created fine abstract collages incorporating vinyl records. Aesthetic potentials will be revealed over time with all our clients, but I like to know something when I start and what pursuits and intelligences they already have developed and enjoy. I foster these as we go.

You want a clear understanding of the problem from the client's point of view. If your client wanders away from the subject, the counselor's/therapist's role gives you the gentle power to interrupt and say, "I think we are wandering, let's go back to..." It may feel awkward but remember this is not a social relationship. You want to be effective as a professional.

As they tell their plight, what senses do their words call forth? Are they painting a picture? Do they see something? Are they moving through something, or is it getting them down? Is it off in the distance, but they can hear it coming? What if they don't feel anything emotional but sense something in their body? You are following along with your imagination, building their world within your mind.

If their body is moving in a particular way, making a gesture, if their eyes shift again and again to an empty spot in the room, note that. Remember, we are always communicating, we are never not communicating. It is your job and privilege to take off the polite blinders of society and look at the whole picture, notice the things that you notice, and bring those things into the conversation, so all of it can be used for the client's benefit.

Do not be afraid to guide the conversation back to an important topic. I say, "Let's circle back to..." or "I'd like to return to..." or "Can I hear more about...?" Since language is a significant part of our work, I may ask a person to repeat a word and open it up. What is the history of this word in their story? What is the linguistic significance? What else is in there; is there another word that would suffice? Do not let details go unnoticed.

Concretize the details and make things specific. Be sure you can follow them. I use the notion of the "memory palace" to visualize the details of the client's story as they tell it. I see the scene in my mind, I let my body understand with somatic experience. Ask for clarification. I ask people to repeat things to make sure I heard them correctly. I sometimes repeat the exact language they used, quoting them, so they can hear what they said. I often act as a scribe and take notes for them that they can take with them. For me, this is an exciting exercise in being in the burning moment as it unfolds and emerges second by second. Although I am relaxed, I am also filled with energy. This process energizes and excites me. It takes all of me; it takes the best I have. That is a pleasure.

Filling-In the Art Analog Way

Usually, the filling-in is a conversation, but not always. If the client has many distressing things, it may be difficult to articulate the most pressing trouble. They may ask for help but be unable to choose what they need help with. In a case like this, I use an art analog method of filling-in, meaning an artful way, but not art-making, using art materials to help organize and clarify the constraints.

STORY: Puddles of Color

Susan came in complaining of symptoms of depression. I could see her downtrodden spirit in her glum face and dragging gait. She came in complaining of feeling tired and angry. Her sentences bounced from topic to topic. I asked what her main challenge was, but she was unable to name just one. She was a self-employed hairdresser, a new mother, and her relationship with her husband was tense because he was not helping with childcare and housework. She resented this. Her income was down. She had previously had some eating disorder issues, and now, post-baby, she was feeling fat. That scared her. She felt overwhelmed. I couldn't address all her concerns in an hour, and neither could she. I asked her to name these issues: lack of help, loss of income, stress of motherhood, negative body image, and so forth. I grabbed my box of scarves. "Show me," I said.

As she named the issues, she dropped a scarf into a puddle on the floor. We walked around together as she decided where each scarf would go. She touched the scarves and made decisions about the colors; green for this, violet for that. We were not in a hurry. She laid them out on the floor, making spaces between some and placing others close together. She created thoughtful piles of color. This was visual thinking. At the end of this exercise, we stepped away from the area of the floor where the scarves pooled. Something became clear to her; she took a deep breath and relaxed. It now made perfect sense that she felt tired and angry—she looked at all she was dealing with. It was understandable and self-evident. It gave us a place to start. This is an artful filling-in. In this case, the filling-in took much more time than usual, but we couldn't go forward until we had a direction. It is cruel to allow a person to stumble and twist in her pain, to go on and on in the narrative of distress. It is my job to offer some kind of clarity, even if that is saying, "Yes, you have too many areas that are out of control." Even that can offer some solace—"I am not crazy; I am dealing with a lot of things. No wonder I am tired and angry."

We accomplished the task required. The filling-in took the whole session. We both understood the complaint better—the reason for the visit was clear. Her issues were in focus.

Small Group—Externalizing the Image: Concrete and Specific

Filling-in also needs to happen with a group. We need a data point for the start of the work, if we want to be able to evaluate it at the end. But how can this be done efficiently? If I took the time to do a complete history with each member, we would never get to the studio art-making. Adapt the task of the filling-in to fit the size and particulars of the group you have.

One way is to offer a selection of items for group members to choose from and use them as prompts for check-ins. Examples of this might include simple musical instruments that they can use to make sounds or prompts to move into a simple posture or gesture. You can use a selection of stones or images on cards. Commercially prepared decks of cards depicting faces with an array of feelings, designed for use with children, are especially appealing. Also, multiple images of doors or windows can evoke a filling-in response from a group of adults. As someone who loves the sky and clouds, I might ask about the "internal weather" of group members. "What kind of animal are you today?" is a perennial winner with children. These methods take some forethought and preparation—gather the stones and bring the cards. Taking the time to have these supplies on hand will be beneficial. You can get a quick overview of the group and can make decisions about the move to the studio space from there.

An Individual Within a Group

Before clients can move into an art-making phase, it is fruitful for them to clarify their current, literal reality. They may need to externalize the problem so that it exists outside of themselves while remaining within their environment or context. If I have noticed metaphors or movements during the filling-in interview, I will mention those. Our goal is to examine the external impediments that people are experiencing, rather than attributing their difficulties to internal flaws.

STORY: The Heavy Burden

During the filling-in, a member of an expressive arts therapy group was saying how burdened she felt by the circumstances of her life. She repeated the words "burden" and "heavy load." Before we transitioned into the art studio, I asked her permission and then piled several relatively heavy floor pillows on her, one at a time, while naming some of the things she mentioned were burdening her. "This pillow might be your job. And these two are your kids who are always asking for your time and attention. These big, heavy ones are your husband and his needs. All these little ones are your school assignments." I waited a beat each time and then asked, "Does this feel right?" This externalization of the problem accomplishes two things: it allows my client to have a physical metaphor of the situation she described, a felt-sense. It also helps me see if my understanding is correct or at least in the right direction. We do not have to know what this means. But it is good enough to know that, yes, this is close to the feeling I have about my life situation. By creating this physical metaphor, it moves out of her—she can externalize it: "It isn't me, even though it belongs to me." It isn't that she is weak or inadequate, lazy, or crazy. The problem was that she was hauling a pile of boulders on her back.

While working with this woman in the middle of the studio, the other members witnessed, surrounding her, in a circle. They served as an amplifier and memory for the situation being explored. It is harder to deny what has happened when you have eight or nine people with you. It helps shift your story and can have important resonance with other group members. After such a piece of work, I ask the working member if she is ready to "take in" the people and look around the room to meet the eyes of the others. This helps to discharge any embarrassment or shame. Then I ask who in the group could relate to this story and how. It is most typical that everyone has some connection. People may have various perspectives, but rarely did anyone have no connection at all and nothing to say. Any specific story usually has some universal aspect to it. We all struggle in the human condition.

Now we had a theme for the whole group: what burdens you? This served as our focus and theme for that evening. This particular group had been together for some time; they could each follow the impulse to explore in whatever medium they chose. Participants would work individually for approximately 30–45 minutes before we reconvened to proceed to the next step.

The transition over the threshold into the next room, the studio, can be difficult for some new practitioners to initiate, especially if the client seems to have lots more to say. It is enough to let the client know that you have an understanding and are ready to move to the studio. Here are some possible questions that might help: "So, do I have it? Is this what is bothering you?" "Shall we see what the art has to say?" "Let's go into the studio and see what emerges." "Ready for something different?"

ROOM NUMBER TWO: THE STUDIO– THE ARTISTIC CONVERSATION

Moving into the Studio part of the session means doing, making, acting.

You cannot rely on tricks or techniques; abandon all formulae and recipes in favor of being present with this person. Allow yourself to be vulnerable, not knowing how you can help, but open and awake, relaxed but activated. Soften your belly and take a breath or two from there. Allow yourself to care. Cultivate an open-hearted curiosity about your client. Admit to yourself if you are scared, if you don't know what to do. This is often true for me, even now, 50+ years later. I take care of my fright by breathing and being as present as I can be (it's not about me). Then training and experience come to my aid. Oh! I know! I can ask, "What music you were listening to when your mom brought you in and you had on your headphones. It was rap? Who? Aha! What exactly do you like about that?" And away we go.

Several tasks are necessary in the Studio.

Task: Sensitize/Attune

The studio portion of the session has several subdivisions, the first of which is sensitizing activity. As adults in a modern world, our senses are often fallow and vastly underutilized compared to their capabilities. Sensitizing is giving time for the cells and systems to awaken, for the ears to open, and for the haptic intelligence of the fingers to come alive. It is time for the eyes to remember how sensitive they are to color, edges, and movement. Sensitizing allows the body to breathe down to the deep corners of the lungs, the diaphragm to relax and do its job, and the blood and oxygen flow to increase. Do you think this is merely a metaphor? It is not. As a personal example, I sometimes check my own oximeter: I can check the saturation of oxygen in my bloodstream before and after deep breathing or movement. It can increase by several percentage points. The skin warms when we move, bringing blood to the surface. When we move, we exercise the sense of balance and sense of the body in space, called proprioception. This also serves as an opportunity to come fully into the here and now. In the Counselor's Chairs, the story of distress refers to "there and then." How they were suffering when they were in their life-world environment. Now we have a fresh start. We allow all of our senses to awaken. If nothing else happens except becoming fully awake and aware in this portion, that alone might lead to some amazing opportunities for change: "I notice how I hold my shoulders up;" "I notice how I don't breathe;" "I notice there is a dull fear within me." These quotes from my clients are all wonderful beginnings or can be sufficient in themselves.

Usually (but not always), this activation is done in the medium you intend to use. Thus, I use movement as a sensitization for dance activities, some aspects of visual art for drawing or painting, working with the notion of 3D for sculpture, sound and silence for music, both instrumental and vocal. Using another sense as primary, in contrast to the main event, can be just as useful. For example, using body movement or drawing as a warm-up for writing is excellent. My bias is that bringing attention to the body is a good awakening for any artistic activity, since all require bodily movement. Adults can have a difficult time moving from ordinary reality into the imagination, so they need this warming-up, tuning-in.

Working with the senses helps create a kind of induction, a space for this transition to happen. People can certainly make art without moving into the imaginal realm. But that misses the point and feels more like "craft" or art class to me, doing a step-by-step with all outcomes being the same and no shift in consciousness. It is when the papier-mâché creature seems to come alive in the imagination, or the dance transforms you into a mermaid, or the drum song becomes a call to the grandmothers, that is potent because we moved from ordinary reality into another reality and different space. Paolo calls this the "alternative world" experience (Knill, 2005, p. 126). It can contain all we need. It is big enough to hold our sorrow and our losses. The sensitization or warm-up is the quickest way to enliven the senses, wake up the imagination, and allow metaphoric materials striving within us to find a form.

I can hardly emphasize enough how important adequate sensitizing is to a good outcome. I give ample examples of the sensitizing phase in the studio of each art discipline later in some detail (see Chapter 4). For now, consider that sensitizing or warming-up is a crucial step for your success. It leads to decentering, a distinguishing feature of the EGS model.

Task: Decenter

Decentering moves us from talking about it to doing something about it. It is "taking a leap and letting go of preconceptions," as Margo Fuchs-Knill wrote to me (personal communication, 2023).

Now that the person has had the opportunity to come into the present with all their attention and senses, we enter what Knill and Eberhart (2023) named the decentering phase. Decentering means moving away from focusing on the problem or being "centered" on the problem. We move away from the idea that the problem is at the center of our work and can begin to consider aspects of a better life without the problem. We move forward. It also means moving away from thinking and talking into doing and making; what we call *poiesis*. Thus, the emphasis is on activating the senses which think and speak in color and line, movement, sound, action, or composition and arrangement.

Decentering results in an aesthetic expression coming from the creative endeavor of the client. It offers a new perspective and resources for solutions. I will explicate these concepts in some detail later. Decentering is where you introduce the aesthetic challenge or puzzle, the experiment or exploration: the art problem. Your invitation is bespoke for your particular client and their particular problem. If the process you propose is too easy, it can be dismissed as "child's play." This is especially true if the clients are teenagers, too close to childhood to want to reach backward to a time of less independence and sophistication. If the process you propose seems too arduous, uncomfortable, or with little chance of success, with too many unknowns, that is also a barrier. Eberhart speaks of developing a "low threshold" in designing the task for the client, meaning it must be "easily accessible and, at the same, time claim the full presence of the client" (Atkins & Eberhart, 2014). If it is too difficult, it will be yet another expression of ineptitude, and immediately discouraging. This requires a light attitude, with curiosity and a sense of adventure.

Task: Aesthetic Analysis

This involves a careful looking at the artwork or whatever emerged in the Studio decentering. I will give detailed examples a bit later.

Third Room—Counselor's Chairs

The next and final room contains a conversation about the harvest— what did they learn, earn? What has changed? What they can take home. I'll detail this a bit later. The harvesting ends the session.

What Goes On in the Studio? A Closer Look at the Heart of the Matter
Methods of Decentering

In decentering, the imagination might catch fire and clients may have an experience of being in a waking dream. The image guides, allowing the paints and paper to be partners. Paolo refers to this as "alternative worlding" or the imaginal realm (Knill, 2017). It is being in service to the image, surrendering to the image. My experience is that this delicate and potent shift does not always happen. People must let go. When I see someone gazing at their clay, or dancing a slight bit to the painting, or mumbling to the installation, it might indicate that they are in the grips of the image. They have established a relationship to it and are in active communication with it. This may not always appear dramatic, but it often looks like they are concentrating and fully engaged. Their imagination has been captured. This is an important and necessary step if we are to have the power of the imagination as a helper and guide in our work.

The three types of decentering that Paolo describes are:

1. *Playing* with the art materials
2. Creating an *oeuvre* or *artwork*
3. Creating and/or participating in a *ritual.*

Let's look at each one.

The First Form of Decentering: Playing with Art Materials

Playing with art materials is a form of experimentation, a process without an expectation of an image emerging. The client experiences what the paint, clay, or dance movement can do. They are fiddling around with the art materials, and immersion in the materials can yield wonderful experiences.

This allows things to unfold and encourages full involvement. This is often the messiest and most unstructured type of decentering, necessary to allow for testing and observation. This experimentation and encounter with materials can be a welcome way to introduce the notion of the "happy accident" and allow the materials to participate in the making. This is the type of decentering to introduce when the client is hesitant to engage deeply with something or finds the whole art-making prospect intimidating.

I find this approach useful for certain clients, such as intellectuals, corporate employees, professors, scientists, military officers, or others who want to know what everything "means," and what I think about what they are doing and how this will help. Although highly successful in the outer world as measured by prestige or financial standing, they may need to let go of knowing. They may need to give up any notion of outcome and be invited to see what the materials can offer them as they play in the moment. In music, we may go from instrument to instrument, hearing what each can do, what kind of timbre it has, and what kind of body involvement is required to make it work. This drum requires a strong arm and back; this bell needs a delicate touch. I remember one student noticing that a certain rattle made a surprisingly robust sound and significant contribution to a group improv with little effort. "This might be good if someone had arthritis or was bedridden," she observed.

Examples of "playing in the arts" or experimenting with the art materials include all the sensitizing and warming-up processes in each discipline.

In visual arts, we can scribble, doodle, and drip paints, tear paper, glue, stamp, and print. We can fold, rip, or crumple wet paper. With clay, we can squish, twist, smash, poke, and roll. We can arrange things, build, or a hundred other actions.

In voice, we can babble, chant, make soundscapes, and engage in simple call-and-response games. We can speak in preverbal language, vocalizing, and making sounds with syntax, but no recognizable language. It was a favorite activity of one adult client to sing what she called "silly songs" that she made up on the spot. These were songs about her shoes or what she had for lunch or other details of daily life. They were usually sung in a high, child-like voice, bobbing her head from side to side, with a sing-song quality reminiscent of children's nursery rhymes with little prancing steps or skipping.

In instrumental music, we can play with instruments in unusual or non-ordinary ways. I prefer to have at least some non-ordinary instruments, home-made or "kitchen orchestra" type of sound-makers which deconstruct the notion of what a musical instrument is. Flowerpot gamelan, anyone?

In dance, the person may move freely with carefully chosen music. They may do body awareness activities, like responding to a list of movement words, or playing with the breath, or using props that support movement exploration. What movement wants to happen; following the impulse to move. How does the ribbon move, how do I move when I dance with it? They may work with the basic elements of dance movement, such as various axial or locomotor movements, but without the idea of making a dance. This is pure exploration; what can you find?

When we are playing with the material, no image or form is expected at all. It is sufficient to notice what is happening and manipulate or play with processes. Sometimes an image may appear, but this is not the aim. What they have done is left a strictly rational world behind in favor of exploring and receiving feedback from their senses and the rich stimulating opportunity offered by the art materials. This experience can have an important, even profound impact on the person. It is not a lesser activity than making a work; it is different.

STORY: Rain of Color

I was with a client who suffered from fibromyalgia who had worked with me for about a year. These were the days when some people thought it was psychosomatic, which felt demeaning to her. She was a serious woman with a serious high-level job and wanted to be taken seriously. She got better, then worse, and better again, a pattern typical for the course of recovery. Part of managing this disease is doing something, but not too much. Too much movement exacerbates the pain, yet no movement increases pain. Much of our work was done in dance/movement. The trick is to move a little all the time, gently, to keep moving. On this day, she came in depleted. She couldn't move without pain. That was discouraging. I suggested she lie down on the floor pillows, and I made a little pallet for her. Then I brought out the bin of bright chiffon scarves. She had played with them many times, they were well known to her. While she was lying down, I tossed a scarf high above her face. The lights illuminated the scarf. It was vivid and gorgeous. It drifted slowly down and landed softly on her face. "Was that ok?" I asked. "Oh yes, it was beautiful. Do more."

I took scarves, one at a time, and sailed them high overhead, allowing them to float slowly down. As several colors mingled, they created combinations and complementary schemes that she remarked upon. Some I repeated at her request. I slowly dragged the scarves off her face when several had landed. It was gentle and soft—a sensuous chiffon facial. This attention to the hues and shades of color allowed her to relax deeply and be nourished while her eyes were focused and engaged. We created fanciful names for the colors: "cinnamon toast," "overripe berry," "stormy cove." We laughed and "oohed" and "aahed." At the end of the session, she was more energized and in much better spirits and less pain. No art product had been made, but a deep excursion into the world of color still allowed her to leave her torment behind and float away on the colors of the rainbow, with very little effort. Her work was attention and the visual involvement that took place. This is one example of "playing with the art materials," in this case, color.

Playing with materials in group

Playing with art materials is a wonderful way to work with groups, especially at the beginning. Any basic element of any art discipline can be used for this "play with the materials" decentering approach.

In my introductory classes, I ask people to make a color square. The instructions: cover a piece of thick paper with one color of a creamy oil pastel; do not draw anything and do not leave any white space. Make a sample of this color. This is engaging, though it doesn't take long. Then, we contemplate the color and remember it in our lives: What specific memories does that exact color bring up? Where does this magic carpet of color take you? This meditation on color goes from coloring to storytelling, to writing, to poetic reduction, and then to a group poem. People are surprised by what emerges and are eager to share. The hardest part is getting participants to be simpler and do less.

In the domain of dance, getting non-dancers to stretch fully, change levels, move with acceleration, and make shapes is a way to warm up. Ask the group to move with an emphasis on one element of dance—body awareness, time, space, or motion. For example, locomotion—all the ways of getting from here to there. Or making shapes in space, or all the things they can do on the low level of the floor. This is dance movement exploration, but it is not dance-making.

The Second Form of Decentering: The Image/Oeuvre: Making an Artwork

Work at the EGS supports manipulating materials until a clear image emerges—an artwork. Paolo calls this the "work-oriented" or the "oeuvre-oriented" approach. Many people respond to something in the world, their personal world, or the greater world. They will work diligently until the piece takes shape. The approach to this type of session may indeed start with playing with materials. At a certain point, it becomes clear that a particular thing is being shaped. An image has emerged. Now they serve the image. The client is working toward an end: a dance or character, a scene or sketch, creating a musical piece, a song, or a painting. These are art research projects. The types of works that can be made are limited only by time, resources, and imagination. The more complex the work, the longer it might take, and it might involve several experiments along the way. It could take several appointments.

STORY: The Microbus

A teenage girl came to me because her boyfriend had died in an accident when hit by a drunk driver. She was a sweet and lovely girl with a seriously broken heart. She was depressed and having trouble in school in part because no one would honor her broken heart. No one to talk to and nowhere to go. Her mother had not approved of this relationship because he was a different ethnicity than the girl, so home was not a sanctuary for her grief either. She had another boyfriend now, but he was shallow compared to Quinn. After our initial meeting, where she shared her story of loss and grief, we went into the studio. I offered the idea of a reliquary, a container to hold some memento of her former boyfriend. She was interested in making something in his memory, but not that. I offered her the notion of making a triptych of photos and other ephemera from their relationship. She didn't like that either. How about a book with their story inside? No. As so often happens, a direction made itself known. They shared a dream of a life together: a VW microbus in which they would travel all over the states. It figured large in many of her memories of him—although they did not have this vehicle.

As she spoke, we both lit upon the idea of the bus as the image she wanted to create. This felt right, but how to proceed? Would it be a drawing or painting? As we scoured the studio for materials, her eyes fell upon a tissue box, full of tissues. It had the right scale and the right oblong shape. So that was the beginning. The two wanted their bus to be light blue, so she began a search for the just-right shade of baby blue. As she found paper fragments, she glued them over the surface of the box. The next time we met she finished the covering the box with the blue and began on the windows. Clear transparency paper was just right for the windows. The next time we had buttons of the right scale and color for the headlights and taillights. The time after that we needed wheels. As uncanny as this may seem, I had large metal badges from a drink-drive prevention campaign. I had four. So, soberly, those seemed perfect. Week-by-week, she created this tribute to their love. She remarked that she liked that it was still a tissue box, to catch her tears as she mourned him. When all the details were done, this "found and embellished" sculpture held as much as any reliquary or triptych could have done. We took it off the art table and placed it on a white plinth to appreciate it. She took photos. On the bottom of the box, she wrote a short poetic phrase. Satisfied with this project, she left feeling their relationship had been honored. It is my fervent belief that, like Romeo and Juliet, teenage lovers can be as ardent and committed as any. This humble tribute held and honored their love.

Image-making in Group

Often in group art-making, every individual makes their own piece and then we put them together in a grid or quilt or in some kind of tableau. During the course of a 15-year ExA group, many of our art experiments were displayed in gallery exhibits: rubber band dolls, blind contour portraits, tissue paper animals with aluminum foil armature, masks, and so much more.

If poetry has been the focus, we speak the poems we have written, one at a time, as a kind of poetry slam or open-mic reading. We do our one-minute dance solos as a recital. Sometimes, we all work on one piece. This can be in any art discipline. Murals can be spontaneous or with a theme. We give resources to students with image research—if the theme of a mural is spring we might look at some flowers and butterflies. If the theme is the ocean, we might research underwater plants and animals. This gives us some basis for the shapes and colors we might want to use. Or not! Large murals come together over time by putting the paper on the wall with the paints and brushes available. Then students or the public paint in response to what is there, and over time things emerge. The time can be an hour, an evening, a weekend or longer.

Working in silence

I usually ask my group members to work in silence. My rationale is that once we are engaged with the material, various things can occur. Every person is having a unique experience, we are both with ourselves and together. Working with the hands with concrete material draws us into our own senses and creative flow, our own imaginal world. So, if I am having a playful time and you are having a sad one, the chit-chat may inhibit the flow of your experience; it may stultify the full bloom of emotion, thought, or memory. Conversation might take me away from my sensory and somatic experience and inner imaginings, and into the room with others. Sometimes, though, it seems just right to have a kind of kaffeeklatch or quilting bee feeling, where we do chat with each other—the kids or grandkids, the travel adventures, stories from school. This can also act as a kind of backstory glue for the relationships in a group. When the group is new the explorations can help the members get to know one another.

As the facilitator, you make the call. What would best serve the clients and the project at hand? Working in silence or with some drumming or music can create a sonic environment and that can help.

Stephen Levine says we must not act as a "demiurge," that creature in charge of the creation of the whole universe (Stephen Levine, 2005, p. 40). We do not want to control the materials and impose our will upon them. I love this humble stance. The paint and paper are your partners. Move or sing until you have made your way over to the imaginal realm, to the play-space, to the "other world" where the paintbrush can speak. Sensitization and warming up can accomplish this.

Our job is to take *aesthetic responsibility* for the experience, to help assist the client in having a satisfying experience, even if obstacles are encountered. This is part of our ethos. Some aspects of this endeavor should be enjoyable. Help people discover that. Your full attendance is critical. Your function as a witness is valuable even if you do not act as an assistant in any other way. Get things people need, like scissors, glue, or that drum, so they can stay engaged. Working like a midwife, you assist in a physical way to get this art-baby born. If they need help with some small technique ("I can't get the eyes in the right place") be the "third hand" as Cathy Moon describes it (Moon & Lachman-Chapin, 2001). Assist.

The Third Form of Decentering: Ritual

Our definition of ritual in this context is simple actions that everyone can do together, usually with an atmosphere of reverence or celebration. In my practice, the person or group determines the need for a ritual or ceremony. It is a response to some event in the life of the group or a group member. These are most often done to recognize a significant passage or turning point, such as a graduation, a birth, a death, a relocation, or some personal success, especially one that changes a person's status. The group creates the ritual. Sometimes in communities, they participate in a ritual that was designed for them—such as the opening or closing of a conference or graduation ceremony. Community members may have input on the design of these celebrations.

STORY: Moving from One Year to the Next

No matter where we were, be it outside in the woods, at the beach, in the studio, or on Zoom, when the first year had been completed, the final presentations had been made, and we were ready to close studies for the summer, we used a ritual. Each time, it had the same basic elements. An archway or some kind of passageway was found or created. One year in a wood, students bent branches of young trees to create an arch and prepared the ground. Last year, we draped long sparkly scarves over some wires suspended from the ceiling. The Zoomers had been asked to find their own doorway or arch. We had put the room in order and made every preparation to have no distractions.

Everyone knew the script. Students found two objects: one for something they would leave behind as they moved forward in their studies and another representing something they wanted to bring with them as they went on. People were silent before we began. I drummed the entire time once the ritual had begun. One-by-one, each student came to the opening of the arch and set down the first object, while saying aloud, "I leave [the object and what it holds for them] behind," and walked through the doorway or arch. Holding up the second object, they said, "I take [the object and what it holds for them] with me." When everyone had gone through the drumming ended. We were silent for a time. Finally, the spell was broken, and we went home.

In Knill's writing about ritual in *Minstrels of Soul* (Knill *et al.*, 1996), he is speaking about the ritual of the expressive arts therapy session itself, the *rites of restoration*. He also refers to the ritual of art-making *per se*. These activities are outside of everyday life, the life of your professional occupation and house-holder duties, the job of child-rearing, and so forth. Thus, they require markers; a beginning, middle, and end. There is a certain sameness to the structure of these events, something to be relied upon. The practitioner constructs and conducts the proceedings.

There is another type of ritual that can be considered a ritual decentering: the ritual constructed or conducted by the client. These rituals are actions taken to serve the client's concerns or community concerns. They might mark some nodal point in the life of the person or group. "I quit my job," "It's time for holidays," "I was admitted to law school," "My divorce is final," "School is over," "I am entering menopause," "My mother died," "We bought a new house." We celebrate these and more in my studio. In my studio, the individual client and I usually create them together on the spot. We talk it out a bit, to be certain that we understand what the relative flow of time might be. We discuss the props that we need, if any. It usually involves some words or actions, perhaps sage or incense or a candle to evoke a kind of special ambiance. Often an object or objects are used, a stone or natural thing like a seed pod or shell, perhaps a small sculpture or image they have created. There is a feeling of reverence. Sometimes I am a participant, sometimes a witness.

STORY: The River Styx

A woman came to me after her mother died. Her grief was not immobilizing or overwhelming her but it was taking up a significant portion of her inner life. She had not told anyone the whole story of her relationship with her mother, which was complex and difficult but not without redemption. She was not married or partnered, was a named partner in her law firm, and felt she had leaned upon her friends enough. So, she came to me wanting to change her relationship with this loss. In that studio, I had a large carpet-covered box/bolster. It was approximately six feet long, three feet wide, and two feet high. Can you see it? It was heavy. I guess it had been part of a display in a retail store, one of the things that Danny, my younger brother introduced in the Preface, gave me.

As we talked through the ritual we were going to create, I grabbed a large, black velvet cloth and laid it on the bolster as a possible prop to be used in some way, maybe. I didn't know what would happen with this, but it seemed like a good prop for any work dealing with a death. I chose a requiem for the music system. We lit a couple of candles on my tall wrought iron candle holders, which she had placed just so. As she considered the layout of the studio, she thought she would start with the bolster in another location and started to push the heavy bolster toward the preferred location. The moment she did that, it instantly turned into a coffin for both of us. She unfurled the black velvet, completely covered the box with it, and began to push. As she pushed, the bolster moved, but only with great effort, slowly. She was going to cross the River Styx. She pushed and wept. It moved toward the other bank of the river, largo. She took her time, but the task couldn't have been done quickly in any event. Each push required her to position her feet, legs, and back to handle the weight of the bolster/coffin. One pass across the floor had helped her contact her grief in a muscular and embodied way. She could feel and experience the depth and weight of this sadness and the significance of the loss of her mother. At the end of the journey, the black velvet was removed and we sat once again on the ordinary bolster to conclude the session.

A second example:

STORY: House Blessing

A friend had just purchased a new house. She had rented for a long time after her divorce, so this was a big step. I went over with another friend to see it and murmured approvals. After inspecting all the rooms and yard, we decided we would have a house blessing. I used a long branch of leaves as a wand and my friend held a burning bowl of sage. We went to each doorway, and I said words to bless that particular doorway, as I waved the branch in and around the opening. We were solemn, but not stiff, some things were funny. We stayed with the form. Afterwards, we had a meal, and pronounced the house blessing "satisfactory." This spontaneous ritual created a moment, a special memory to commemorate this new phase of her life.

Group ritual

STORY: Holy Water

A training class had been together for a year and we were parting for the summer. We decided to have a formal toast. The students chose water as the libation. We set up a centerpiece with flowers and candles. There were eight women in the group and at each place setting there was a "crystal" goblet. A pitcher filled with water was in the center. After the ringing of a bell, each woman held the pitcher and said a wish or a blessing for our time apart. We imagined that it "went into" the water. After it had made the rounds, we filled our glasses. Then we drank this dedicated water together. We sat for a few moments, looking around the circle at the faces we would miss over the summertime. I rang my ting-shas. A feeling of love, friendship, and unity filled us. Our faces were open and warm. We left the room in silence. This marked the end of our year together.

WORKING WITH THE EMERGING IMAGE
The Third

Paolo referred to the emergent image as the third "person" in the room (Knill *et al.*, 1996). He wrote about its emergence as akin to a spiritual experience, something ineffable. Certainly, not all image-making results in such a dramatic occurrence. When a person works with the material at hand, something develops. It can hold clues to the inner resources of the person, which is useful. It can be worked with in the methods I describe below. So, the object is also called the Third. The Third, then, refers to both the object and an event. When it comes as a complete vision, little needs to be done to gather the fruits of this manifestation. Often, it is best to allow the messages and wisdom of the image to drop gently into the lap of the client. The only requirement is being receptive. People may feel things deeply in the body and must wait for that experience to be translated into words, if it can be. My job is to remain present and quiet, not mute, but also not bustling with questions, poking and prodding. The Third is felt. Tears often accompany this experience.

STORY: The Crone Came

In a workshop with Paolo at a San Francisco conference, an image grabbed me so strongly that I had to take a little nap, right there in the workshop. We were moving and developing a character. My character, the Old Woman, came on so strong, it was shocking. I was in my 40s at the time and this Crone character was not entirely welcome. The message she brought touched me deeply; it was personal and profound. While others continued to move and work, I was in a corner, napping for a few minutes. Fortunately, the room was large, and this did not disturb others. Such is the result of the Third as an event. I could not avoid it, unless I popped out of the workshop experience and went to the bathroom or other distraction. No, I wanted to stay in with the image and the group, but it took time to digest. You could say the image knocked me out.

Most work doesn't come from this type of transcendent event. Still, the images and experiences that develop can have a significant influence on the person, can carry important messages, can touch them, and point to resources.

Crystallization Theory

During studio time, numerous methods and techniques help the client deepen their contact and relationship with the image beyond completing the work or project itself. These are not always necessary, but they may allow a client to have the fullest possible experience of their efforts. Perhaps the best outcome is *crystallization*—the coalescence of our psychic material into an image (Knill *et al.*, 1996).

An image comes into being from playing with the materials. It emerges and holds the entire situation of the client, like a hologram. The image arrives, it stands up, and tells its story. An entity, with its name and place of origin, its message. It comes as a visitation or even a vision. It is powerful and cannot be avoided, gripping a person, and capturing and holding their attention. It contains the entire situation of the client—it crystallizes the issue. Now the client can see the externalized situation, held by the artwork.

The crystallization event results in a tremendous "aha!" as it comes into sharp focus. It takes place between the therapist and the client. "Crystallization theory finds interpretation and meaning phenomenologically, through artistic differentiation in a poiesis indigenous to art that is, in words that are imaginative, particular and precise" (Knill, 1994, p. 322). This feels like a surprise; the sharp intake of breath. Your issue is externalized, and now you are with it, it is no longer inside you. Crystallization is a result of "the basic human or drive to crystallize psychic material; that is to move toward optimal clarity and precision of feeling and thought" (Knill *et al.*, 1996). It is satisfying to have the canvas or dance or whatever medium you were using suddenly reflect your primary concern, in clear and beautiful imagery. Sometimes this requires additional help.

Serve the Image

We think of the image as an entity. Or, so as not to sound crazed, as having a kind of life or presence that is not merely a projection of the artist. At some point, an image begins to emerge; something is happening. It has its own energy, it is a thing by itself. When that occurs, we surrender to the imaginal reality, we serve that image. What does it want or require? What should happen next? The logic of the imagination now can assist: does the robot need two eyes or just one? Does the evil guy win this time or is he thwarted? This is the logic of the imagination, not of literal reality (Knill, 2017). If we have crossed the threshold into the world of the imagination, then it is imagination that guides and decides. We usually know when it is complete. Or the clock might tell us it is time to stop.

Framing

Framing refers to the instruction that the facilitator gives concerning the restrictions or limits of the experiment or project. Not anything goes; not everything is available. It is a way to shape the art-making portion of the session. This presents a type of "art problem." Each session is a kind of art-based research. This is novel and stimulates creative action. It requires limits. We call those limits and agreements the frame.

Clients usually look to me to provide a task or frame for the art-making. For example, shall we paint or shall we dance? This is a mutually agreed-upon task, but I am usually in charge of shaping it. I make suggestions based on my observation in the filling-in and I also ask directly, "What appeals to you today, big paper or small?" "The relationship with your boss might be explored in a role-play, what do you say?" I take a new client around the studio pointing out the various options—the drums, the drawers of paper, the paint cart, the costume rack. "What strikes a note, what grabs your attention?" Clients often ask, "What shall I do?" even when they know what medium they would like to work in. This is part of our high sensitivity—we need to create on the spot an art task, a "directive," and an art challenge. It could be close to their story (theme-close) or not connected to their story at all (theme-far). New clients frequently create something to "show me" their pain; something that helps them experience their painful situation in a metaphoric way. "This is my eating disorder." "This is my grief." Some examples of this are breaking a scale or working on a dinner plate for an eating disorder; making a reliquary for a dead friend or loved one or writing them a letter. These things have their place. We meet people where they are. There is a learning curve to becoming a good ExA client! Yes, we are learning from each other. They learn how to get the most out of their time with us, and we learn about their lives and their inner resources. This type of activity can let someone know you are interested in the shape of their suffering and that you will hear them. At some point in the course of therapy other choices will lend more potency.

STORY: Diptych of an Authentic Life

She was feeling stuck in her own creative life, although she was satisfied with her work as a costume designer at a local theater. This was our first working meeting. We previously had an interview to see if the way I work, my schedule, and my fees were acceptable to her, but this was our first working session. She was a professional woman in her late 50s, with a history of gambling and perfectionism. Because of the COVID-19 pandemic, we were working virtually. During the filling-in, themes of interest were discussed. I suggested several questions we might pursue, telling her that this was a collaboration, and I wanted her input. As we turned over the possibilities, we discovered all the themes were a kind of grief—a loss of either an actual thing, an ideal, or an opportunity. She decided that the overarching theme was the life she was raised to live versus the path that she had discovered for herself, and the tensions between them. This sounded right to us both.

She decided to create a piece that would hold both themes. I asked her to get some art materials (which we had previously discussed) and to tip the camera so I could see her hands working. I told her I would remain silent for the time it took to complete this small art task.

She gathered her materials and began to work. She chose the form of a diptych, one piece with two equal sections. As the collage took shape, we looked at it carefully in an Aesthetic Analysis. There were several unusual qualities of the materials she chose and the way she used them. Naming this delighted her. She was surprised that I had seen so much as I watched the action of her hands. I could report back to her several noticings about her process, even though the session was virtual. But the big "aha" was that this first attempt gave her an overview of her entire situation—her conservative family life and the self-determined artistic life she was choosing. Everything about this image told the story, from the form of the diptych, to the materials used and the composition. The satisfying surprise is an excellent example of crystallization. There it was... her life's largest metaphor contained in this small piece of art.

Dialogue with the Image

Dialogue means a two-way conversation. The client speaks to the clay piece, sculpture, painting, or object, then we listen for its voice to speak back. Ask people not to talk *about* the object but speak to it and have the object speak back and tell them things in the voice of the Other. For many, it can be tough to even get the concept, and tougher yet to do. Nevertheless, persist. As a kind of priming the pump of imagination, I might say, "I hear the horse talking. It says..." This requires a surrender and a willingness to play. Think of the sculpture or painting as a puppet. Change the voice, like you would for a puppet. At its most basic, puppetry is animating an inanimate object, usually to tell a story or forward some action. Shaun McNiff wrote of dialogue with the image early on: "When talking with an image, I engage it as a new arrival in my life and I continuously acknowledge and discern its physical presence" (McNiff, 1992, p. 105).

STORY: Dialogue with Face of Yellow and Blue (An Example from My Illuminated Journal)

An image caught my eye; an abstract face painted yellow and blue, holding a book also of yellow and blue. I pasted it into my journal. Some time later, I decided it was so striking and I was so attracted to it, I wanted to see what it might reveal about itself and its relationship to me.

Dialogue with the Face of Yellow and Blue:

JGE: Hello, Face of Yellow and Blue. You came to me. Why?

Y&B: I came because you asked me to.

JGE: I don't remember doing that.

Y&B: It was indirect. You struggle in your mind whether to do your writing or to attend to others. It is easier for you to take care of the needs of others than to show up for yourself and your work. You prioritize others.

JGE: I suppose that's true. Oldest and only sister of five brothers, Mormon family—role of the female, old habits, and so forth.

Y&B: New habits can be born. In fact, you have the discipline of a dancer at your disposal when you call upon it.

JGE: Also true. But it feels pretty hidden, and rusty, and out of reach right now.

Y&B: Do you see the book I hold? A book of yellow and blue—half in shadow, half in sunlight. Very much like your creative process. You don't have to abandon the care of others to pursue your own work.

JGE: It's hard to keep the balance. I get discouraged. Appointments and commitments take over my calendar. Plus when it comes to my own work, I can be lazy.

Y&B: You must plan your time. That is where your discipline comes in. You can be organized for yourself as well as for others. You can bring your "A" game for yourself as well as for others.

JGE: Hmmm. I seem to have no real refutation for that. I guess I'll just let that idea percolate and see what happens.

Y&B: Percolating equals procrastinating. That is not enough; thinking and feeling and waiting and wanting are not sufficient. Make a concrete plan, make an appointment with yourself. Keep it like you keep other appointments. You must move into action with yourself.

JGE: Okay. Yeah, I understand, and I get it. Thank you, Face of Yellow and Blue. Sound advice.

Y&B: Don't think I will merely disappear. I will be attending to your progress.

JGE: Like Big Brother?

Y&B: No, like Anam Cara, the friend of your soul.

Superimposition

In the graphics, digital, and photographic arts, superimposition refers to laying something on top of something else, so both are still seen. In the expressive arts studio, superimposition refers to any action that is additive to an original artwork, often performative work. In music, an example might be sampling or a mash-up, layering sounds over the original. In dance, it can be adding music, text, costumes, lights, or other elements to the original score. In theater, it can be all of the above as well as additional characters, scenery, soundtrack, or text. See an example of superimposition in the story below.

STORY: Pinky Does a Dance

A woman in her early 30s came to me with body image troubles. A serious and scholarly person, she had struggled with an eating disorder for years, but her appetite and eating had returned to a healthier state. Now the struggle was accepting her body; she wanted to feel better about herself physically. As she moved to the decentering phase, she was searching for lightness. She was trying to find the physical expression of light emotions, maybe happiness or joy. Her shoulders bounced up and down, and that led to some skipping and intermittent, small running steps. In this case, she wanted me to witness only, but I could comment on what I observed. I spoke about the quick and light gesture of the shoulders and feet. Her fingertips flicked and her wrists flexed and relaxed in a quick rhythm. She bobbed her head and her hips moved right to left in small wiggles. Her whole body eventually took on a bouncy motif. As she came to the end, she was smiling broadly and came back to me from the dance space.

Talking about the movement, we wondered if I had any music that would support this happy little dance. I thought of Penguin Cafe, which was light-hearted music, and not too fast. She loved it. She tried again for one or two minutes to allow the music to support her, without pushing. That was big fun for her, and the session ended here. In the next session, the urge to move with light and cheery gestures remained a desire, so we used the music we had found, and this time she wanted to add a piece or two of costuming—to bring this sweet little dance into focus even more. Pink was the color. It had the "just-right" feel to it. A voluminous pink boa made an appearance. Each time we added a layer to the dance, it added a layer of gravitas to the endeavor. Serious play. We were dance-making. She had several takes to get it just right—no take over about two minutes. The superimposition helped this serious woman realize something new in her repertory of movement themes: something sweet, light-hearted, and cheerful. I believe that working with these themes for several visits and adding the superimposed elements helped give her time to accept this important theme. It might have been too big a leap to do all at once, might have felt strained and false rather than organic and authentic. Doing it a little at a time, she could grow into the message of the sweet pink happy dance.

Intermodal Transfer

This means moving from one primary communication modality or sense to another, such as moving from a full-body kinesthetic sense like dance or theater, to a primarily visual one, like drawing or painting. Moving from a poem to a painting or dance is another example. An intermodal transfer can be made from any communication modality to any other communication modality because all the senses are always present in any art communication. Put another way, you can go from any art discipline to any other art discipline. There is rhythm in painting, movement in pottery, colors can be loud or soft, lending an aural dimension to primarily visual work. Find the elements or qualities of the first art discipline and see if they are good transfer vehicles. Are the colors in the painting bright or dark? How might the voice make bright sounds or dark sounds? Are there rhythmic, repeating elements? Can that transfer to the feet? I have always found that people can do this easily, returning to the synesthesia of our infancy, especially if I point out a few possible points of entry into the transfer from one discipline to another. In my Liberty Station studio, I had hand-painted silk curtains from floor to ceiling. There was a panel with bright reds, oranges, and yellows. The design motifs were roughly like fire, little flames. Another panel was light blues and light greens, with undulating lines, watery and wave-like. Even with completely new students, it was possible to have them "sing" the curtains. The only prep was for us, together, to notice the bright colors versus the soft colors, the sharp design elements versus the smooth and wavy elements. This never failed. Then I could ask them to add movement—even with just their arms. The red curtain resulted in flicking and punching movement, the blue curtain in wavy and undulant movement; the red curtain was faster and more energetic, and the blue curtain was gentler. People will do this effortlessly when given the least bit of instruction.

Example of an intermodal transfer:

STORY: Lover Man Where Can You Be?

We had been writing poetry during the Institute class. After reading a poem to her absent lover, a class member mentioned how much she missed him, and how her sexuality had suffered because she had no one to receive her. "Would you like to dance it?" I asked. "Yes!" she said Suddenly, the studio was a flurry of activity: people scurrying everywhere setting up a scene, a boudoir of sorts with sumptuous fabrics of velvet and silk, adding feathers and beads, adjusting the lighting. The entire class was involved and all the elements were added simultaneously, people shouting to each other, "Get the fur," "...and the velvet curtain!" Meanwhile, the poet/dancer was at the costume rack, adjusting her clothing into something "more comfortable," and conferring with peers as to the best soundtrack for her exploration. When we had settled on the music, she proceeded to give a steamy rendition of a lover's longing. This was first an intermodal transfer from poetry to performance, and then a great superimposition. It was as satisfying to the whole class as it was for her. The poetry held the image, the performance gave it embodied power.

Intermodal transfers are not required for every session. It is most useful when the first effort is good, something is coming, but something is missing. In that case, examine the first offering, see what other art disciplines are implied. Is there a bird? Maybe it has a song. Is there a door? Step through it. This transfer from one communication modality to another usually brings something new and adds to the first image.

Takes

A "take" is going once through the score or a specific section of the score. This technique is used with performative material. Most often, after the first time through or first take, the person or group receives feedback from various witnesses about what could be improved and what might be best left out. Then the performers do a "take two." When working with the students at the EGS, I will do several takes, depending on the complexity of the score, or takes of the various pieces: the encore or this particular duet. Even in small groups, people can be encouraged to do a take two, especially if something falls short of their best effort. This is when the voice can be enhanced, as in, "Why not stand so your diaphragm and breath can support your voice? Let's try that." Movement or music can be edited, for example eliminating the big drum in favor of a smaller one or deciding to have a soloist perform the opening movement instead of the quartet. The "takes" move the effort of the artists in the direction of clarity and strength of the image. It brings things into focus. It is always a collaborative effort.

Reduction/Expansion (Microscope/Telescope)

It is possible to reduce or expand any work. This can mean going from a small painting to a giant one (or the other way around), or a big looping dance move to the same gestures in an axial stance. Commonly, I ask people to stand and share their poetic utterances in full voice. "I want to hear you in the back." Poetic reduction is a fine example—eliminate all the unnecessary words and write it again. Boil away the excess. Get to the essence, then you can add words back in the language of the senses—what is the fragrance or odor in the poem? What sound is present? What quality of light? Adding these words would be an expansion of the original.

I call this the "telescope" and "microscope." Step back and look from a distance; the image may take a distinct shape obscured when looking closer. If you want to see the details, you can step closer. This can lead to further work: if the microscope reveals a tiny opening, go through it. Example of the microscopic details opening up:

STORY: The Microscope and Red Dot Aperture

She had painted a complex abstract with the idea of exploring some aspect of her life. As we looked at it together, we noticed a red dot. To me, it held the same attitude as the red-tipped push pins that get stuck into a map to say, "You are here." We examined the entire piece but kept coming back to the red dot. So, I asked her to enter the red dot, to go through it as an aperture or as the rabbit hole in Alice in Wonderland. See what was inside or on the other side. This led to an examination of smallness—a theme for her. As well as painting the red dot as the central image, she moved with the image. Making her body small, squeezing it into a tiny shape, feeling crowded and crushed helped her experience the sense of constraint she felt in her primary relationship. It was one thing to know it "in her head," she said, but another thing to feel it in her body. This gave her three-dimensional and embodied knowing. It informed her.

Example of the telescope opening up details:

STORY: The Telescope and the Compass Rose

In a recent training group I asked students to make an exploratory collage I call the Compass Rose—which is the symbol or legend on a map that points to North, South, East, and West. They had been introducing themselves and this was a further way to share what directions their lives had taken and the journey they had been on before coming to the Institute. We were practicing the Aesthetic Analysis, the challenge of phenomenology, staying on the surface looking at what is actually there, what you can point to. After doing this, I asked the class to turn the piece upside down and in other directions to change the perspectives. From the back of the room came a yelp, and I could see why from across the studio. When her Compass Rose was turned upside down, an undeniable creature was smiling back at the artist, as if it had been put there intentionally. This happy accident now became the focus of her inquiry. Who was this, what did they have to say?

FEEDBACK AND VALIDATION
Five Types of Feedback.

Paolo said every expressing person deserves feedback (Knill *et al.*, 1996). Feedback, as I am using it here, arises from the aesthetic experience and perspective of the witness. It has to do with how the offering was received, not a critique of the offering. When someone performs, or a visual piece is seen, there can arise within the viewer or witness a feeling of being moved, or touched—this is what Knill called the *aesthetic response*. We transform the old critique session that focuses on what failed and did not work into a focus on what works, "from a position of aesthetic responsibility toward the emerging work." In my studio, I use five types of feedback: artistic-homage, emotional-aesthetic, phenomenological-descriptive, what I learned, and what surprised me.

Artistic-Homage Feedback

Artistic-homage feedback is a small artwork generated as a response to the client's piece. Homage means honoring or respecting someone or something, praising. This type of feedback demonstrates that respect. You might "dance back" some portion of a dance performance. Of course, you can give dance movement feedback to other artworks like paintings or poetry. Other forms of artistic-homage feedback include a short poem, or song, a quick sketch, or some musical phrase. It also is effective to repeat some of the words of the performer as a chorus or chant.

Emotional-Aesthetic Feedback

Emotional-aesthetic feedback refers to any feeling or emotion that the witness felt during the sharing of the piece; emotions felt while in the presence of the artwork. "When you did... I felt..." This can include everything from "It moved me," to "I was scared when you went under the table," or "This large, bright blue splash reminds me of the beach, and I feel happy."

Phenomenological-Descriptive Feedback

Phenomenological-descriptive feedback means describing what you saw, heard, or felt. Although obvious to others, performers do not track everything they do when performing, nor see everything they have created in a visual piece. Thus, saying what you saw or heard provides great concrete feedback. "I saw those great leaps and then the toes wiggling." This can bring a great surprise, even if it only confirms that you were engaged.

What I Learned

Delightful and informative, this feedback form is especially useful in exam situations, but can be used at any time.

What Surprised Me
Give voice to the things that are unexpected.

These are merely examples of methods used to expand and intensify the client's contact with the work. I encourage you to be fully present and trust what wants to happen. Find your own responsive actions. Make up your own frames and structures.

Honoring the Image
The following vignette illustrates how a seemingly trivial dot can be "honored" as a serious artistic event.

STORY: The Amazing Dot
I had an individual session scheduled with a reluctant young man. He came to the appointment, slouching into the room and his resentment was visible. I was unsure of myself. Most of the teens I worked with did like me, at least. He made it clear I was no favorite of his. I offered him a blank piece of paper and an array of pencils and markers. Looking back, I would not offer such an open-ended, unstructured frame now. I would have offered a smaller frame, or done something with him, or offered something that had more shaping. But then I was beginning and that was a model I knew. He took a regular pencil from the pile of choices and in a quick and spontaneous gesture he jammed the pencil down on the paper, leaving one dark mark. So forceful was his gesture, it left little crumbs of graphite. He looked at me triumphantly, with chin held high, eyes narrow, face defiant, as if to say "There! Whadda ya think that means?"

I had many feelings—I was a bit shocked. It was a quick, powerful gesture. I was slightly anxious—not that I feared him, there were people right outside the door if things became rough, but how to respond to his question? I had no idea what to do. So I took my time. I took a deliberate slow breath. I looked at the mark closely. I saw the tiny graphite crumbs. The force of the mark made a little dent in the paper. Then I saw, to my utter surprise, that this gesture had somehow landed in the dead center of the page. I wasn't certain he had even looked at the paper when he slammed the pencil into it. Yet, there it was, as if measured. So my first comment was, "Look! It is in the exact middle. Wow!" Now he also looked. He became interested and considered his mark. "That is incredible," I said. "How did you manage that?" I didn't expect an answer, but this gave me time. I talked about the force of the mark; how bold and strong it was. He was looking at the mark. I was on a roll. I said how tiny the mark was, given the size of the paper. How, being in the exact center, it might want to be noticed, maybe even admired. That was when I won him over. Now his face softened.

That was my cue to give the dot a narrative, about being lonely there in the middle of the big page, with no other marks close by. He entered and we discussed the life of the mark. It had an uncanny parallel to his own. At the end of our session, we found a place on the wall that was "just right" to honor what we called The Dot. He was warm and friendly when he left. We didn't make great art, but we had an aesthetic experience and made a great start to a therapeutic relationship. Take what is given and treat each effort with love and respect. Take your time. I made a therapeutic relationship that day by slowing down and not assuming that the dot was a waste of my time. I accepted what he did as our material.

Curation as Validation

If a work has emerged, it needs to be treated with respect. We curate it as a means of validating the work itself and, by extension, the author of the work (Knill *et al.*, 1996). The curatorial process involves selecting artwork for exhibition, or content for inclusion in a collection of poetry, or otherwise choosing things that fit the group's mission or aesthetic. It generally connotes a winnowing, an editing process, so the most shining examples remain. It also implies that attention will be given to how and where an object is viewed. This culminating experience is an exciting activity, one filled with delight. At the end of an expressive arts class, we arrange the objects that emerged with some care. At the end of a course of therapy we have a kind of gallery show to celebrate what occurred.

Paolo believed that validating both the process and the product of art-making efforts serves multiple objectives. By validating a piece, one endorses the process in which it was created, as well as the piece itself. It honors the fracture of the work, meaning how it was made, the method and material. In this way, the piece and the person who made it are given dignity. It reinforces the value and worth of the activity. It honors the product and its contribution to the overall work of change. Validation says that what the client did was worthwhile and, by association, the client is worthwhile. One can do this with an individual client, but also with groups, small and large.

When you validate the work you treat it as an art product, rather than a test or psychological diagnostic. This choice continues to keep the art product in the domain of art, aesthetics, and metaphor instead of slipping into the domain of psychology, as this change would be detrimental to our arts-based way of working. Art is art, no matter who makes it or where it takes place—a school, a doctor's office, an artist's studio, a kindergarten, or the street. It remains a product in the domain of art. It must always be treated as art, that is, seen as art. This is the *continuity principle* Knill *et al.*, (1996) are referring to—keeping the art and all that transpires with it in the aesthetic domain, not transporting it to another domain. It is important to examine ideas and objects within the context of their origin. Thus, curation takes a tradition of the art studios and galleries and uses it in the expressive arts context, with an expressive arts attitude, keeping us within the domain of arts and aesthetics.

Paolo asks, "How do you receive this work? You are gifted with its presence; how do you receive it?" Create a place for the objects to be received. But how can we do this? How should the ExA practitioner proceed? We don't want to overtly praise the person or the project. We know that praise can be discarded and easily comes off as being insincere or fawning. "You want me to feel better but telling me my painting is good will not do it." It also may go against the client's own feeling about the project. If they dislike it so much and you "love it" you might not be trustworthy. You could be trying to flatter; perhaps you are insincere or easily fooled.

In "The Studios" section of Chapter 4, we will explore how to name and talk about the work in artistic and aesthetic terms, keeping the process grounded in artistic tradition. Is there anything beyond that?

Depending upon what has emerged, the practitioner can raise the level of interest by "honoring" the efforts. The act of honoring demonstrates the respect, the interest, the open-hearted curiosity that the facilitator is experiencing toward the artwork.

Strategies like these are not completely spontaneous. Have the needed equipment and supplies on hand. In addition, you should be familiar enough with these procedures to make them second nature. "Oh, let's put it on the easel." Or "If I turn the light like this, we can see it better." Or "I would like to see how that works when we move the chair to the center of the room and have everyone else step back. What do you think?" I have dozens of examples of how my taking initiative with suggesting these moves has a powerful impact on the person working. These actions communicate the fact that I take them seriously as art-makers (which I do) and I take their product as worthy of considerable attention (which I do). I also know they might not have the experience in the arts to know how to do justice to the work. That is our job.

Yes, we might also do this during the decentering and art-making processes. In superimposition we add music and perhaps a costume piece to the dance. We add a prop to the monologue. We reconfigure the room around to create a more conducive environment for the activity we are engaged in. We watch from a certain perspective: "Stand here in the stairwell and listen while I sing at the bottom." These superimpositions and finding the just-right placement are part of the work. I don't mean to make a bright line demarcation between that and the notion of curation. However, curation usually occurs when the work has emerged and is considered "finished." We want to honor it, see it better, and share it.

Speaking of sharing: Knill asks, "Does the work want to be shared?" There is an ethical question here. Having people share their work in various venues and capacities demands that we do not abuse the work nor the author of it. Sometimes even a fabulous thing is not for sharing. When I ask a client/student to consider sharing a piece either in our annual exhibit or in another way, I take the time to make careful inquiry. Besides making sure all the release paperwork is in order, we talk with the image. "Are you ready to be seen by the eyes of the Other/Strangers?"

STORY: Danish Masked Ball

At the Expressive Arts Spring Symposium in Denmark in the early 2000s, the Danish Institute hosted. During the four-day symposium, everyone attending the symposium had taken a full-day workshop on making plaster masks and performing with them. This method of mask-making involves wet plaster strips laid on the face until dry. When the masks come off they are embellished. At the closing ceremony, all the masks, 80 or so, were placed around the centerpiece in the large community hall. It was sumptuous with flowers, candles, colorful scarves, and these rich, vivid masks. As we moved around the center, music was playing and every person picked up a mask, but not their own. We moved and danced together in the big room, meeting our mask as danced by someone else. I could see myself coming toward me. It was bewitching. We danced for a long time; it was a big group in a big room. At the end, we unmasked, then carefully placed the masks around the centerpiece. We then proceeded to close the symposium.

Each studio requires its own manner of curation. I discuss specifics of each art discipline in Chapter 4 on the studios.

AESTHETIC ANALYSIS

In the Studio portion of the session, the final task is the Aesthetic Analysis. This is a sensitive activity where the work is looked at carefully. It is reminiscent of the critique in studio arts, but serves a different purpose, as we shall discover.

SuPER

Knill's acronym, SuPER, assists you in remembering all the ways you can encounter and deconstruct the art-making experience and the emergent object to encounter the message and significance it might bring (Knill,

2005). It is a time to have surprises and the sweet moment of "Aha!" It is the time to consider what happened from the aesthetic point of view.

- Surface: This refers to looking at what is concretely present in the language of the art discipline used. The client has the opportunity to describe their work phenomenologically, and "through this description, the client gains additional perspectives about the work of art" (Fuchs-Knill, personal communication, 2023). This is a conversation between you and the client about what appears concretely and specifically in the work. It is the same in the performative arts as in the visual arts, which I will unpack later.

- Process: This is the step-by-step experience that the client had. The first thing we did was this, and then this. How was that for them? What impediments and difficulties were encountered? "What stands out, how have difficulties been tackled?" (Margo Fuchs-Knill, personal communication, 2023).

- Experience: This refers to the emotions, sensations, associations, thoughts, and memories that the client had while doing the work. These can be difficult to capture, so give it time. "What was your experience when we added the hats?" Often the question is asked as, "How did that make you feel?" I don't prefer this construction because it is not only emotions that comprise experience. I like to allow for the full range of possibilities, and I often name some other qualities of experience, such as body sensations or memories.

- Reflection/Round-up: This step is most often a summary thought or a title of a work. In this step, we are wrapping up the work, not moving forward with it. This is not an intermodal transfer, it is a conclusion, an ending.

This is a comprehensive way to assess the process and the work, but it is not the only way. The crucial point is that the process and the product will be considered from an artistic point of view. Lead the client to the first step, "describe what you notice," and listen. Noticing, allowing oneself to know and acknowledge what attracts attention, is a big step in development of the authentic self. Instead of noticing what I'm "supposed" to notice, I notice this other part. One phenomenon is observed in a variety of ways. Leaving contradictory possibilities together is fine. No need to close it down and choose just one. After the client has spoken, you may add something if it seems important. It is a kind of dialogue, but the client is the lead. This is where deep listening is required—listen with your heart as well as your head. When the client says something that strikes you, repeat it back to them. When I am looking with a client, I might use my finger or a stick to touch the surface and trace along the area I am drawn to. In my small notebook, I jot down words or phrases that seem important to this client. I might refer to these later in our harvesting discussion.

Although this formula gives guidance as to the order of things, it doesn't tell you what might be important for the client. For example, reviewing the process step-by-step may be profound for some. "I haven't cut out paper shapes since I was child, and now it hurts my hands, arthritis, so I couldn't cut, I had to tear." For others, the experience holds importance: "While gluing I thought about my tattered relationship with my daughter. How I wish I could glue us back together as easily as I glued this collage paper." There is no way of knowing *a priori* what might be important, what the boon of the experience might be. Again, your job is to help them distinguish what is significant from what is trivial.

As Atkins and Eberhart say in *Presence and Process in Expressive Arts Work* (2014, pp. 137–138):

> Using art-making within a therapeutic, counseling, or consulting context usually has the purpose of overcoming the limitations of everyday language, often painfully experienced by clients and professionals. Working with the arts can be understood as dealing with another sort of expression, a totally other language... And, it is important to realize that the logic of everyday language has dissolved... Therefore, art-making in a therapeutic or counseling context usually has an opening and freeing effect. This normally is experienced as beneficial and pleasing or even a blessing.

When I am demonstrating a session, my students have often remarked that I return again and again to the work itself. It is my resource, my co-therapist. Unlike some other approaches that use the art images as a jumping off point, I use it as an anchor. Everything I need is right there, in the art; by this I also mean the performative and written arts.

An Aesthetic Analysis is the last task in the studio room, the second room, and is an opportunity to evaluate what exactly happened during play, art-making, or ritual. No matter what form the decentering has taken, we need to consider it carefully or value may be lost. We keep the Aesthetic Analysis within the tradition and discipline of the arts. Look at the finished piece (or as far as we got) within the context of the art-making, within the traditions of the arts. It should be in the "studio time." This is not a psychological exercise; it is an artistic one. Remember "critique" time in an art class? This is the therapeutic version of that. We look at the art as art. Use your extensive vocabulary and knowledge of art processes and history here. I will speak more about this later. For now, suffice it to say that you will undertake a close and sensitive looking (or listening or watching). We look at both the overall gestalt and the details. Allow the client to speak first, but don't be afraid to add what you see. Remember, if they were in an altered state, in the imaginal realm, they might not remember what they did entirely. They might not see what they made. This is not at all uncommon. It is important that you not usurp the power or autonomy of the client by imposing your own interpretation of what emerged.

In this procedure you review, remark upon, and stay with the work in the traditions and language of the studio. Include the difficulties that the client encountered. Allow them to be articulated in a concrete and specific manner, in the vocabulary of the arts. Also include the satisfying moments of ease, the happy accidents. This conversation takes place in the tradition of the studio, in a descriptive vocabulary. To emphasize—this is not a psychological analysis of the work, nor a diagnostic tool. We look to the senses and the images and metaphors that have arrived. If the client insists on giving meaning to the work at this point, accept what they say and draw attention back to the image. I often say, "And what else?" I say this so frequently my students once gave me a coffee mug with "...and what else" inscribed. But the power of decentering is lost if we stop at one message. The value of decentering is that we can entertain many messages, even conflicting ones. In fact, it is not at all uncommon for an image to contain both a depiction of the problem as well as various resources and solutions to that same problem.

A common mistake early practitioners make is to panic. The client may ask: "Well, what do you think it means?" And the new practitioner might take the bait. They are professionals, they get paid, they should know something. All the clichés of symbolism come to mind. But wait! They do know something—they know how to proceed with the process. I have a suggestion: When this occurs take a slow and deep breath. Say something like, "Yes, let's take a look." Remember, this thing in front of you has never existed before. No one has ever seen it before. Give yourself and your client time to consider it. It deserves that, your client's effort deserves that, you deserve that. "Let's take a look" says we will proceed together and the first thing we will do is look. Keep your eyes on the art; glancing once is not sufficient. Then lead the client into a review of the work itself.

Group Decentering and Aesthetic Analysis

To take a look at the Aesthetic Analysis in a group setting, let's step back to the decentering process.

After the checking-in or filling-in with a small group, I get their consent to move on, to go into the art studio. Whether you actually move or not, conceive of this portion of the session as changing your role. Now, you assume the aesthetic responsibility for the entire experience of the client. Now, your duties shift—you are still required to listen with all your senses and make mental or physical notes of important nodal points, but the main charge here is to help your client move away from the narrative of distress and into contact with the imagination through the art materials. We move from the story they are telling into the sensitizing and warming-up of the senses to prepare for the aesthetic endeavor to come; into a creative or expressive opportunity. It is by engaging the senses that the client can also move away from what troubles them and come into contact with the world as it is, here and now. The senses, all of them, any of them, are avenues through which the imagination can enter into the play and contribute its part. Ten thousand doors to the imagination, and their keys reside in the body.

It is your aesthetic responsibility to ensure that the client has a satisfactory experience. This is tricky. You cannot do it for them, although as Moon and Lachman-Chapin (2001) say, you can be the "third hand" and assist at times. We know that they will encounter frustration, disappointment, blocks, failure, or other unpleasant feelings, because any art-making may contain these or other unpleasant experiences. Maybe your client will get a paper cut or stub their toe. They might splash paint on their pants. The clay will not cooperate and stays a lump instead of becoming a head. How will this turn out to be a satisfactory experience?

ExA has less an emphasis on technique and skill of the maker and more on the exploration and exploitation of the expressive possibilities of the materials. Knill and Eberhart call this "low skill/high sensitivity" (Knill, 2005, p. 100). It means art that communicates and feels satisfying can be made with little technical skill when undertaken with heightened sensitivity to materials and to the person. I sometimes suggest "do less/feel more" when encountering the materials. This is why we need that warming-up sensitizing time. This is what makes the "low skill" capable of revealing wonderfully expressive work. We increase their sensitivity by acquainting them with the materials, and the practitioner must be highly sensitive to the entire process: the client, the room, the materials, the whole situation.

Since the checking-in and filling-in for a group is less detailed than with an individual, the group quickly moves into the sensitizing activity.

It generally takes a group longer to both settle down and get energized for the activities ahead. It might take invitations and reminders. I use side-coaching to help keep a group on track. I also call this "talking to the wall" where I share my observations to the whole group without mentioning anyone in particular. These instructions can be about things that are working well (most often) but also about dangers that might be imminent. The Aesthetic Analysis in a group can be done person-by-person, or better yet, between partners. Depending on the circumstances, you can pair experienced people with less experienced people. You can also provide a step-by-step formula on a flipchart or white board. If it is done in pairs or small clusters, I move around to listen in on how it is going. Sometimes I demonstrate with one person and have others repeat. Doing this perfectly is not at all the point, but rather to look closely, to consider, to let the multiple messages of any given image come forward and be heard.

On Image Abuse—A Caution

Before we move back to the Counselor's Chairs, let's take a look at the dangers of standard "intuitive" interpretation and a rough history of symbolism.

Human beings have left markings and messages from prehistoric times. We no longer know exactly what they were telling us, but the people of the times knew what these markings communicated. Some written languages began as pictographs, letters that looked like the things they were signifying. In that case, an image did mean a specific thing. During the Middle Ages, religions developed symbols that could be understood as signifying their domain—the cross, the Star of David, the crescent. In Europe, many paintings of this period served as a kind of bulletin board for the Christian message; precise symbols in the paintings about Jesus's divinity but also other bible stories and aspects of doctrine. These symbols include the position of the hands, what they held, the colors used, and what else was in the painting like animals or plants. These aspects of the painting did mean one thing, whatever it was. In England, the portraits of the monarchy also had specific messages and stories to tell. Later came the notion from Freud that only a person with special knowledge could decipher symbols. That would be him, of course! This special knowledge extended from dreams to all images. The notion that images mean one thing still has traction today. Dictionaries of symbols, tarot cards, animal wisdom cards, and any preordained symbols make it much harder to do our job. This is the rubble that we step over with our phenomenological, descriptive Aesthetic Analysis. The legacy of symbolism and the force of folk wisdom is where we begin. Add to this the fact that many people want us to tell them what it means. Sometimes the first thing out of their mouth is, "What does it mean?" I cannot tell them, even if I knew (which I never could), because that would diminish their personhood and empowerment. I can only explore it with them.

Stephen K. Levine has contributed to righting this wrong. In his essay, "Image Abuse and the Dialectic of Interpretation" (Stephen Levine, 1988), he gives a fuller accounting of a psychoanalytic approach to symbols, in dreams and art. Importantly he introduces the notion that the image is a dialectic, a "both/and." He asserts our images contain both the sacred and the profane; they are both teleological and archaeological (pointing to the future as well as uncovering the past). He asks us to trust the image itself.

Ellen Levine in the Afterword of *Tending the Fire* (2004) cautions us not to flatten images by keeping them in the literal reality as signposts to underlying meanings, but to allow them to soar on imaginal wings. Follow them where they lead into the dance or the music, the poem or the painting. Our images come from our inner life and have the most power there.

ROOM NUMBER THREE: MOVING BACK TO THE COUNSELOR'S CHAIRS— THE THIRD CONVERSATION

Room Three returns practitioner and client to verbal reflection; here, we are harvesting meaning and plan transfer to daily life.

Substitution Theory: Art Solutions Can Suggest Life Solutions

Knill's Substitution Theory suggests that changes experienced in art-making can generalize from the art encounter into ordinary reality. The lessons from art-making can be transposed (substituted) into ordinary life. This is what Knill and Eberhart call "harvesting" (2023). We see evidence of change, which is the point of the whole endeavor. The majority of changes fall into one of 13 types or categories, listed below. A good harvesting starts at the check-in, at filling-in. Yes, way back in the first room. Get a grasp of the problem; this is what your summary statement in their first room is all about. You will then be more able to help your client notice changes.

Now, after the art has emerged and been worked with—by whatever technique or method—after the Aesthetic Analysis of any kind, we try to understand the take-away message of the whole endeavor! Only now. Not before. Now we can ask: "What did this process have to do with your life, with the problem you came in with? What art problems did you solve? What does it say to you about what is helpful?" This is the time when the metaphors or processes and procedures of the art-making can be reviewed to see if they bring any resources to the client to relieve the trouble the client came in with.

Help them remember the difficulties they encountered and their narrative of distress, how they described their situation. By doing so, you will be able to determine where to look for possible changes. We call it harvesting because we can let it come to us, we don't need to dig and prod. This is usually obvious after reflection. The useful metaphors should be readily available, right there in front of you. They are "low hanging fruit"—easy to reach.

The harvesting is based on the assertion that the art-making will reflect in some way the troubling situation of the client and will offer resources or solutions by way of metaphor (Knill & Eberhart, 2023). It operates like the supposition behind homeopathy; a little bit of the hair of the dog that bit you will bring relief from the bite itself. So, solving a small trouble in the art-making session could bring attention to resources and tactics for solving the big trouble in the life-world. The art situation is a substitute for the life situation. How does the message of the art translate into life? How do the resources or solutions translate? Did this extravagant art-making excursion bring me any relief from my oppressive divorce or chronic illness, or stressful living arrangement? Has anything changed at all? Is art actually a change agent?

Some people immediately begin to name the changes that occurred to them through the session. They feel different and they can name it. They see instantly that this part of the dance can be said to be analogous to that part of their life. It is my experience, though, that some people can have dramatic changes and not notice them, not hold onto them securely enough to articulate them. Or, have no language to speak about them. So it becomes my job to both gently and carefully listen to the changes they have experienced and also to help the client collect the beautiful moments into their basket.

The simplest harvesting technique is to ask: "Did this help? And if so, how?" Or, "What changed for you?" Or, "Did you get a response to your question?" These are especially good for group sessions, where you cannot witness everyone and a lot is going on. We can always ask: "How did you handle that art problem?" whether with an individual or a group.

While the client is thinking, feeling, remembering, and tries to put things into words, I stay quiet. This is hard work, they might be trying to say something they have never said before. Let them work. Now you are all ears! Now your antennae are up, being as sensitive and patient and present as you can be. Silence is not something to be feared. At the same time, don't be afraid to share, but let them decide for themselves what is significant.

It is critical that you do not shield your client from encountering the frustration and disappointment that comes with all art-making. Artists speak freely of the fear of creation, the necessity of failure and its role in success. They know doubt can haunt a project, how many attempts it can take to get something right, not perfect, but satisfactory. Encountering these difficulties and overcoming them is what builds resilience, and makes art happen. It is also what helps us create solutions to our challenges.

Solutions to the art problem suggest a parallel solution to a life problem. It feels incredible when this occurs. The dialogue goes like this: "When I tried to build this mountain higher, I needed some help from you. Maybe I also need to ask for help from someone with my situation at home." Or, "I tried so many times to get that fold just right. Finally, I just threw it out and went with something else. In the end, that was a better solution. Maybe I can stop trying to make my current job fit me, throw it out, and get something else entirely that fits me from the start." Although it is best when the client makes the connection, the expressive arts practitioner should not hesitate to add what they have observed, in a phenomenological manner. Your supportive input is critical because you can see into their blind spot.

"What if they reject the whole session? Cannot find any parallels?" the skeptic asks. This is possible. Although it is rare, I have had it happen. Since I cannot make anything happen, but can only allow things to take place and support that emergence, I need to acknowledge the experience of the person with grace. "Well, maybe next time the image might reveal its truth." There is no need to pathologize this occurrence and no need to apologize. No blame, no shame for you or for them.

Using "From...To" in Harvesting

Less complete, but still useful, is "From...To" Each individual can keep track of desired changes in a personal way using From (this)... To... (that). Judy tracks her physical energy "From" sluggish "To" energized. David tracks his anxiety "From" medium anxiety "To" less anxiety. Or maybe the thing they are tracking stays the same or moves in the direction of worsening. One quick and simple way is to ask group members to contrast and compare how they feel now, after the experience, with how they felt at the beginning of the experience. "I went from feeling really sad to feeling less sad." "I went from worried about the big empty room to a simple dance about my elbows." People can share these with a partner or in smaller groups. They can write these responses into a journal. You can ask who would like to share and have some people share aloud. It is possible to do a demonstration of the Aesthetic Analysis with one member of the group, then have the rest of the group do it with a partner or work in trios with the third person working as witness or scribe.

Dire Straits

When clients are ensnared in negative behaviors, thoughts, or emotions, Paolo refers to this as being in "dire straits," a nautical expression reminiscent of treacherous channels like the Strait of Gibraltar or Strait of Magellan.

These narrow, perilous passages demand careful navigation. In the days of sailing galleons, ships could become trapped or wrecked within the straits, losing their ability to navigate. This metaphor signifies a dangerous state where change seems impossible or even unthinkable.

The following categories are places where you and your client might see discrete changes but the categories and the changes overlap. This is a guide, but not a recipe.

1. In the Area of Ability

In the **Dire Straits**, the client is unable to do what they want to do. You will hear "I can't." Their ability is missing or weak; they are "dis-abled." There is an inability to make the changes they want for themselves.

In the **Art Studio**, there is ability. A change in the sense of ability from "I can't do anything" to "Look what I did!" This aspect is dramatic and yet common and core to our work. People who have never danced or painted come into our workplaces and dance or paint, or play with the elements and materials of the dance or of painting and see that these activities are not beyond their reach. Do not fail to notice this; point it out. Doing what you have never done before is exciting, taking us to the edge of our growth. I often say to adults "When was the last time you did (something like we just did)?" As in, when have they last painted or made music or whatever we have done? The most frequent answer is "in childhood," but often it is "never before." In my view, if you are doing something in your adulthood that you have never done or rarely done, that alone is worth noting.

The ability to do something you thought you were not able to do is evident in the art process or product. You did it! It means you have the inner resources to create that kind of change but may need help to access it. Growth continues.

2. Perspective

In the **Dire Straits**, the client has a narrow perspective, one view, especially a dim future or constrained vision, either of the current reality or especially of the future. The foreshortened future is even a sign of suicidality, so very important. The master narrative of society also plays a much larger role in people's lives than they sometimes realize. These old views about the way life "should be" are confining and restricting. They should be challenged by the notion of a self-determining life—one that is unique to the individual.

In the **Art Studio**, there are benign views, multiple views, new visions of possibilities. "I thought my life would be so much less interesting after menopause, it represented so many losses. But now I see how things are opening up, how possibilities are coming my way; I can be vital and vigorous for years to come." Or, "I was afraid that being divorced would be lonely and dull, but things don't look that way to me any more. My horizons are open and I see lots of good changes coming my way. I see it in a new light." Going from a narrow perspective to a wider vision or even multiple views. "I was only looking at this one way, but now, after dancing, I see many possibilities." "I felt that everything was a mess, but now I see that many things are working well."

3. Embodiment

In the **Dire Straits**, the client is "in their head"—thinking only, trying to create change by only changing thoughts—having the same thoughts over and over again—cognitive spinning, automatic thinking, fragments of thoughts that aren't fully formed but recur. Sometimes it can seem like the client has been thinking cogently, but it is often bits and pieces of the same old thoughts.

In the **Art Studio**, the body is activated, sensation and emotion activated. The person takes action, allowing the corporeal self to begin to speak and embodied knowing to emerge. A change in the sense of bodily aliveness can occur, and a shift of energy, from sluggish to upbeat and ready for what's next. "When I came in, I felt draggy and dull. Now, I feel energized and alive. It was partly the hopping and stretching, yes, but it was also just getting my vitality galvanized."

This is a change in the mind/body split, going from only thinking about the issues, to now noticing and allowing emotion and sensation, the felt-senses. If the emotion that comes is sadness or frustration this can be difficult for the client. You can help frame this. Allowing our emotions to guide and influence us is one of the great mysteries of being human. All possible emotions are part of the human experience. They are expressions of life in contrast to deadness, being frozen or shut down. It is not uncommon for a client to say, "These are sad tears, but I do feel better knowing what I've been holding." Or, "These tears are my truth." Or, "This doesn't feel good, but it feels good to know." Acknowledging their less pleasant experiences, they enlarge their personal world.

4. Resources

In the **Dire Straits**, the client often experiences their own limitations, a lack of resources, and feels limited. They might be bankrupt, without capital or equity in some area of their lives. Whatever it is they think they need, they do not have it.

In the **Art Studio**, we use what we have. The artistic attitude is "with just a few resources, you can do a lot."

Clients go from a sense of limited resources to a sense of expanded opportunities. The feeling of scarcity is replaced by one of abundance. "With this old cardboard box, I made this wonderful dragon." We all have limited resources, thus we need an unlimited imagination. As Bucky Fuller suggested we can do "more and more with less and less." It is not at all uncommon for people to list and name many helpful people and opportunities bearing on their situation after an expressive arts session. Reusing and repurposing materials or using recycled materials in the studio gives a sense of history, but also emphasizes that none of us has unlimited resources yet we can have wonderful experiences and create.

5. Social Standing

In the **Dire Straits**, the client feels lonely and alone. "Just me, all by myself." I've had clients complain about their aloneness only to discount the friends they did have. "Oh, just her," and "Sure him, but that's all." Or, "No one calls me." "Do you call them?" "Well, no."

In the **Art Studio,** while interacting with the practitioner and/or group, the client is in dialogue with another. This is especially noticeable in small group work, but possible in any setting. Clients may move from feeling isolated to feeling connected. They may come to appreciate the connections they already have. They go from "I am alone" to "We work together." A sense of social embeddedness may come from valuing relationships with loved ones who are dead. If possible, divide groups into units—duets or trios—to strengthen connections. It is often by reflecting on their web of relationships that people notice they are active as a member of a group, getting and giving feedback. They may notice it is more pleasurable working with others.

6. Focus

In the **Dire Straits**, the client is focused on the past, looking backward. "This happened..." I call this "getting your pants stuck on the fence as you try to move forward." That snag pulls you backwards.

In the **Art Studio**, the focus is here and now since that's where the action is, no matter what the aesthetic task may be. What am I doing with the paint, the flute, my feet? What emerges? Art-making gives concrete examples of how attending to here and now serves change and gives a sense of unfolding, moving forward, and rearranging things. It can bring the excitement of "what will happen?" Looking for the image to emerge takes the focus off feeling unsatisfied with the past and places their attention on the image, on "what I serve" right now. Important, since "now" is the only time we can make a change.

7. Sense of Purpose, Self-Efficacy

In the **Dire Straits**, the client feels hopeless, ineffective, with no future, at a dead end, no sense of purpose.

In the **Art Studio**, the art-making is learning by doing. "Look what I did." "I can't believe I did that." The art brings forward the "wow effect." The client is rewarded for staying with a project. They experience success. "I did it. I overcame a challenge, solved a problem, I wasn't thwarted or stopped." "I can do it." Rarely is someone truly disappointed with a project when they stay with it because the materials and imagination provide delight and surprise. "If I can do this, what else can I do?"

8. Emotion, Mood

In the **Dire Straits**, the client says, "I hate it! I can't stand it!" They have a limited emotional range, possibly a toxic mood. They find it hard to shift, or may even cling to the negative mood as proof of their suffering. The self-talk is self-deprecating and critical.

In the **Art Studio,** while in the art experience, there can be relaxation, meditation, an opportunity to find flow or be in the "zone." There is enjoyment. "I create joy, or it emerges and it comes to me." Or, "I approach it; it waits there for me." Most people feel better after an expressive art session. In all my years, there have been less than a handful of exceptions. It can be soothing or exciting, but it is a mood changer, up from depression or down from anxiety. It allows for a greater range of emotions, playfulness, delight, awe, expressions of grief or sadness, joy, fun, tenderness, concern. Art can hold the emotional range of a human being. It is a great companion to our existence.

9. Action/Behavior

In the **Dire Straits**, the client can't take action or won't take action. The client is focused on failed past action and has given up. Or the client is caught in a negative behavior loop: "I know it won't work, because it didn't work before, but I do it anyway."

In the **Art Studio**, action is a neutral word. It means what you do or do not do. The client can have an expanded range of play and action, or *Spielraum* (play space). The client can now make new decisions, do the unfamiliar. "No mistakes in art" is the motto of the studio. As art-makers we learn when we fail. Clients move from failure to discovery. There is the iterative nature of repetition: each time you try, you learn something. In the studio, we turn "failure" into research as a resource for learning. Increased *Spielraum* is something we wish for the client: to explore, examine, play with, and improvise with the materials of the arts, be it words, sounds, movement, actions, or colors. The client may increase their tolerance for ambiguity, failure, accident and learn to incorporate these elements into their play. This internal play space or attitude helps the client stick with something. This immunizes against discouragement and giving up.

10. Language
In the **Dire Straits**, they tell the old story, with the old vocabulary and impoverished language. They can sound like a "broken record." They repeat the same old story told in the same old way.

In the **Art Studio**, they enjoy an expanded use of language. Not only aesthetic terms, but also concrete and specific language, such as descriptions of processes like printing or sculpting; names of products, such as gesso or paste; specific tools like putty knife or bone folder; and techniques, such as impasto or repetition. There is a move from the anesthetic to the aesthetic—from numbing to beauty. Here again knowledge of schools of art and history are a resource. When people discover that they participate in life in a similar way as an artist or musician from another era, the horizon of their life expands. They begin to notice new things in the environment. This concrete and specific language can be used to describe how they are succeeding in life instead of glossing over the things they do well.

11. Identity/Role
In the **Dire Straits**, the client identifies with the label of their problem, i.e., homeless/battered woman/depressed/victim/drunkard/mentally ill. These labels are fixed, negative, and limiting. They are unidimensional versus multidimensional.

In the **Art Studio**, the client can be the songwriter/artist/dancer/poet. We break down the singular identity and role of distress. We believe that what we do describes who we are: as in the musical *A Chorus Line:* "God, I'm a dancer, a dancer dances." There is a change in a sense of identity from a person who can't do anything right to an art-maker who made this lovely thing. These shifts can come slowly over time, but they can also come quickly. A person enters into a new tribe, with a new role, and at the same time adds a dimension to their identity. Perhaps there is nothing as galvanizing as a more dimensional or expanded identity.

12. Relationships
In the **Dire Straits**, the client is stuck in User/Used relationships that are flat and toxic.

In the **Art Studio**, there is a chance for collaboration. When we don't "need" someone, there is the possibility of an "I/Thou" relationship as detailed by Martin Buber, which refers to authentic and reciprocal inter-actions between individuals that go beyond transactional or utilitarian relationships. The client can build an alliance, with you or with others in a group. You can be the example of a good-enough partner/collaborator.

13. Philosophy/Menschenbild
(The German term, meaning "image of humanity," refers to one's beliefs about the nature of human beings.)

In the **Dire Straits**, the outlook is problem focused: "All my good work comes to naught." "My life is defined by my problems; it's too late to live the life I wanted." This denotes a delimited horizon, perhaps even a fore-shortened future.

In the **Art Studio**, they can experience pleasure in living in the here and now. They can participate in the joy of creating and can have fun. Even if only for an hour, they can accept their circumstances. It was in one of my darkest hours that I decided to take *amor fati* as a personal motto. It trans-lates to "love my fate." Although I was in a low and dark time, I was alive and would not surrender to an invitation to get stuck. I wrote, painted, and danced. I communed with my favorite trees. I was devastated, but I knew the sun would rise and I would go on; this is an existential orientation. "Life is good."

Concluding the Harvest
The Harvesting phase concludes with a review of how the art has been beneficial, as suggested above, and how these noticings might apply to their life. Allow the client to immerse themselves in this new awareness. Do not hesitate to provide feedback on what you have observed. Many of the changes are subtle and so novel that they may take time to solidify and become recognizable.

I encourage individuals to journal about their experiences. Not every-one does, but those who do often understand more. Journaling serves as a commemoration of the work undertaken, acting in its own way as a witness that individuals can incorporate into their life-world.

Any of these changes may indicate a teleological function of the images—that is, they can point to a future, suggest a new vision, or unveil new possibilities (Knill & Eberhart, 2023). Anxiety can be considered a fear of the future, a negative use of imagination, whereas studio experiences draw us into an absorbing present moment.

COMMUNITY ART

Like art, revolutions come from combining what exists with what has never existed before.

GLORIA STEINMAN

Expressive arts practitioners working with communities, that is large groups, do so within artistic traditions. At the EGS this usually looks like a dance/theater process, or a musical ensemble, choir, or any combination of these performative arts. We have also made community art with poetry, visual art, paper sculpture, and clay work.

I love group work, and particularly community art. Without doing anything overtly therapeutic or pointed, I have seen people change dramatically over time in expressive arts groups and in educational settings, like the training I offer at my Institute. People encounter themselves, learn, and grow. It is non-threatening, cost effective, and can occur under numerous auspices and within many venues.

Community art is a way to help promote changes for individuals, couples, families, groups, teams, and other large groups. It is a beautiful form of helping. Not just because it uses the arts, no. One could have a harsh dogmatic approach to art-making; or a judgmental approach to discussing the art; or an authoritarian relationship between the practitioner and the students or clients. Every aspect of this practice must be aesthetic: the process of curating, the relationships, the methods, and handling the outcome. All guided by an eye and ear tuned to the possibility of beauty at every level of the project.

When Paolo discusses community art he is bringing people together to create some type of performative work. The people come in not able to do what they will be doing, and they leave having done it. From "I can't do this" to "I did it." That is a profound change. He defines a community as a group of people who have a job to do together, some work to bind them, some common goal or objective, some shared purpose. It can be a team in a company, or it can be the students and faculty at the EGS, which will serve as my model here.

Architecture of a Session in Community Art

Does community art use the architecture of a session? Yes, but it is greatly modified. The first conversation in the Counselor's Chairs must be short. It is the time for the facilitator to give a shape and direction to the participants. A type of filling-in may be done by individual participants without direct interaction with the facilitator. The majority of the time and work takes place in the studio section, including the various ways of working with the images and themes, and the Aesthetic Analysis. The tasks of the third room, the harvesting, is also done as an "individual within the group" which can then be discussed in the larger group or in break-out dyads, trios, or other smaller groupings.

Filling-In for Community Art

I have used many types of filling-in or checking-in: a single word check-in; a movement for your mood; show me where in the room you would best like to be right now, then say one phrase about it; find the image that speaks to you today (when I present a collection for them to choose from); choose the color that says something about you; find an animal (again from a pre-selected assortment) that attracts you today. Even more efficiently, I say to the whole community: "Take a few long, slow breaths and note your mood, level of energy, present concerns." I limit the checking-in because in a larger group the decentering activity takes most of the time. Yet, this notion of arriving and having a personal basis of beginning to work is essential. The check-in is a data point for comparison when the group is over. Then they have a "From... To" and can experience for themselves any shift or change that may have occurred.

My course, Didactics of Community Art, has a lab portion in addition to the classroom portion. All the students and faculty come together several times during the summer session to create something, under my guidance. Until the summer before his death, Paolo did this.

When I facilitate community art I want to come from the poetic mind—the metaphoric perspective. I will not be putting people through a dance camp—showing steps and creating a large group dance in that way. It is more precise and, at the same time, less definite than that. The practitioner must ignite the group's curiosity and their cooperative impulse so they can become an ensemble, to move from ordinary reality into the aesthetic domain, together. It cannot be my dance, it must be our dance. Can ordinary people with no dance or theater experience actually create a piece of dance/theater together? Especially as an emergent improvisation? They not only can, but do. And it is spectacular!

From Then and There to Here and Now

There are as many ways to do this as there are communities. At the EGS we will recognize the homeland, language, and position at the university at the very first gathering; the "there and then." Next, we will begin the welcoming and weaving of the current student body. It is important to orient all the participants to what is actually happening in the life of the group as well as other considerations of the here and now. This comes clear in situational analysis: who are we, where are we, why have we met, what events are important to us?

From Me to We

In community art, the facilitator leads the individuals to a sense of their belonging in the group or team, going from the "me" to the "we." While you cannot plan a real step-by-step, have your score in mind *a priori*. You must have thought it through completely with this exact group, time, and place in mind, a thorough situational analysis, with the understanding and ability to yield to whatever emerges. Your score is the map, it is not the territory! The score will be improvised and the facilitator improvises along with it. Some sections will expand, some contract, some will be abandoned, and new things added. Like a musical score, the performance score guides the facilitator from here to there. There is notation on both the timing (first this, then that) and also the action (first the low singers, then the running dancers). The score itself evolves over time as the people transform into an ensemble. It has a kind of destination but not an exact goal.

Improvisation

Improvisation is my main methodology. What is improvisation? Well, first, what it is not: Improvisation doesn't mean "anything goes" or "do what you want." It doesn't mean losing yourself in the group or within your own world. Each member of the group needs to keep aware of the group. It is a double-vision: What am I doing and what are we doing? This means keep your eyes open and the score in mind, but not rigidly. Relaxed and alert.

It is up to the facilitator to clearly set out the basic material; the themes and manner of investigating it, as well as the timing. Materials can be given, but the shaping of them depends upon the improvisation of the group. Things then emerge that are surprising and unexpected.

Everything depends on the skill of the facilitator. Paolo says the leadership of community art must engage curiosity and motivate discovery (Knill, 2005).

Usually at the EGS the community art takes place in the largest room, the plenum, which is semi-circular, with an exposed wood beam ceiling fanning out from a center point. Numerous windows look out onto the alpine Swiss landscape, the larch forest, and the flowering meadows, grazing cows, the neck-breaking peaks of the frozen Alps. The room is large enough for a group of 80–100 to move in. In the summer of 2019, our community was about 90 students plus faculty. Several sessions were three hours in duration, others were 90 minutes. Some students knew each other from previous summers, but most did not know anyone. They came from across the globe. In this session, we had students from the USA (Oregon, California, Texas, and New York) and from Canadian provinces, including Toronto, Vancouver, and the Northwest territories. Participants from Europe hailed from Germany, Italy, France, Spain, and the Nordic countries of Denmark, Finland, and Sweden. Russia and the Georgian Republic were there. Asia had representatives from Hong Kong, China, Korea, and Japan. Several states in India were there. The African continent was represented. Australia was represented. Israel, Palestine, and Turkey also. Many languages and dialects were spoken, with English as a second language. Some were PhD students who were graduating from course work, some were first time MA students. Some students had recently completed their BA degrees, while others were embarking on a second career. There were parents, divorcees, widowers, those never married, not to mention queer and BIPOC people. What might bring these various people together? They had all made the trek to Saas Fee, the Pearl of the Alps, coming to study intermodal expressive arts at the university Paolo founded. That alone is a lot to have in common; it tells me how important they think and feel the role of the arts is in the process of change. We shared something of an ethos, perhaps a vision.

Safety

Creating a sense of safety is paramount to having a good community art experience, and there are several ways to achieve that. First, I give the entire group various permissions: To sit out if they need to for any reason; to become a witness. Do not drop out completely and go on your phone but stay in the structure in a different role, stay connected. I don't know their physical limitations, so they have to be in charge of doing things they can do, and refrain from doing things they cannot do safely. Note, however, that there is a difference between feeling safe and being safe. No one can enter the mind and experience of another to ensure absolute safety. Trust is the foundation of safety and trust is built over time. Any breaches in the relationship need to be repaired as soon as detected. Acknowledge it and seek an opportunity to mend. Articulating the process as each new step is taken also builds trust and safety.

Knill had acronyms regarding community art. These let people know there is a structure and, even if it is not totally obvious all at once, it is there guiding us. The reins are in hand. Instructions are neither capricious nor arbitrary. One of Knill's acronyms for guiding community art is MORE (*POIESIS*, 2005, p. 140).

MORE

"M" is for "Materials." Easily manageable with simple shaping, says Paolo. In this case, the students were my material, but for them the material was dance movement. I introduced the concept of the personal space or reach-space of the body on its axis. When I am working with a large group that I don't know well (only a few know me and they are mostly strangers to each other), it is paramount to allow the notion of personal space to be articulated. In this safety bubble we breathe and stretch gently, allowing the range of motion of each joint and limb to be explored. Eyes open. By turning on their axis, the students can observe each other, see each other move. It communicates something about the animal-self. You know them in a different way. Then, I have the group move through the space somewhat slowly—moving from the edges in through the middle. I am side-coaching throughout. I say things like, "Go in both directions. Don't make this the Del Mar Racetrack." I invite the students to explore the room, so it becomes familiar to them. While they are moving, they are looking. They are increasing the energy and flow of their own body. I might suggest meeting the eyes of others in a gentle, non-social way. "This is not a cocktail party. Just look, with soft eyes, like animals do" This helps decrease socially imposed expectations. At some point I have the group begin to "run for pleasure." Not to get away from something, not to get to someplace, but to run the way animals do, because they can and it's fun and it feels good. This gentle running increases the energy of the individual bodies and also of the group as a whole.

I say things like, "Use the body you have today, use the energy you have today." Allow participants the freedom to step back if they need to. I say, "You have to take care of yourself. Perhaps you have a headache, or a hip that is acting up. I cannot know about all these things, so I trust that you will do what is right for you." This "easy in, easy out" attitude contributes to the sense of safety people feel. No one wants to be coerced. Over the next few meetings, I introduce various types of movement. The whole group tries these in an exploratory playful way, seeing what they can and cannot do, what they like or don't like. I tell them that I would like everyone to try these movements on, but not everyone will do them in the final project, only people who want to do a certain part will do it, no one will do everything. This gives them permission to be a part of the whole thing without damaging their body or sense of involvement. We move forward in this manner each time.

"O" for "Organization." Possible structures for organization of the ensemble include solos, duets, trios, ensemble, double quintet, and so forth. Organization also means considering the element of time, such as the duration of crossing the stage, or slow and quick paces juxtaposed. We try various elements upstage or downstage; this theme first and that one last. We can manipulate and arrange the composition. The ensemble chooses among various elements: Shall we do this or that? They help decide and therefore help develop the piece. It gives them authorship. The communication is between equals with different roles. Remembering what American documentarian Ken Burns said, "Communication only happens between equals," they become co-creators and help shape the final piece.

"R" is for "Restricted frame." Give simple and clear directions. Each time we meet, I take a step back and repeat some of the things we have done before. We will use this material and not that. This allows the ensemble to become increasingly familiar with the material and develop their own mastery of it. I use knowledge of the body as the instrument of dance, naming the body parts like sternum or sacrum. I describe how the body moves: axial (in place), locomotive (through space), and so forth. I also use the language of dance—time, space, and motion—and give examples to explore. Gradually the dance is taking shape. Some of the elements require greater skill, all require great sensitivity. Some of the moves all can do, some moves only a few can execute. I have given them a wide variety of movement choices to play with.

"E" is for "Explore." Allow the ensemble to try things out. Play and explore with the materials we are working with. If some people are not able to participate, I ask them to witness and give feedback, observe this or that aspect of the movement as the dancers perform, requiring them to use the vocabulary and terms of the dance, which I have introduced as we move through the process. The dancers need concrete and specific feedback. This is critical for helping us move from ordinary reality into the imaginal place where we are a company of dancers making a dance. It expands the role of the participants and reinforces their knowledge of this art discipline. When you can clearly see the dance, your perception of the world will never be the same.

This is serious play. Deep play. I take it seriously, but with a light touch. When the group is large, I might divide the entire ensemble into the various parts (those who roll on, those who kick, those who leap, and so on) and while the leapers are leaping, the rollers can observe. Learning to make community art is one part doing and one part observing and reflecting. Like all expressive arts processes, there is an in-breath and an out-breath. After the evaluation, we are ready, with that feedback in mind, to try it again, to do a "take two."

Sensitive musicians are invaluable. Especially those who are experienced improvisers and willing to provide whatever is needed at a moment's notice.

STORY: Singing in the Small Room

On a particular day, the plenum was not available, so community art had to be held in adjoining studios. It was a much less aesthetically pleasing room than the plenum where we usually met, and much smaller. We could not comfortably do movement-based work, so I chose to use voice. We did have an upright piano and guitar. This activity fit the space and the size of the group. Ninety people could easily sing in this room, but not easily move. We began the sensitizing process by focusing on our breath—allowing our bellies to soften so the diaphragm could function properly, individually experimenting with the depth of breath. Then, I asked if people would be comfortable being touched and, if so, to allow a partner to touch their back and sides—to better feel the movement of the ribs, which only move by means of the muscles between the ribs (intercostals) and the diaphragm. Next, we whispered as we milled around the room and then hummed. I asked people to listen to each other and find hummers who were in a similar or compatible tone as theirs, to linger with them and enjoy the hum. It was time to find a center tone (a tone that everyone in the whole community could reach and hold easily). We began to play by moving up and down from the center tone. To help the group stay connected to the tone, our musicians played chords that supported the singers. We moved up from the center tone in steps and down from the center tone in steps. After doing this for several minutes with me leading it, I let the singers do it on their own, with the instruction that they come back to the center tone before going up or down and end on the center tone. By now we were well warmed up.

Next, I introduced the notion of chant and song from the idea that "we are all musicians as we speak." This sentence has a distinct rhythm as every sentence does. You can make a rhythm out of a sentence by eliminating the words and speaking the rhythm. In the life of this community, the graduation classes were going on a trip to Italy the next day. They were excited, and we needed to acknowledge that. They had finished their exams and were jubilant—everyone had passed. So, I asked each group to come up with a phrase or sentence that reflected their mood or focus that day and to use the center tone to find a little melody that went with the phrase. The theme was graduation. Within a few minutes every group had something. We listened to them sing their songs individually. Then we tried all together. The musicians were there to support the rhythm and tone. Everyone sang, from the experienced singers (we had about six), to the people who never sang. There were a couple of adjustments needed in terms of rhythm, but after one or two takes it worked wonderfully. We sent the graduates off full of humor and high spirits. The songs had honored their work and their triumph.

Benefits of Community Art

Art-making has many health-building or salutogenic qualities for human beings. These are amplified when we are in groups.

Large group or community work is one way to bring the change-making power of the expressive arts to people who would not otherwise have the ability or opportunity for such an experience. Community art addresses the necessity for people to feel a connection to other people and to their own creative selves. Forming ties with like-minded individuals where the focus is on art-making at any level restores the humanity needed to go on; the juice for a meaningful life. There is wonder and softness, rigor and daring. If the facilitator can create a sense of safety and provide that "just-right" amount of challenge, people get excited about working out the mystery and puzzle of art challenges. We need to see each other being brilliant, magnificent, taking chances, warm, and radiant—not merely working, shopping, or driving.

This is a particularly good approach when working with teams, or working groups. The change-making possibilities can occur without the need for therapy or counseling. People can see themselves in different roles, doing different things. This helps bring to life a change within themselves. I remember Knill saying that community art is a much better formula for workplace team-building than, say, bowling or a ropes course. He notes that those replace the competition of the workplace with the competition of a game: who got the highest score or who did the best. Activity in the arts can avoid this. The arts demand that people work together, cooperatively for a good result for everyone.

STORY: Carnival!

Let me give you an example of a community art session that Paolo and I did in Bisbee, Arizona, at a Harvest Symposium. In order to see how this works, I'll break the story up into the various rooms and processes that correspond to the architecture of a session; revisiting the tasks that need to take place in the Counselor's Chairs (Fill-In), Studio (Sensitize, Decenter, Working Through (if needed), Curation (if necessary), Aesthetic Analysis, and back to Counselor's Chairs (Harvest).

Bisbee is a desert mining town in the Mule Mountains of Arizona, the site of the four-day Harvest Symposium. In the structure of the symposium, the participants went as a cohort from studio to studio, spending an entire day with one teacher or set of teachers and whatever theme they were working with. Paolo and I were leading one of the all-day workshops. We had chosen Carnival for our theme.

The First Room: Fill-In

After greeting our group members—maybe 25 people—we resourced and oriented our participants by sharing photos of different folk festivals and our rationale for choosing it as our theme. We shared something about the history of Carnival, and the notion that what happens at Carnival stays at Carnival, a time for wild unfettered Dionysian activities before the constraint and sacrifice of Lent. Resourcing the group can help them focus and ignite the imagination. We discussed the varieties of this mid-winter festival from the perspective of an assortment of societies and cultures. Paolo and I were excited about the possibilities. Our image suggested music, movement and dance, costumes, and, in general, a day filled with festive fun, celebration, and a rowdy rogue-ish flavor!

Even if a participant had never heard of Carnival (which was not the case), they would end this section of the workshop with enough familiarity to be acquainted with the theme and the look and feel of the ensuing activity. We sat in a circle so everyone could see everyone, as is the ExA custom. We allowed people to share briefly how they did or did not connect with the theme. We approached this as art-based research, with everyone having their own question.

Moving on to the filling-in task of the first room, we quieted the group with a short time to breathe quietly while the participants wrote in their notebook or journal something from their "real life" they would like to release, exorcize, let go of, change, or celebrate. We did not ask anyone to say what that was. After a few minutes we asked them to tuck that away. We would revisit this at the end of the workshop. Then, we turned our attention to our sensitizing activities before we could begin to create our Carnival performances, the costumes, the songs and dances that we would perform for each other and the entire community.

The Second Room: The Studio
Decenter

From there, we crossed the threshold to the studio activities into decentering, which begins with sensitizing and warming up. First, a general warming up, getting the breath and bodies moving gently. Then more theme-focused movement; for example, if you had no cares in the world, how would you move? What if you had something intoxicating to drink? How would it look in the lower body, in the upper body? What would the rhythm be, the pace, and so forth. Then the group broke up into clusters. People continued to mix, meet, and regroup. At certain points small groups self-organized, chose themselves, to meet and create a song that reflected their boisterous mood. After these were reduced and refined, the costumes came out. Then people dressed each other in various pieces from my studio costume rack. I brought everything black or red with accents of gold or silver, including long gloves and headpieces. It was dramatic. We did several takes until it felt just right. We performed these small ensemble works for each other, with much shouting and laughter. Later we performed them for the entire community.

Aesthetic Analysis

At the end of the day, we gathered back into our circle—sans costumes—and reflected on the process and experience of the day. This is a version of Aesthetic Analysis. We went over the step-by-step, the warming-up, the group selections, writing the lyrics, the costuming and musical development, the development of the movement pieces. We remembered both the problems we encountered and the overall high jinx and hilarity in the creation. People spoke of their experiences and their associations to those. We talked about all the theatrical choices we made, how the image of Carnival guided us. Once the event had been deconstructed and critiqued from an aesthetic point of view, we asked people to dig out their papers from the morning. It seemed a lifetime away.

Third Room: Back to the Counselor's Chairs—The Final Conversation
Harvesting

Now was time to see what, if anything, changed for the participants, the harvesting. Paolo was always clear that this was an experiment. Maybe nothing changed for anyone. But maybe something changed for someone. People spoke about the shifts and changes they experienced during the process of making. Paolo and I framed those experiences with the substitution model of change. Very gently, forcing nothing, but asking: "What happened as you struggled to find the lyrics? Was it easy or difficult to work with others on this project? How did you solve the 'art problem?' How did you manage the uncomfortable things that arose in the process of making the performance? Where were the changes located—in your social self, your performative self, your song-writing self, your corporeal being? Did you change perspectives? Do you feel more enlivened now?" I was happily surprised that so many wanted to share what occurred to them and what delightful changes had taken place during our Carnival.

As it happened in this particular case, we "curated" the experience later by sharing it with the whole community. We gave it as much framing with the lights and entrances and exits as we could manage with the space we had. It was bawdy and extravagant, the witness/audience were wowed, and they cheered, which was gratifying for Paolo and me and the participants. Carnival!

Group Immune System

Community and large group work can increase the resilience of any group. Resilience, as I am using it, is the ability to activate resources and mobilize coherence. It is a word related to qualities of physical movement—an ability to bounce back, to return, to stretch, to compress, and then recoil. If you are resilient, you can come back if you get "bent out of shape."

Making art together strengthens the immune system of a community. Groups or teams can shatter and splinter without enough strength and respect to hold difficulties and differences.

What does that metaphor/image of the immune system suggest? How can dancing together or singing or making art together help us as a group? What is the metaphor of the group immune system? If community art is to keep or develop a healthy immune system for a group, how can that be accomplished?

A group is both the individuals within it and also the whole organism at once. A group has its own "body." Separate individuals make up the group, and comprise the group-body. Members of the group act and function in certain ways for the group. For example, you might have the thinkers and planners, the active doers, the initiators, the reflecting critique-ers. It is common to see people who jump right into an activity and those who hang back, those who feel comfortable right away and those who need to warm up to the idea. So, if we consider the group as a body, what would constitute its immune system? How would it operate?

To increase the immunity of the community, the members need some measure of trust in each other. Circulation and interaction between and among the members fosters group familiarity. It involves observing others. It is the freedom of personal choice that a community art-making event should have, even within a structure, for the community overall. It is the opportunity for different people to come to the fore as leaders or shapers and the permission for others to wait until they feel ready to enter or to hold back, allowing another person to speak. I call these positions "the head of the snake and the tail of the snake;" someone will be first and someone will be last. These are ensemble members, not soldiers.

How does the metaphor translate from the physiological system to a social group?

- The immune system keeps illness away. In a group the seeds of illness are stereotypes, mistrust, gossip of a nasty flavor, exclusion. It can show up as judgment. If I have been playing with you, I am less likely to harbor resentment, suspicions, prejudices, stereotypes.

- The healthy immune system means circulation of energy. Community work breaks up "cliques" and subgroups, such as all the men, or those who have done it before, or seniors, people from Scandinavia, or other divisions. A well-planned community art experience will circulate and mix the larger group. It will subdivide again and again to blend and to ensure some measure of familiarity. Like cutting egg whites into flour, gently and consistently mix and fold and turn and mix the group members together in various combinations for greatest incorporation of acquaintance and comfort.

- Letting everyone see each other in the aesthetic environment and activity increases the healthy group immune system and safety. This enables everyone to connect to some degree. Those who in normal social settings take a quiet role may be the ones to sing the loudest. An aesthetic environment allows people to change their ordinary role and their usual strengths. It helps to change status assignations. The dean of the university is on the floor and a student is standing on a chair above her. We can do this in the dance environment, but rarely in a normal social situation.

- The healthy group immune system softens "common tensions" when individuals meet each other in a creative context. We learn new sides and aspects of people we have known in other settings and roles. I didn't know the quiet student was a singer; I didn't know the old professor could dance. There is a different focus—the art we're making.

- We are drumming together, and it doesn't make sense to hold back. We help each other with the music. We have playful encounters— smiling, laughing. When we are at ease, our bodies move differently, conveying our comfort, aliveness, and joy. The soft open face, the smiling face, the concentrated face conveys emotions and messages different from the workplace face. This allows us to change our perspective and interactions with an individual and the larger group. When we are "all in," we see each other differently—our opinions are modified, more accepting, less judgmental.

- We make something together, greater than we could make alone. We have depended upon each other in a non-demanding way. This section won't work if we don't cooperate. We see the creativity of others, which is wonderful and astounding. Our dependence on others for the fulfillment of the piece is highlighted.

- We create beauty—"then follows love" says Paolo. We become part of the tapestry or mosaic, part of the symphony or mural. We can see and appreciate that we are all "a part of."

- Art-making creates a pathway for appreciation and acknowledgement of our place "in the universe of things." "I was needed, and you were needed."

- Art-making greatly increases self-experiencing. When I do something new, I experience myself in a new way, I am bigger, my vision is greater. Therefore, I have more to offer, and so I can and do offer more. I am a useful member of the group.

- Understanding increases sense-making beyond words. I can have novel ideas, fresh feelings, new knowledge that is difficult to put into words. I am not judged, therefore I am less likely to judge.

- We discover the possibility of new resources in the new situation. I use myself in a new way. I allow others to see me and use me in new ways. I contribute.

- If safety is maintained in the new situation, it will increase a sense of trust—in self, in others, in the situation altogether. Where trust is built, more trust will build. It is recursive. When we trust, we can take risks. With risk comes experimentation and the possibility of surprise and new ideas. When we all take a risk, the comfort zone is expanded.

- We surprise ourselves. Adults need new experiences to bring new ideas, new emotions, to create new memories and alter identity. We feel expanded and this expansion often brings a sense of hope—I can change, and therefore my world can change. For adults, the world is often routine, so allowing for change can be thrilling as well as a little scary.

- Our roles change. When I see myself as a musician, working with other musicians, I realize the many possibilities I have not yet experienced in my life. My horizons widen, my eyes see further down the path.

A group or community with a strong immune system may be able to hold tension without splintering into fragments or deteriorating into arguments, and may be able to celebrate differences, not merely tolerate them.

Community art can build cohesion among and between diverse groups through aesthetic play—which brings out the best in people and allows our cooperative impulses to be expressed. Community art asks us to work and play together with a focus and a purpose. This is an artful way for us to practice these life skills. I urge you to try it.

CHAPTER THREE

THE FLOWER OF EXA

STORY: I Invented ExA—Sort of!

Out of necessity, I invented my own version of ExA. As a registered dance therapist with degrees both in dance/theater and in dance/movement therapy, as well as years of experience performing and teaching, I worked in my own private practice in my own studio. I was comfortable adding music to my sessions because of my experiences with John Cage, the Harry Partch Ensemble, Organic Dance and Music, and more. I had a tremendous collection of recorded music that provided sonic support to movement explorations, ranging from contemporary to classical, microtonal, opera, world music, jazz, folk, pop, world music, and you name it. The studio also had instruments like rattles, drums, bells, and simple flutes so we could create original music; voice was always present. As a journal writer and ardent poetry lover since childhood, creative writing was included. I read poems to my clients if they spoke to the situation. It seemed necessary to include drawings as a way to leave an artifact, a trace and tangible memory of what had been done. While dance was the necessary primary modality, it was not always sufficient. So, there I was, doing expressive arts therapy in the margins, before I knew it had a name! My mash-up was well intended and my background in the arts was a deep resource. I was endeavoring to serve my clients. The work they did seemed to call for other art explorations. What I lacked was an understanding of the principles of intermodality and polyaesthetics; why moving from one art discipline to another was helpful, and how to accomplish such a thing gracefully. Now I know.

Think of expressive arts like a flower. First, there is the doubled center of the flower. Surrounding this center are five petals representing the arts disciplines. Next, there is a second layer consisting of eight petals representing interdisciplinary influences. Further out are nine philosophical leaves. Here, I share with you how these elements contribute to my current practice. Your flower, however, will be different.

A. THE CENTER

At the center of this blossom lie the twin principles of polyaesthetics and intermodality, which distinguish this way of working. Unlike other theories and methodologies, these principles are founded on the fundamental understanding that all art disciplines are interconnected through the senses, and thus, all sensory communication modalities are likewise connected. These ideas recognize the synesthetic quality of our sensory-motor system and the manner in which we communicate through the languages of the arts.

1. Polyaesthetics

Polyaesthetics refers to the cross-pollination of all the art disciplines, how all the art disciplines are implied within each other and work together. It encompasses many kinds of beauty. All art disciplines share an inherent connection and belong together, by virtue of their origin in the body. They interpenetrate, overlap, and merge, continuously feeding each other. Because they are all bodily expressions, we cannot separate them, except in a theoretical way. We can have aesthetic experiences that emphasize diverse aspects of beauty: tactile, visual, auditory, kinesthetic, or verbal. Different experiences move each of us. The intricate carving of a woodblock can surprise and astonish us, the tender composition of a lullaby, our delight in a tactile environment made from large woven hangings, the inspiration of a poem, all these speak to us.

2. Intermodality

"Inter" refers to something situated between two or more things, while "modality" refers to the channels or modes of communication: i.e., speaking and communicating with words; pictorial communication with visual signs or symbols; or physical gesture as communication. All communication modalities we use "in real life" are also present in our imagination. For example, I can see in both, I can hear in both, I can move in both, and I can feel in both. In a recent dream I touched someone and could "feel" the touching. The most basic explanation of intermodality is that each art discipline is exalted in its own unique way. When Paolo discusses intermodality, he refers to the manner in which communication occurs and the means through which expression is conveyed (Knill *et al.*, 1996). Through our senses, we speak to the world and are in dialogue with it. We take in experiences and information from the world and express our responses, much like the process of inhaling and exhaling. Human beings are constantly communicating through various modes, including visual, auditory, and physical channels. These aren't languages *per se*, with syntax and grammar, but they are forms of subtle communication. The messages cannot be reduced to a single meaning, yet it is significant.

Often intermodality is discussed only in the context of the intermodal transfer. Paolo was clear that this was not a necessary step—unless it was called for or indicated. It is the sensitivity to "what happens between the modes and disciples..." that is the essence of intermodality (Knill, quoted in Stephen Levine, 2017, p. 58).

The arts give voice to our human condition. They encapsulate and convey who we are and what we experience. I dance because it allows me to communicate in a way that I cannot achieve through any other means, first to myself and then to you. Dancing brings me clarity. Music, poetry, and painting are ways of knowing through which we can express our human experience. Our relationship to the arts is profound. They encompass expression that cannot be directly translated into words. They help us acknowledge the complexity and messiness of emotions by providing containers for our feelings and experiences. The arts provide a fulfilling way to respond to our lives, to our existence.

It's important to note that intermodality is distinct from interdisciplinarity. For example, after a dance movement exploration, we might make sounds and utterances—though not words—thereby transitioning from physical expression to vocal expression. This represents a step into the basic elements of language, in this case, preverbal language, which is the basis for poetry. In doing so, we have transitioned from one communication modality to another (movement to sound), but we have not moved from one artistic discipline to another (from dance to poetry).

B. THE PETALS OF THE ART DISCIPLINES

Surrounding the center are the petals of five mother-art disciplines: dance, drama, music, visual arts, and language arts. Each petal represents an art discipline, each with its own rich history, traditions, variations, and specialties. For example, visual art includes both 2D and 3D forms. It encompasses drawing, painting (such as oil and watercolor), photography, small scrimshaw carvings, the Elgin Marbles, and anything where the primary mode of appreciation is through the eye. Dance as an art discipline includes everything from hip-hop, ballet, modern, and jazz, to folk dances from all nations, ranging from the street to the stage, and diapered babies on Tik-Tok, bouncing to the beat. Each art discipline includes many traditions and techniques therefore; these reside in the home discipline. All these petals connect to the same center, the principles of polyaesthetics and intermodality, showing all sensory experiences are actually present in all art disciplines, even if one might be emphasized above others. It also implies that an intermodal transfer can go from any art expression to any other art expression. More on this later.

The arts serve as both our sources and resources. They comprise the medium for our exploration, the traces and trails of our creative process, and the final products of our artistic labor. The arts reveal the metaphors that hold the potential for the change we seek, serving as a bridge from the art to our inner selves. Chapter 4 on the Studios delves into these concepts in depth.

C. THE PETALS OF INTERDISCIPLINARY INFLUENCES

The outer layer of the flower consists of petals representing other interdisciplinary influences, in addition to the five art disciplines. These petals depict domains of knowledge with strong influences that can be incorporated into ExA work. They are enriching, not essential. These fields interpenetrate and add strength to our view of the world, the arts, and society. Let's briefly consider the contributions of these interdisciplinary influences to the practice of ExA. While these influences may vary from practitioner to practitioner, I offer you my perspective. Yours can be different.

1. Sociology

STORY: Shelter from the Storm

It was nighttime. The house was dark, except for the lamp that illuminated my desk. It was quiet, but my ears strained to hear something, anything. When leaves rustled, I startled. I was afraid some guy would clamber through the back door, looking for his wife, who was probably upstairs. It was my first overnight shift at the safe house of Casa de Paz, the first shelter in San Diego for battered women, and I was one of the first counselors to work there. When they hired me, they provided some domestic violence specific training. First, they presented the stark fact that 85% of domestic violence victims are women, and one-quarter of women worldwide will be victims. Second, the training covered several key areas, including understanding that domestic violence included not only physical violence but also psychological abuse, encompassing coercion, stalking, and sexual abuse. The training underscored the factors that increase the chances of domestic violence, including being younger, having a higher education than the man, alcohol use, low family income, military families, and others.

I learned how to handle the crisis hotline and address the situation and needs of women who were our clients. We taught them what was then called "the cycle of violence." We needed to comprehend the psychology of the perpetrators because the shelter also provided treatment for them. We had a program to respond to the needs of their children. When children observe domestic violence between their parents, they are more likely to become either the victim or the perpetrator, so the cycle of violence continues intergenerationally.

In those days, if the police were called to a domestic dispute, they wouldn't do anything—they called it a family matter and left. But intimate partner violence was not simply a personal problem; it was a social problem. Our legal team conducted training for the SDPD to educate them on the impact of domestic violence. It was there I met my lifelong friend Victoria Del'Aquala Garcia, who worked in the legal department while she finished law school. She and I have championed the rights of women ever since. We sought to understand the factors, personal and societal, that contributed to domestic violence and to explore ways to address and mitigate those factors from a societal perspective.

That night, I finished a required text, *Battered Women* by Lenore Walker. As the night dragged on, I looked at the clock frequently, waiting for my shift to be over, waiting for violence against women to be over. I'm still waiting.

Sociology examines the relationships between individuals and the societies in which they live. It encompasses the study of social problems, such as crime, poverty, human rights, race, and gender, as well as the theories that seek to solve these problems. Sociology also provides a broader perspective on identity, culture, and the development of human societies. Through the study of sociology, we gain insights into, and can address, societal challenges, even those affecting populations that may not realize their interconnectedness.

How does sociology relate to ExA? Many ExA practitioners work within community centers of various kinds, primarily existing to assist individuals facing similar challenges. Interns at the Expressive Arts Institute in San Diego have worked with diverse populations, including survivors of torture, victims of domestic violence, individuals in prison halfway houses, people in alcohol and drug recovery programs, and children in the juvenile justice system. Additionally, ExA services are provided to asylum seekers from Haiti and refugees from Afghanistan and Iran (as classified by their legal status according to the government). All these underserved populations receive services from nonprofit organizations, whether they are private entities or those operating under the umbrella of social services in San Diego County or City. Sociology offers insight into the broader movements and struggles of people—issues that go beyond the personal but ultimately impact each individual (Levine & Levine, 2011).

2. Neuroscience

The field of neuroscience is concerned with the study of brain function. It teaches how to provide an optimal environment for our brains and how to maximize our potential in terms of brain health. Furthermore, recent research advancements have given us a better understanding of how trauma affects both the brain and behavior. This knowledge aids in observing and identifying the symptoms of neurological distress that arise as a result of various stressors. Thanks to neuroscience, we are now better equipped to recognize and support individuals who exhibit the signs and symptoms of trauma, and we have interventions that enable us to better treat trauma. As it turns out, ExA is an excellent treatment choice since it is holographic, uses the whole person, enacts and expresses emotion, and allows for the *better ending* to inform the person of choices that they might make.

As a result of these understandings, we can reduce victim-blaming and develop treatments for conditions such as post-traumatic stress disorder and shift to post-traumatic stress growth. It is essential for every ExA practitioner to know how to recognize and accommodate individuals who are experiencing such suffering. ExA sessions can be conducted in a trauma-informed manner, and resources for this approach are readily available online for practitioners whose training programs do not provide this information. While individuals may experience significant suffering, they can harness that suffering as a springboard for personal growth.

3. Embodiment

Perhaps the most auspicious decision I made in my young adult life was to study dance as my major for my bachelor's degree. As a result, I began to pay close attention to my physical self, considering questions such as: Was the foot beveled? Was the sternum lifted? Was the diaphragm descending to accommodate the breath? Over the course of my lifetime, this intimate connection with my body has served me well. Every inch of a dancer's body, and every muscle group, is brought into consciousness, allowing them to be trained to execute the precise movements needed for a particular composition. This understanding and control were particularly beneficial for an asthmatic like me.

My dance education included study on human cadavers. Through this hands-on approach, I gained a deep understanding of anatomy and was able to identify muscles, nerves, tendons, joints, and organs within a real human body. I touched the vagus nerve, and indeed, what they say is true: it is as thick as a shoelace and wanders extensively throughout the body. This was a transcendent experience for me, even as the reek of formaldehyde permeated the room, my clothes, and my nose. The body was laid bare without life, impulse, personality, the stark thing of it. My cadaver had only one leg, so an extra leg was thrown into the casket. The indignity of it, the randomness, the sadness. And my gratitude to this person, whose name I never learned.

In the studio, we did deep meditations on the organs, using imagination to locate and recreate our insides. This was in addition to studying kinesiology and corrective exercise. My program encompassed all the dance techniques offered at the university, including ballet, modern, folk, and ballroom dance. Each tradition had its own movement traditions, vocabulary, rhythms, and use of space. There were many other topics that a dancer/composer needs to master, and my decision to study dance offered me much. These included: self-discipline, trust in my developing body awareness, physical intuition, and an appreciation of diverse cultures through their music, dance, stagecraft, and an indelible understanding of our embodiment.

"Embodied consciousness" refers to the notion that our consciousness resides within our flesh and emerges from it. "I" am not enrobed in my flesh, I am my flesh. The body and the mind interact as one; the division is only a conceptual and artificial one. It is both a paradox and a truth that we have a body and are a body. We can only understand our world through our bodies, our senses. They are conduits of the flow of information and sensation both inward and outward. We give out and take in impressions: sounds, smells, images, movements.

Consciousness is not the province of our brain alone but emerges from the complexity of our brain and the interactions with the rest of our organs, muscles, the shape of our anatomy, the origins and evolution of our form—the totality. The study of consciousness suggests that we perceive and think the way we do because of the type of body that we have. Our brain extends itself via its fluid all the way down our spine, and then its couriers, the nerves, travel out to the farthest reaches of ourselves, and those outposts send messages back. But traveling at the speed of light (as nerve impulses do) through a body of 5 feet, 2 inches, the communication is instantaneous; it is not useful to think in terms of "out and back." Our physical form influences the way we think. This gives weight to the idea that all of our senses have ways of knowing about the world because our consciousness is distributed. Our eyes can see light from galaxies light years away and a candle 30 miles away (under the right conditions). We can detect around a million colors. Our fingertips can perceive textual differences between weights of silk and something as thin as a tiny hair. We have the capacity to detect an estimated trillion different smells. Our sensory abilities are remarkable. It is through these extraordinary sensory capabilities that we understand and interpret the world around us.

You are flesh. You are matter. That is both source and receptacle of your consciousness. The work of Mark Johnson (2007) reminds us that we can "know" things about ourselves and our world that can never be translated into words. Christopher Bollas (1987) called this type of knowing the "unthought known"—something we know, but not by cognition, not by thinking, but from the body. This bodily source of knowing is found in the writings of many thinkers and writers from Heidegger, Piaget, Vygotsky, John Dewey, to George Lakoff, Eugene Gendlin, and Mark Johnson.

Contemporary theories of embodied consciousness suggest that a significant portion of our thinking occurs outside our conscious awareness. For example, certain sensations that we are initially aware of may fade from our consciousness over time; when we first put on our shoes we notice them, but after a few minutes, we may no longer be aware of them. Every day, we demonstrate our capacity to understand aspects of our experience without conscious thought.

To emphasize the importance of this concept, pay attention to the studio or decentering phase of the session, especially the sensitizing phase. Allowing people to come to stillness and silence while attending to their breath and the pull of gravity on their bodies is never a bad beginning. Doing a brief body scan helps people come into the here and now. I provide numerous examples in the studio section of the book. It's important to remember that embodied consciousness is not an either/or phenomenon—it comes and goes and can be learned.

4. Ecology/Environmental Philosophy

This is the study of living organisms, their physical environments, and the interactions between and among them.

STORY: Dark Night Sky

The star-filled night sky brings me a profound sense of peace, as my anxieties and fears soften and melt away, if only for a while. Glittering and gorgeous is the Milky Way—the milk of the goddess, sprayed across the darkness on the curve of the arm of the spiral galaxy, the place our little solar system calls home. Contemplating my place in time, the beautiful universe somehow relieves me of angst. I'm not sure why, perhaps because it is so vast and magnificent, and I belong to it. It is my only home. Often, I weep, but it isn't sadness; it's more like gratitude or reverence, as well as an acute understanding of my short lifespan. The desert elicits similar feelings in me. Landforms reveal geologic time, the eons of upheaval and chaos the earth endured. Vast silence and emptiness bring relief to my smallness. Tiny, no-name human, a speck on a speck, somewhere in a blip in the eons of time, in this singular now. Hallelujah, I got to be here.

Carl Sagan (1994) told us we are made of star-stuff. This is not a metaphor; it is a fact. The universe, including us, is made from the detritus of the Big Bang. The same elements that make up the universe make us. In a sense, there's no separation or difference between us and the universe. Our life form is like all the other life forms on Earth, carbon-based. We grow and reproduce, like all carbon-based life forms. We are fabulous, wonderful creatures, along with the rest of the fabulous and wonderful creatures that inhabit our planet. I won't catalog all the compelling creatures we share our planet with, but you get the idea. They are made of star-stuff, like us.

Kurt Vonnegut (1963) called us the "Lucky Mud" that got to sit up and look around at creation. I liked that metaphor, especially because soil and living things are composed of the same elements, including the human body. We are made of the elements of the earth, and our breath keeps us alive.

Because the Earth is our home, our connection to it is a vital part of our comprehensive health. We seem to be re-awakening to its necessity and benefits. Popular now is the Japanese concept of *shinrin-yoku, forest bathing*, or being in the company of trees to be restored and rejuvenated. It is expanding to contemplate our relationship to trees, whose out breath is oxygen, our most vital nutrient. My favorite place to walk and sit in Saas Fee is in the larch forest. Larch needles are soft and bendy, not hard and pokey. They invite you to sit for a while, draw, lie down, breathe, rest. Rocky formations around them suggest fairy gardens with tiny wildflowers and mosses. The sound of rain is a known soporific. On platforms like YouTube, one can find dozens of options for such calming sounds, including rain in a camper van, rain on a window, rain on a tin roof, and rain on a tent.

Morning sunlight helps the pituitary regulate circadian rhythms of sleeping and waking, light and dark—a rhythm observed even in single-cell organisms—and profoundly central to life on Earth (Huberman, 2022). Negative ions, which are known to have both physical and mental health benefits, are found abundantly in natural environments, such as near the ocean, waterfalls, and forests (okay, your shower does this too) (Howard, 2000).

All of this is to say that we are creatures of nature, and being in a natural environment is good for our physical and mental health, otherwise known as *health*. I suggest you practice weaving yourself into your environment. Put yourself into a relationship with other beings who live there—when you see the lizard, the lizard sees you. Be nourished from the particular beauty of your sky, trees, grasses, or stones, whatever is noteworthy or unique about where you live. Looking at the horizon of the Pacific Ocean as far as I can see, or into the miles of vast badlands of the Anza-Borrego Desert, I resonate with the long view. This is just true for me; I didn't try to make it so; I didn't choose it; it chose me. These were the vistas available to me. ExA offers a way to contemplate climate change and the human-caused destruction of the natural world. It provides avenues for dealing with that knowledge and its consequences. In my work, it means taking people outside and bringing natural objects inside. To be in the presence of nature, whether a forest or a flower, is to reconnect with the beautiful and forgiving natural processes of our planet. When the destruction ceases, the healing processes begin. We have lots of evidence of this in the recovery of our oceans, coral reefs, forests, and waterways. Connection with the planet can help us heal our own despondency. Then we can take action to further contribute to the forces of healing.

What is the best way to honor our relationship with the Earth? First, we need to know it. It is said that we care about what we love, so loving your landscape is not trivial.

STORY: Women's Wildflower Retreat

Annually for ten years, my friend and fellow dance/movement therapist Betty Backus and I held a Women's Wildflower Retreat in the Anza-Borrego desert. This long weekend included educational elements about the wildflowers, their cycles of bloom and dormancy, the fragility of the desert—especially its patina, despite its rugged appearance. The abundant life: jackrabbit, coyote, cougar, kangaroo rat, tortoise, and the many birds and insects and the vibrant beauty of the wildflowers transfixed us. Those flower seeds evolved over 80 million years ago and changed the Earth. How they evolved is a great mystery in botany (Eisley, 1996). They emerged from the Earth herself, and now, in springtime, California poppies are so abundant that they cover acres; they can be seen from space. They were never planted; they simply emerged. Our casual studies included a look on the desert geology and an acknowledgment of the native people, the Kumeyaay, who have lived here for thousands of years. When you know the landscape you walk through, you walk through it differently; you belong; you are not a stranger. We danced under a large, eight-sided canvas umbrella, our Hexa-Luna. In this shelter, we sang, drew, wrote, and recited poetry. We slept under the stars, knitting ourselves back into a relationship with the place. We experience the beauty of this sere landscape as early peoples might have.

We evolved alongside our planet, composed of the same materials as the Earth itself. Our bones contain the same minerals as stones. Our senses are in the embrace of the Earth and sun, moon, and stars. Your eyes have a tiny opening, the pupil, through which light—a wavicle, both wave and particle—enters the aperture and reaches our retinas. The sound of a voice or any tone enters the ear and causes the tiny membrane known as the eardrum to vibrate. This vibration sets in motion the ossicles—the hammer, anvil, and stirrup—within the middle ear. The coiled shape of our inner ear, known as the cochlea, resembles the spiral shape of a nautilus shell. This spiral pattern is echoed in natural phenomena, such as our spiral galaxy, water swirling down a drain, hurricanes, and even our own fingerprints. The pattern of five phalanges or digits is found in the limbs of mammals, reptiles, birds, and amphibians. All the food we consume ultimately originates from seeds, which absorb water and nutrients from the soil and grow toward sunlight. In essence, we consume sunlight made tangible through the process of photosynthesis. Patterns found in nature are echoed in our bodies: the flow of rivers can be compared to our bloodstream, the branching of trees to the branching of our bronchi, the structure of clouds to our lungs, and lightning to the electrical impulses of our nervous system. We are intrinsically connected to the natural world—we are earthlings.

5. Medicine
Medicine is the study of the human body and all its physical processes, including the means of restoring health. Also, a compound or chemical substance taken, or procedure undergone to relieve pain and suffering.

STORY: I Honor Dr. Percy Lavon Julian
At the age of nine months, I was diagnosed with a chronic illness that still affects my bronchi and lungs. Some of my earliest memories include hospital visits and time spent in a croup tent. During Black History Month, I take to social media to express my gratitude for the chemist Dr. Percy Lavon

Julian, who isolated the compound that has allowed me to breathe more easily and continue to live. Since a baby, I have had an intimate relationship with doctors, hospitals, medicines, and machines. Part of my struggle has been learning how to live with a chronic condition without allowing it to define my life, accepting both the limitations and the opportunities it has offered me. Many medicines and medical people contributed to my being here, but it was his work that allowed me to live. Thank you, Dr. Julian.

In America, health care is a vast system involving people and businesses that deliver care. ExA practitioners may work with individuals who have acute or chronic illnesses, so it is beneficial to have a balanced view of medicine. This perspective acknowledges that the delivery system may have flaws and instances of power abuse. The medical model used to treat mental illness follows principles similar to those used in treating physical illnesses. We live beside the medical model and need to understand the benefits it proffers, even as we offer an alternative.

The problems with the current medical model are numerous, including limited access to care. Perhaps more relevant to our topic is the reduction of a person to a diagnosis. "Diagnosis" in Greek means to distinguish or discern, to look closely, but that is not usually what happens. Often, a person is seen as their disease, as their identity. They are reduced. For example, I am "an asthmatic." It serves giant medical corporations and insurance companies to standardize the treatment of certain illnesses; "take two of these and one of those." This leads to abuse of power and greed-driven decisions, diminishing the person with the illness. This approach makes the person smaller. It is efficient for the medical machine, but not for the individual. Without a diagnosis, many insurance companies will not pay for treatments, and most of us could not afford to pay for medical treatments out of pocket. The insurance companies stand between the patient and their doctor, as they must approve the course of treatment. This layer of complexity allows for another layer of profit to be made. This is especially egregious in the United States.

Having said that, physicians can be helpful, giving the patient a sense of being seen and cared for. Sometimes a diagnosis brings relief: "My suffering has a name. I'm not the only one." Based on medical science, careful history taking, and scrutiny of possible treatment approaches, the Western medical model can be life-sustaining—as it was for me. A CT scan can look inside you, and an MRI can do the same thing in a different way. This offers an unprecedented view of internal organs and functions. For many individuals, the benefits of medication allow them to live without unnecessary suffering. Still, there are other ways to approach illnesses. The physical aspect of illness is not the end of it: there is always a person who is experiencing the dis-ease or dis-order. ExA can be a valuable adjunct to medicine in the treatment of many conditions. The body affects the mind: If you are suffering from a chronic or acute dis-ease process, it will affect your mental state, emotional state, social standing, and behavior. Likewise, when mental suffering is paramount in a person's circumstance, it will manifest in the physical and emotional aspects of their life. We are a united field. These are recursive elements of our lives. Not only do our mental and physical lives correspond, but our environments, both physical and social, also influence us, even as we influence them. We are semi-permeable to everything in our surroundings.

ExA looks for the "origins of health," a concept known as salutogenesis. Aaron Antonovsky first coined the term in 1979. His research question was: "What created health." The medical model and the salutogenic model can coexist. ExA therapy can be adjunctive to a medical model approach, so the practitioner must have a certain knowledge of how that system works. The language of the *DSM* (*Diagnostic and Statistical Manual of Mental Disorders*) is a *lingua franca* for the mental health system, and the ExA practitioner working in environments where it is used should be familiar with it.

At the same time, we should bear in mind the perspective that this "bible of mental illness" is also a political artifact and a profit center for the American Psychiatric Association. It is not "objective truth." Remember, homosexuality was listed as a mental illness until 1973. Women, in particular, experience gender bias in the *DSM*. Although well-intended, it has become an end in itself. Most college courses that study the *DSM* do not explore the financial or historical dimensions of this influential document. Thus unexamined, it has greater force than it otherwise might. Unexamined elements of a system exert undue influence because they are invisible. Like many things, state licensing and insurance payments have both advantages and disadvantages. If you have health insurance it can help with the bills; if you don't, you are precluded from certain levels of care. If you're a practitioner, the insurance company tells you what you can charge and how many times you can see your client.

In ExA, we provide an alternative approach, salutogenesis, or health-building. We challenge these systems of labeling. We can conceptualize the things that constrain and trouble us in more humanistic ways. We can take into account the individual's situation and environment, their strengths and weaknesses, their relationships, and the resources available to them: educational, financial, social, physical, their character, their history. Postmodern health care tries to determine what is impeding the full functioning of the client.

This establishes the environment/situation as a contributor; the "illness" does not lie exclusively within the interior of the person.

6. Complexity Theory

Also known as Cha-Org, or systems theory, complexity theory examines the relationships between components of a complex system, such as a couple, a family, a work team, a group, a department in a hospital, or a governing body. Multiple and interpenetrating relationships exist.

This concept, which originates in physics, can serve as a metaphor for understanding change processes in complex systems, such as those named above. According to complexity theory, chaos and order are interconnected and predict one another; chaos resolves into order and order dissolves into chaos. When things are overly ordered, they tend to become rigid, stagnant, stale. That rigidity will necessarily lead to change, a breaking down of the order. When things are chaotic, they will tend to begin to organize in an autopoietic way—this self-organization is organic and can be surprising and unpredictable. These are two sides of the same process, two sides of the same coin. They imply one another. This understanding brings an end to the predictable universe. This might be scary and it might be a relief. It heralds the end of the black-and-white world of Descartes' universe, where mind and body are separate, and all things can be "either/or." We enter the understanding of stochastic or random occurrences in our lives. Here, things can be "both/and."

Professor Dr. Jürgen Kriz explored the relationship between order and chaos as a theory of change at The European Graduate School (2006). It is my preferred metaphor for change. It asserts that in order to change a system that is rigid or "stuck," the change agent can introduce energy into the system. Knill called this introduction of energy "perturbation." The perturbing element in our case is the art, either playing with the art mate-rials and elements or making images. Perturbation suggests that when the stagnant system is disturbed, it will become activated, more chaotic at first as it lets go of its former structure, but then it will reorganize, taking into account the elements that were left out or unacknowledged. It reorganizes at a higher level of complexity, which is a good thing. This chaos is the precursor of change, and art challenges bring that chaos. We can't know exactly what will happen when we make art in the expressive arts manner.

In the studio setting, people can be afraid of chaos and the change it might bring. It is unfamiliar and might feel disorienting. Order creates a feeling of safety, even if the safety is suffocating. It is important that all other issues of the session are organized and transparent, so that when we get to the art-making, people can endure a certain amount of "not knowing," and tolerate that little bit of chaos.

Beginning interns typically follow a structured plan of art activity. This strategy is an attempt to control randomness, the fear of chaos. As they develop expertise, they move more into the moment and respond to what is present or might emerge, allowing the art materials to lead, following the client.

Chaos is all around us, every day. It is part of life; this changing, one might say, is life itself. Even though it is constant, it can be scary. It's difficult for human beings to comprehend how complex our situation is. Things are so intricate that they can appear to be random. We organize our time and days, trying to ignore the random factors. This randomness is called "stochastic." The word originates from the Greek, meaning "aim, guess." It suggests that systems change because of random occurrences, and we can only speculate about the outcome. We live in a stochastic universe where nothing is predetermined. It is characterized by random events and probability so complex that the pattern, if any, cannot be discerned. This marks the end of the predictable universe.

Chaos operates on the principle of random attraction, analogous to the concept of gravity in physics. Matter attracts matter, forming planets and universes. If you prefer "this" slightly more than "that," it "attracts" you, calls you. Attractors gather value because you are slightly more inclined to like one thing over another. My art—visual, verbal, movement—tends toward the themes of the moon, women, and the desert (and a hundred other things, but you get the idea). These are attractors for me. You might refer to them as my themes, leading ideas, or my "familiars." There is no other grand secret to it; it's about our aesthetic choices. I like the orange one; you like the red one. Period. This is the principle the universe uses to create galaxies. Isn't that both beautiful and astonishing? This bit is more "attracted" to that bit, and together, they are more attracted to those other bits, eventually forming a planet. In our case, it is metaphorical.

Clients can find themselves stuck at either end of a complex spectrum. On one end, suffering emanates from disorganized thoughts that fluctuate constantly. Lives may be characterized by ragged disarray, with undone projects, numerous false starts, disordered eating, fluctuating relationships, or careers in turmoil. Overwhelmed by excess, they can't discern the top of their desk or even identify whose laundry is scattered about. This is the pain of a life caught in a whirlwind of chaos and ruin.

On the opposite end, clients may become rigid and unimaginative, trapped in stagnant relationships and habits that no longer serve them. They endure a sort of soul death, as James Hillman termed it in 1973. Stagnation prevails, as the song goes, "same as it ever was." Devoid of new thoughts or experiences, they slowly decay in boredom, paralyzed and perplexed about what is wrong or how to instigate change. Repeating failures, they suffer the pain of a petrified life, numb and senseless. Both extremes are equally agonizing and unsatisfactory.

Yet, it is possible to inject energy into this stagnant system through art-making, disrupting the status quo. The process of creating art opens doors for transformation. Though initially chaotic, even to the point of unexpected delight, this turbulence can catalyze rearrangement and new possibilities. While the system's ability to change is certain, the direction of that change remains unknowable. Nevertheless, change will bring new openings and opportunities, affirming an intrinsic part of life and living.

7. Anthropology

Anthropology studies early humans and evolution. It also includes the study of the arts in their culture, as well as areas such as race, gender, colonialism, and postcolonialism. Anthropology verifies the heritage of humankind as an image maker.

STORY: A Neanderthal Mother Was My Midwife

An image of ancient mothers helped me give birth. Let me explain. I experienced an entirely natural childbirth with no medical interventions at all; I was alone, all by myself. And also, I gave birth to my only child, my daughter, in Womack Army Hospital in Fayetteville, North Carolina. Both these statements are facts. Here's how that happened. After my water broke, I was informed that I needed to go immediately to the hospital. There, maternity nurses placed me in a room and left me. Apparently, I wasn't dilating quickly enough for them to be concerned about an imminent birth. I was not shaved (which was the practice at the time); I was not given any medication at all, no IV fluids, nothing. After several hours, I began to have bearing-down contractions, and with no medicine onboard and my first pregnancy, it was painful in the extreme. I moaned with every contraction. No medical assistance was offered, no one came to check on me. As they intensified, I groaned, cried out, twisted, and wrung the sheet that was over me. I gripped the bed rails and clawed at the wall. I even bit my own arm. Seriously! I feared my body would split.

At a certain point, I had a kind of daydream or vision: I saw the whole spinning world, every country whirling by; it was populated with three billion people at that time, and I saw masses of humanity on every continent.

A deep and profound understanding came over me: all these people came through the birth canal of a woman. (I realize that's not how it literally is, but this was my vision.) No one came into this world except through the body of a woman. Somehow that sustained me, uplifted me, giving me courage. Ancient women had no medicine, and they did it. All those ancient mothers, that lineage of women, my ancestors—if they could do it, I could do it. My heritage as Homo sapiens gave me that capacity and ability. I felt I might burst; the pressure and pain were excruciating. I now knew why giving birth is likened to going to the gates of death. But all those mothers were with me, somehow, giving me courage. All women linked by this searing pain and singular power. "Let this life inside me burst forth," I yelled at last, "My baby is coming!" A nurse stuck her head inside the door and said, "Quiet down, Mrs. Essex, you're scaring the other women." She said my baby wasn't coming, but when she looked, she saw that, indeed, the little girl was here. The nurse tried to get me onto a gurney and into the operating room, but Gwen was fast, and she was born before we got there, her little red fist in the air. The statues of birthing women, the birthing huts with the stones to push against, and the stories of non-medicalized birth sustained me and served as a resource. They helped to conjure up the images of the ancient mothers. Those images attended me vividly; I was not alone. It was an unexpected initiation into motherhood. Blessed be.

Our ancestors were artistic and expressive. We have evidence of their paintings, and we have evidence of their musical instruments; it makes sense that they danced and sang. We also have evidence of their burial ceremonies; the archaeological record confirms this. This knowledge brings to ExA practice an underlying understanding of the innate artistic potential in all of us, both our clients and ourselves. There is no question that we can all create art that is satisfying to our situation and adequate for our lives. Our aesthetic nature is an intrinsic part of being the species we are. By virtue of our evolutionary development, we all possess the ability to see colors, hear sounds, and move and manipulate materials in ways that constitute the basic elements of art. If these abilities are not utilized, we suffer from what I call the "aesthetic wound." When you have an ability that isn't used, it atrophies, and therefore you suffer. You are less than you could be.

In *Principles and Practices of Expressive Arts Therapy*, Knill wrote:

We have a special challenge in confronting the anesthetizing mechanisms in the world today. Could it be that genuine beauty has absented itself from our daily life to such an extent that we have to anesthetize ourselves in order to protect ourselves from abusive realities? Perhaps concerns about abuse in contemporary therapy should include those which result from an anesthetic everyday life; certainly then the aesthetic response would have political implications. (Knill *et al.*, 2005, p. 138)

Yes. Anthropology demonstrates the importance of beauty from our earliest records. The qualities of cave paintings are exquisite, and they move us still today. Pigments dating back nearly 300,000 years have been found. Archaeologists have discovered bones covered in blossoms, providing evidence of ritual burial. Shamans, the first aesthetically active healers, practiced healing based on beauty and employed a variety of art disciplines. These included dance, drama or storytelling, both instrumental and vocal music, visual elements such as costumes, and various kinds of painting and image-making, as well as environmental shaping and land art to help restore health to tribal members (Rimell, 2016). The Australian Aboriginal culture has a continuous lineage of at least 65,000 years. Their oldest rock art, a six-foot-long kangaroo, is dated at 17,500 years old. Their dance traditions, where everyone danced, are thousands of years old. All Indigenous cultures incorporate the arts as part of healing and celebration. ExA practitioners have a direct lineage to those healers through the use of metaphor and imagery. This inheritance belongs to all of us.

8. "...And Many Other Things as Well!"

Theories and methodologies of expressive arts can draw influence from a wide range of domains. Those mentioned above are a few that have been particularly useful to me. As you explore the field, you will discover your own areas of interest and influence. ExA is open to change, and to ideas and practices that can help support, elucidate, and articulate its approach.

There is significant overlap and interconnection between and among these contributing fields. The relationships are complex and multifaceted. I did not attempt to compartmentalize each aspect into neat categories. I wanted to show that the foundation of this field is broad, as old as our full human history, and as deep as human thought and experience can be. These fields are intrinsically connected to the way human beings live, and they also help support and extend the reach of expressive arts practice. This approach has life-changing implications for all of us, individually, and in our intimate relationships and in our societies. Our work is not a small and separate activity done in a small and closed room.

D. THE PHILOSOPHICAL LEAVES

Philosophy is not the reflection of a pre-existing truth, but, like art, the act of bringing truth into being.

MERLEAU-PONTY (2012)

Continuing with the image of a flower, let us now focus on the leaves. The leaves of a plant serve as the powerhouse of photosynthesis. They turn sunshine into sugar, and this feeds all other parts of our flower: seed, stem, and blossom. Like the leaf, philosophy is involved in all aspects of our work and serves to feed and support it.

All methods of working with people originate from or reflect a philosophical stance or attitude, even if it is not explicitly articulated. Practitioners may not have asked themselves questions, such as "What ideas and traditions support my practice? Why am I choosing this approach instead of another? Where do my ideas come from?" That is what philosophy does; it orients us to our beliefs and "why" we do something a certain way. In order to have rigor and grounding, it is important that we understand, at least rudimentarily, how philosophy makes a difference. Philosophy prompts us to reflect on our thinking, challenges inherited ideas, and provides orientation to our work.

Here are some philosophical questions to contemplate:

- What is a human being?

- What is the value of art?

- What about race and culture?

- Do you believe that a person discovers or invents their identity?

- Can the truth be known with certainty?

- What can be done to address and alleviate suffering?

- In your view, what role does beauty play in human life?

- Do you believe there is a universal meaning of art?

- What do you think about the body—its nature, its rights, its significance?

- What is the difference between truth and fact?

These questions call upon your personal philosophy to formulate a response. Your answers to these questions will shape and influence your perspectives on your duties, your role, and how you interact with people. Many of these ideas may have been inherited, unless you have undertaken the extraordinary work of critically reviewing them, both independently and through conversations with others. It is a privilege to engage in introspection, reflect upon your own thinking, and be open to change.

The philosophies that have influenced me came to me through my lived experience. I didn't go looking for them and, in some cases, I didn't know the things I was experiencing were part of a philosophical school of thought. Here are nine philosophies that have contributed most to my practice today. Yours can be different.

1. Phenomenology

STORY: Passion and Love

Simone, a Parisian woman, had come to the Institute after completing an art therapy training program. Standing in front of the class, looking at her painting that was taped to the wall, she was talking to the class about the passion and love she saw in the painting. I asked her to stop; to really look at the painting, see what was there on the paper. "Passion and love," she repeated. "Look again," I said. "We can see colors, lines, light, and shapes, but we cannot see passion and love because they are concepts—not visible. What do you see on the paper?" "That is what I see," she said and laughed. We all laughed with her and her gentle infectious giggle. What was literally present on the canvas were colors, lines, and some abstracted images that reminded her of passion and love in her own personal imagination and iconography. Learning to see what is on the paper takes both unlearning and new learning.

Phenomenology is based on the premise that reality consists of objects and events, "phenomena." Phenomena are those things that can appear to us, that our senses can perceive, and that can be said to exist for all of us, even if we experience them differently. These are the things themselves, without an overlay of personal interpretation. This is the philosophy behind our method of looking and commenting on what has appeared in the art.

A profound influence on the way we interpret and interact with the images that emerge in the work, both performative and visual, is this phenomenological way of looking. It is difficult for students to come to grips with the fact that they see the world through a lens of their own making and often do not see what is actually there. The truth of a thing is best understood through how we perceive it. It is shining right in front of you, don't go to the book to look up the meaning—this is not the time for that. Just dwell with the thing itself, and try to see it as it is.

The phenomenological approach teaches us to encounter the literal world—the "thingliness," as Heidegger refers to it—of what is before us. To see, hear, sense what the world is offering us and not to depend upon past stories and encounters, but endeavor to see freshly here and now. This one principle, of being with what is, has become a kind of discipline or mind training practice for many people.

2. Existential Philosophy

Existentialism emphasizes the existence of the individual as a responsible agent determining their own development. Existentialists are concerned with the act of living and how to do it in the best way possible. They took on the big questions of human existence: What is an authentic life? What is worth doing? Should we avoid conformity? Who decides what a good life is? How shall we face our death?

In an existential frame, individual freedom and personal choice is valued. Sometimes referred to as "self-determination," this concept reminds us that every person should have the autonomy to make their own decisions to the extent that they are capable of doing so. We create our lives from our actions, from this moment. We must take responsibility for our own lives even though it is difficult to deal with our many fears and failings. It is not easy to cope with our fears, self-doubt, and especially our anxiety about death. Even if it may seem absurd at times, we are obliged to strive to live an authentic life and be willing to accept the challenges that it may entail. If we are to make a meaningful life for ourselves, it matters what we do.

Existentialism suggests that there is no hidden "essence" to be "found" or discovered within us; instead, there is the awe-inspiring possibility that we are actively creating ourselves as we live. As we walk, the path appears. We experience both the pains of conformity and the pains of authenticity. Amidst the challenges of living, it can be difficult to distinguish between the two. Nevertheless, this is solely the responsibility of each person. This suggests that ExA practitioners must not interfere with the impulses and decisions of the client. We can guide, we can prime, we can offer and frame, we can inspire, demonstrate and be an example, but we are required to promote agency within the client. In the times of reflection, we can review and be thoughtful about how things turned out. What emotions and experiences did the client have? Were their impulses fulfilling or inhibiting? And how does this relate to their decision-making in "real life?"

Existentialism posits that we all have a fundamental human right to make choices. Even if a client wants to relinquish that responsibility to the therapist, those working within an empowerment model gently, and perhaps with humor and patience, redirect the responsibility back to the client without reservation. This conviction of self-determination runs counter to the idea of a diagnostic chart of things to do: If depressed, do this; if anxious, do that. If the existentialists are right, then every session must be bespoke for that person or people. We know that each of us must design and determine our own life and its direction, all within the constraints of the time, place, parentage, and privileges or lack thereof of our circumstances. We make choices, even when not all options are available to us—which is always the case.

An important element that existentialism brings is the sobering understanding that not only are we responsible for our lives, but it will end; we all will die. We are required to be courageous enough to look at this fact and then pull back from the moment of death to this moment right now. Empower yourself and your client to take responsibility and set sail in the direction best suited for this life. Even as the winds blow this way or that; even if the winds die and the sea is still for a while, no matter what we encounter, fair winds or foul, we can learn to steer our own barque, to look to the horizon and stars for guidance. There is no other way. We all must do the same. Existentialism suggests that life has no pre-existing meaning or grand scheme waiting to be discovered—there is no overarching authority greater than ourselves to tell us what to do, how to live. Life simply is. Hand-in-hand with this notion of freedom comes the experience of anxiety. Angst is part of existential philosophy in this way; in seeking your destiny, how do you know you are making the right choice? Which is the right way to go? Without a divine blueprint, which path is best? When we take on the reality of our aloneness we can become overwhelmed. So, the excitement and eagerness for the freedom of choice are tempered by worry and dread. Since I am responsible for my choices, what if I make a wrong one? To what extent am I responsible for the illnesses or misfortunes that beset me? It would be a distortion to presume that we have caused everything that happens to us. Life is more random than is comfortable for most of us to acknowledge. Still, we do make choices with consequences and fail to make choices, which also has consequences. What turns did I take, and what turns took me? Choice and chance. Existentialism asks us to face our mortality. That is daunting and scary. Many poets and wise people have noted that knowing life will end can give relish to our days. Certainly, we grasp—no matter how unappealing and unpleasant it may be—that our life will end, and we will have passed through the river of all the lives on the Earth. Poet Mary Oliver asks: "Listen—are you breathing just a little, and calling it a life?" This perspective can help us make decisions about what is useful and necessary. It can also help inoculate us from the overwhelm our clients might feel as they face the perspective of their own demise.

We live in a world where anxiety, alienation, and estrangement are prevalent. Being alone doesn't have to mean being lonely! It means we live our own lives; no one can live it for us, make the choices we need to make, or do the work we need to do. Guarding against detachment becomes part of the job of being responsible for your own life.

One of the great existentialists, Jean Paul Sartre, said: "Existence precedes essence." This suggests that before someone's life has meaning, they exist; in other words, there is no precious "essence" of a person that is given, hidden, or that we can "discover" waiting within. Rather we design our life and its meaning emerges—we make it as we go. It's an improv. At the end of a life, we can see its arc, its trajectory, its themes. Having lost many people I love, I have come to see that the way a life unfolds is itself an action, a statement, an image. Day-by-day we work on our tapestry, our opus. I could easily see at the end of a life the threads and themes that were prominent, which actions were pivotal, and what influences were primary. Lives have a dramatic arc, like a play.

How can I fashion a meaning for my life when I can barely get my laundry done? And how can I do so with no blueprint? There are some givens.

Referring to Uri Bronfenbrenner's ecological developmental systems theory, we see that many aspects of a person's life are predetermined—such as whether they have good health or a troubled body; their sex, the year and place of their birth, the status and situation of their parents. What opportunities and resources do they or do they not have as a result of either a "lucky" birth or an "unlucky" one? Their inclinations and preferences are also part of the shaping. So, life isn't a blank slate. These predetermined factors are the givens from which one begins to fashion a life. As Heidegger said, "we are thrown into life"—a life that we didn't create and cannot fully control. Our most authentic act is to respond to what is given. This making a response and working with what is given; this is *poiesis*. It might sound corny, but we are response-able. We can respond, and each response is a choice. Choice by choice a life is made.

In a simple way, allow people to make as many decisions in the session as makes sense. Encourage them to tell us their story, to make decisions about the direction of the therapy. Yes, it is a partnership, and we have our opinions and ideas as well, but it is up to us to listen deeply with our ears and our hearts, to make certain the dignity of the person is preserved and enhanced. This is especially true when we are working with people who may have difficulty with such decisions or are immature or impaired in some way.

Fragile or elderly individuals, people with mental illness at certain stages, children, individuals with mental challenges such as traumatic brain injury, and those who have suffered from severe depression are more vulnerable than others. To uphold their "self-determination," we must understand how central this principle is to human dignity and champion this idea. Restoring a person's sense of agency is a wonderful and healing experience, both for them and for you. We approach them with open-hearted curiosity, eager to understand their world and, within that context, design aesthetic experiments for them to explore.

3. Feminism and Humanism

The basic premise of feminism is that all people are equal; women are equal to men and deserve both equal treatment under the law and equal opportunity in education, work, sports—everything. It makes me sad to have to type that. Our world is so blatantly not there yet. For example, as of this date, 2023, women earn 15.5% less than men. According to the World Economic Forum, it is estimated that the global gender pay gap will take well over a hundred years to close. How to fix this? This is a job for Xena, Warrior Princess.

STORY: My Daughter, the Dean

I am a champion for women. I encourage each woman to make her own decisions, pursue work that she loves and that uses her abilities, have the type of relationships she prefers, and get an education that allows her to shine in her chosen field. Stay the course, get through the rough patches. Many of my clients and students have turned their lives around, discovered their true direction, created jobs, or returned to work for the first time in 20 years, pursued careers in the arts, had children or decided to not have children. These changes happened when they began to listen and recognize the voice that was their own. There is no better example than my daughter Gwen (the other Dr. Essex, we like to joke). After 20 years as a professor at UCSF, she took a position as the Dean of Academic Affairs at California Northstate University, a private medical and dental university. I couldn't have predicted any of that. Coming out of high school, she didn't want to go to college right away because she didn't know why she wanted an education. I thought she would go to Portland to become a Shakespearean actor—she was that good in drama. But, when she saw her vision, she followed it. She began to work with intention. She took math and science classes that might have scared her before, but now they were just a hurdle to jump over. Despite her parents' messy and contentious divorce, despite poverty, despite numerous other challenges, or maybe in part because of them, she persisted. My smart, funny, queer daughter persisted and triumphed. I am bragging, I admit, but I am also saying hold tight to your aspirations and dreams when they arrive, be not deterred. Believe in yourself. Persist. Climb the mountain of your choice. Take advantage of both your own genius and what is within reach, what the world offers you. There is a place for you.

Feminism has a mission to establish political, economic, personal, and social equality for all people. This includes advocating for educational and professional opportunities for women that are equal to those for men. Feminism examines the role of gender and addresses issues such as sexism, racism, oppression, ageism, and sexuality—topics that are so vital to life that we cannot ignore them. Feminism honors knowledge gained from living in specific situations, giving us the perspective of the "Situated Knower"—an expert with lived experience. Feminism also addresses notions of independence, domination, and agency—especially as they pertain to women, but ultimately relevant for all people.

According to feminists, societies determine what is considered knowledge. This is influenced by how we are raised, and the cultural and social context that surrounds us. This determines what questions are asked and what questions are overlooked. Thus, stories and narratives play a significant role in shaping a society.

For much of human history, female people have had a kind of second-class citizenship. Feminism grew out of the recognition of the oppression and subjugation of women, first for suffrage, the vote, then for economic and educational opportunity. We still haven't passed the Equal Rights Amendment in the United States. How does this impact the practice of ExA? First, it involves understanding that many of the so-called symptoms of mental illness are manifestations of distress and oppression. Women in my practice are often reluctant to view themselves as oppressed or to voice complaints. However, the recent #MeToo movement has validated what many of us already knew—that a majority of women have experienced sexual harassment or worse. Women still face financial discrimination and are underrepresented in governments. The greater responsibility for child-rearing and housekeeping falls to women. As a popular meme suggests, "I'm a woman and I'm tired!" Our autonomy over our own bodies is not always respected. Thus, ExA practitioners need to recognize that part of what causes depression or stress in individual women may be rooted in systemic issues, especially those stemming from patriarchy. As of 2022, the fight goes on for dominion over our own bodies and health care decisions, which, with the overturn of Roe v. Wade, sustained a blow.

Reproduction is one of the most central issues to women and their lives. It has been undermined in the USA by decisions of the Supreme Court, mostly made up of men. When given agency, women will choose to have the number of children they are capable of caring for. A woman's development should not be held hostage by her fertility.

To highlight the overwhelming patriarchal nature of our own country, I conducted a meditation exercise with my students to explore how different our world would be if women had equal access to power in the US. What if there were an equal number of women on the Supreme Court? Or as Justice Ruth Bader Ginsburg said:

> ...when I'm sometimes asked when will there be enough [women on the Supreme Court]? And I say when there are nine, people are shocked. But there'd been nine men, and nobody's ever raised a question about that. (Bader Ginsburg, as cited in Filipovic, 2012)

How would the world be different if at least half of the heads of Fortune 500 companies were female? Currently, only 10% are. What if God was a woman? God the Mother versus God the Father. Would Big Goddess religions be different? If our legislature were 50% female, would our foreign and domestic policies, especially concerning education, health, and ecology, remain the same? These questions resonate powerfully. Like me, you might wish for all children to have access to adequate shelter, food, clothing, education, and health care. Why not? The domestic budget of the USA has been overwhelmingly allocated to military spending. As President Dwight D. Eisenhower (1953) said:

> Every gun that is made, every warship launched, every rocket fired signifies, in the final sense, a theft from those who hunger and are not fed, those who are cold and are not clothed, this world in arms is not spending money alone. It is spending the sweat of its laborers, the genius of its scientists, the hopes of its children.Would this be different if women were in power? It's important to note that not all women are feminists. While that is a topic for another day, the experience of carrying a zygote, an embryo, a fetus, and then a child, and nurturing that child at one's own breast, leads to a different perspective on the world, especially if one's bodily experience is not managed or interpreted by pre-existing ideas.

As a resource for my practice, I need to see and know what women have done in the arts and sciences throughout history. This can take some doing. In histories of all kinds, if women are mentioned, they are typically defined by their relationships to men as adjunctive figures such as wife, mother, or daughter, rather than as agents on their own. Even highly gifted artists like Frida Kahlo, Remedeos Varo, Jo Hopper, Lee Krasner, and Elaine de Kooning were subjugated to their husbands, or not recognized as artists in their own right.

As a feminist in your own practice, fulfill your role and potential as a human being. Nothing is more important than the example you set. Take good care of yourself so you can last. Getting older means living longer and that means more experience, more knowledge, and more opportunities. Use it. Set an example of being active in whatever way suits you.

Defend a woman's right to pursue her opportunities. Encourage your female students and clients to create and go after their dreams. Encourage them to "make their luck" by taking risks and chances. Encourage a woman to get her own education, pursue what she is interested in and good at. Know resources in your area for "first-generation" women who are the first in their families to go to college. Support the notion that she can have her own money and financial independence—own property if she can, as a safe harbor.

Be aware of the issues that often go unspoken because of the shame associated with them. When working at Casa de Paz, the first battered women's shelter in San Diego, I saw how learned helplessness cripples a woman's ability to make choices. Be cognizant of this, recognize and name it. Making choices in the art studios can transfer to making choices in life.

Understand and articulate the limitations and barriers placed on women's ambitions and dreams. In being solution-focused and strength-based, notice and make comments on the strengths you perceive. Understand and articulate the hardships of marriage, child-rearing, and household responsibilities. No woman can live up to the idealized image of the mythical Great Mother; instead, we can strive to be the "good-enough" mother as described by D.W. Winnicott. Many women have unreasonable expectations of themselves in these demanding roles. The culture encourages it. Foster reasonable expectations.

Encourage your female clients to think through the issues of pay and opportunity. Pay is not the only definition of successful work. Work can sustain our lives as well as pay the bills. A beautiful life has time for pleasure and personal pursuits. Encourage women to be politically active, to vote. Encourage them to exert the social power they do have.

Be open-minded about sexual expression—examine your ideas about what constitutes sexual health. Be informed by WHO (the World Health Organization), for example. Know the signs of sexual harassment; be aware of the personal and political dimensions of this issue. Women and little girls are sexualized by a patriarchal culture. The #MeToo movement exposed the depth and breadth of the female's sexual harassment experience. This is not limited to females but it is an overwhelmingly female issue.

Look at the body not as an object to be weighed and measured, but as a creature who wants to move and do. Rethink the male gaze by calling it out. Define feelings of safety; how do you know when you are safe? How does your body feel when you know you are safe, in your breath and belly? How does your mind feel? Support organizations that support women like Planned Parenthood and the National Association for the Repeal of Abortion Laws. Subscribe to feminist publications, like *MS.* and *Bust*. Consider reading literature by transgender and lesbian authors. Look for her-story: female artists and scientists as nourishing images, such as Isadora Duncan, Madam Curie, Madeleine Albright, Rachael Carson, Artemis, Sally Ride, Loïe Fuller, and Queen Tomiris. We need heroines, their stories and images. Have a bookshelf full of feminist literature. Myth, metaphor, and image are our tools. I have collections of images of women as leaders and change agents, both literal and imaginal, from goddesses across time and place, from Lt. Uhura and Captain Janeway from Star Trek, to the pink pussy-hatted women in the 2017 Women's March—the largest march ever, and without violence. These images feed the imagination of women and can act as goals, reassurances, and signposts.

4. Aesthetics

Beauty has an important role in human existence. We have plenty of evidence in the archaeological record that humans made things beautiful. We do so to this day.

The goddess of beauty and love in ancient Greece was Aphrodite. The sound associated with her is laughter, so pleasure and delight is associated with beauty. One of her magic powers was in her belt, also called her girdle, which other goddesses asked to borrow, so embrace your love of costume and body adornment. Another power was in her magic cream. This is a woman I can relate to.

Aesthetics is interested in what is considered beautiful and what beastly, especially the history of these ideas and how they inform human life. The word "aesthetics" comes to us from the Greek, meaning "perception," so right away we know that beauty and human perception are connected, that beauty is not separate from the person doing the perceiving. When we are making art with ordinary people who are experiencing difficulties in their lives; it is good to remember that perceptions are individual, not universal.

Our understanding of aesthetics now includes the grotesque, the dark, and ridiculous aspects of art and life, as well as the charming, funny, light, and gorgeous aspects. Think of the rugged beauty of a rock wall, or the twangy sound of the country banjo. What about the drag aesthetic or a leather bar, steampunk, or Japanese street aesthetics? All cultures and societies across time have their own ways of arrangement, preferred palettes, textures, and symbols. The traditional Japanese aesthetic, wabi-sabi, embraces the beauty of imperfection, impermanence, and incompleteness, the rugged old stone fountain with freshly blooming daffodils. Picasso's Guernica reveals the horrors of war, but in a compelling aesthetic manner. These different kinds of beauty reflect their cultural origins, but we all respond to them.

Aesthetics in the postmodern world suggests that it is the experience of a thing that makes it beautiful. Beauty is a personal phenomenon—I respond to things that resonate with my history, culture, education, taste, and so I like them. I have noticed that as people are exposed to more art, their tastes and tolerance for images expand. Same with music; it takes a lot of listening to appreciate the high-energy jazz of John Coltrane or the microtonal compositions of Harry Partch. With our tasting palate, we become accustomed to various tastes and textures in our food; our art appreciation is similar. We learn how to listen, what to watch, what to look for, how to see. We develop our "ear" and our "eye," as in "she has a good eye;" or "he has an ear for gamelan." Thus, it is absolutely necessary that the ExA therapist have as wide and deep an appreciation of the arts as can be managed. This is a lifelong education that we must engage with in an ongoing way, and in our own art-making practice.

Poiesis comes from the philosophy of aesthetics. It is the notion of shaping our world in response to what is given, as introduced to ExA by Stephen Levine. In expressive arts therapy, our aesthetics allow images to emerge as we shape them. This is a critical point. It is important to bring this to bear early in the ExA relationship; we are not going to imagine something in our mind's eye and try to reproduce it. No. As Steve says, we must not impose our will upon the materials. Allow the paint and the paper to be our partners, allowing for the "happy accident" to inform the direction of the work. This principle is the same in dance or music; see what can happen, see what "wants to happen," and discover how that can be incorporated into the overall piece. Paolo called this "serving the image." Thus the importance of the sensitizing phase of the session, getting warmed up to the elements of the endeavor and discovering the qualities and preferences of the materials themselves.

I have wondered to what extent the human capacity for beauty can be stretched. Could a single person perceive the beauty in all cultures across time and space, if that were possible to arrange? I like to think so. I believe that a person equipped with heart and imagination could perceive the human record and recognize the beauty therein.

The understanding and pursuit of beauty is moving us toward an aesthetic life, as opposed to the anesthetic life we are offered by the "one size fits all" consumer culture. When asked about how to cope with the devastation of climate change, terrible weather events, conflicts in the world and other situations, Paolo said, "Look for the beauty." I might add, "create beauty" as a way to nourish and sustain ourselves, so we can continue, one day at a time.

STORY: Helen and the Leaf

In the last year of her life, my mother, Helen, was bedridden. She could no longer walk and spent all her hours in bed, except when she was wheeled into the shower. I visited frequently, and almost always brought her a small gift: flowers, hand cream, new socks, a favorite candy. One visit, I got to the door and regretted that I had nothing to offer. It was either October or November, and there was a bright yellow leaf on her porch, fallen from one of her trees. So bright a yellow it was almost neon. She had a lovely garden but now she was no longer able to see it. On impulse, I stooped down and picked up the leaf. The color was exquisite, I thought she might like it. As I climbed the stairs I felt a bit foolish, picking up a dropped leaf. But she liked nature and the seasons, so...

As I presented the little leaf, her face broke into a wide smile. My mom had a famous smile. She took the leaf and turned it, carefully examining both sides. She commented excitedly about the bright and vivid color, twisting and twirling it like a tiny flag. She danced it in her hand. We remarked upon the tree it fell from and the change of season she couldn't see any more. The leaf animated her, bringing her a piece of herself. It tickled and delighted her. She enjoyed this leaf as much as anything I had given her. It was a spot of beauty.

The aesthetic nature of human beings needs to be acknowledged, as Ellen Dissanayake (2001) did by renaming us Homo aestheticus. We all come from ancestors who expressed themselves artistically and creatively. Early humans used all aspects of the arts to shape their lives. Your own ancestors were among the first to use pigments from the earth and plants to decorate burial sites, to use shamanic enactment for healing, with chant, songs, and story. Your own ancestors, if you go back far enough, were using their aesthetic abilities to survive and thrive, to create community with ceremony and shared myths. We were cooperating with each other and making things beautiful with symbols and embellishment.

5. Postmodernism

Postmodernism is both a philosophy and a period of time. As the name suggests, it comes after the "modern" period and is a reaction against it. For our purposes, think of the modern period as between the 17th and 19th centuries, with postmodern coming in the late 20th century, say the late 1950s—although threads and aspects can be found long before, especially in art.

Modernism and postmodernism coexist in a state of vibrant tension. Modernism subscribes to the notion that there's a truth, the same for all of us, discoverable and "out there somewhere." Postmodernism posits that truth is always local—your truth, my truth—and that it can change. It doesn't promote a "grand narrative." Bear in mind that "truth" is different from "fact."

The modernist stance has great faith in technology and science, believing that they can solve our most vexing problems. Progress is always possible. The postmodernist would cast doubt on that ideal, pointing to the failures and problems that technology brings, the repetition of dangerous trends, and other ways that circumstances can get both better and worse all at the same time. In the USA, we've made wonderful progress with medical issues, but we are still spending the majority of our wealth on military needs, thus neglecting our social needs.

Largely, modernism is the mainstream myth, the technological "fix," and picket fence dreams. Modern art is serious and experimental—think writer

T.S. Eliot, dancer/choreographer Martha Graham, and painters Picasso and Frieda Kahlo.

Postmodernism brings us the music of Meredith Monk and John Cage, the art of Judy Chicago, Cindy Sherman, Andy Warhol, and Keith Haring, theater from Samuel Beckett, and Harold Pinter, and the writings of Toni Morrison and Margaret Atwood. Postmodernism embraces contradiction and mixing genres in all the arts. It is irreverent, like Burning Man and the Fringe Festival.

Philosophy can attempt to distinguish clearly between the two: Modernism is more serious, while postmodernism is more playful. Modernism is characterized by righteousness, whereas postmodernism is marked by doubt. Modernism believes in progress, while postmodernism can lean toward pessimism. There can be no clear timelines, although modernism can be roughly placed from the late 19th century to the mid-20th century, and postmodernism from the mid-20th century to the present. Modernism has not abandoned us, and elements of postmodernism can be found much earlier. In individuals, these attitudes and preferences can also blend.

In the ExA studio, how is the "po-mo" philosophy helpful? In so many ways. First, people can be trapped by the idea of looking for an all-encompassing "big truth"—a singular, authoritative narrative or belief. This could be the belief in religion as the road to happiness, or the capitalistic myths of how money brings safety and security. It is important to have an ear out for how our clients and students impose rigid expectations or "shoulds" on themselves. I find it helpful during times of life transitions to combat the notions that "I should be here by now" or "As a mother I should be doing..." "If I don't do (*fill in the blank*), I will never make it!" Helpful when working with a person's sense of sexuality is deconstructing "normal" or "moral." The only truth that counts in these personal matters is their personal truth. Unless other people are harmed. Knowing this can ease so much suffering. People create their own stories and make their own truths through art, and the attitude of the postmodern therapist can serve as a helpful guide in that process. It also helps to laugh. Absurdity is a "po-mo" point of view: Things are ridiculous, preposterous. How did we get here? What crazy thing can happen next? Allowing for humor can be helpful to uncork the bottle and let off some pressure. We can take big ideas apart and look at things from another perspective. As I see it, both these characters are alive and well in the world today.

6. Archetypal Psychology

James Hillman was a psychologist who disliked psychology. I like him already. His writings seem to meet the criteria for philosophy: thinking about thinking. He studied with Jung, and later refused to label his own approach a "school." Hillman brings us an important leaf for our philosophy flower—the importance of images in our lives. He suggests a definition of soul for the postmodern person—a way of living. "By soul, he does not mean a substantial, underlying entity, but the quality of existence that gives meaning and vitality to our experience" (Hillman, 1975, as quoted in Knill *et al.*, 2005, p. 53). Hillman's notion of "soul" parallels the African-American vernacular sense of soulful vitality—something or someone can "have soul" or lack it. Soul for Hillman dwells in the depths, in the dark, obscure places of the psyche, especially in its pathology. "Beauty, not knowledge, is the ultimate therapeutic goal for Hillman," said Levine. For Hillman the person is not a self, but a character: "Convivo, ergo sum," "I party, therefore I am." Now there's a philosophy I can get behind.

7. Educational Philosophy

Education is a pathway to change, as well as therapy or other endeavors. Both the EGS and my Institute use an adult learning model, androgogy, recursive or experiential education, where an emphasis is put on learning by doing. This is part of a progressive educational philosophy. It includes portions of the educational experience that take place in "alternative learning frames," such as trips to museums, internships, fish-bowl sessions, practice sessions of all kinds. It welcomes cross-generational classrooms, and studio time.

These four have contributed to my understanding of education as a change process. First, John Dewey with his emphasis on experiential learning by doing, interdisciplinary studies, and discussion. Maxine Greene with her concept of wide-awakeness, and the arts as a way to enrich and inspire the social imagination. She also taught that learning should be an outgrowth of the teacher and students meeting, not a generic canon. Elliot Eisner preferring a rigorous arts curriculum on the same level as all academic subjects. The arts, he argued, teach about having more than one solution, having multiple perspectives, that we know more than words or numbers can tell. Finally, Paolo Freire, who emphasized the democratic aspects of adult education and interaction between students and teachers; a learning community. He wanted students to take charge of their own learning, to become autodidacts in a sense, and to be aware of and critique the power structures of schools. These four, and others, contribute to the educational philosophy that is the aim of the EGS and my Institute.

Many of the graduates from my Institute comment on how this education changed their lives. Progressive education is rooted in questions that arise from the interaction of the student with the world, including interaction with the environment. My educational experiences helped me begin to move away from a small, closed-family system to a larger, more open community. It put ideas in front of me that I could accept or reject, and could grapple with on my own.

8. Embodiment

Our body informs and shapes our being and experience. Since we are made up of the elements of the earth, our design follows the design and evolution of previously existing animals. Our lives are decided by our flesh, which includes our organs, like our brain. But we are not merely our brains. A key notion of embodiment is that all knowing and learning are deeply grounded in the flesh of the body (Lakoff & Johnson, 1999). Lakoff and Johnson call us central nervous system beings. Your body is your brain. All our human experiences, all states of consciousness take place in our human body. According to Merleau-Ponty, the body is the ground of reason and there would be no philosophy without the body. The myths against this truth are numerous. They get repackaged and passed around every generation, which does us an injustice for several reasons. First, they imply that we can disregard the suffering of the body without consequences. If you honor the body as the ground of your knowing, you might deal with your suffering differently. Think of your suffering as a source of knowledge, even wisdom. That kind of knowledge cannot come from anywhere other than your flesh. Go toward your body when it is in distress; learn what only you can know.

Second, these myths promote the notion that what happens to the body is trivial, that it is "just" a husk, that the most important parts of us are doing fine. Except that all parts of the body coordinate and interact with each other. When discussing the relationship between my allergies, asthma, bronchiectasis, air quality, traffic, rugs, and dust, my pulmonologist said "It's all connected." Yes. What happens to the body happens to the whole person: It can have effects both physiological or psychological. It can have social or even intellectual effects. Shall I give you an example? Say a person has acne, a common skin disorder. It typically affects the face but can include the back and chest. With this red, purulent face, having a social life is instantly more difficult. It may persist for a lifetime, having an impact on years of the person's life. The cysts can be painful and require strong medicines that can have an effect on other organ systems. This could easily mean missing school or work, with whatever consequences come with that. Looking into the mirror when grooming becomes more difficult. Our face carries the most information about who we are, so this is a challenge to be confronted at least twice a day, and self-esteem may be affected. It can leave deep scars. Can you see the cascading consequences of a relatively simple example like acne? It is a social liability.

Third, disregarding the body, treating it as a meat puppet, allows demeaning self-talk. Self-talk needs to be kind and responsible. Talk to yourself with honesty and kindness—like you would a beloved child: truthful and at the same time, kind. Yes, the body is messy and mysterious. Yes, it changes for reasons unknown. It participates in the great riddle called life.

In summary, many of these philosophies are recursive, looping back on themselves: Both feminism and postmodernism value the individual narrative and pay attention to intersectionality. Existentialism and feminism both emphasize the importance of the lived experience and taking responsibility for our choices. Postmodernism and existentialism both ask us to tolerate uncertainty. Both complexity theory and postmodernism allow for unpredictability and ambiguity. Embodiment and feminism regard the body as central to human experience. They honor the changes the body undergoes throughout the lifetime, as does existentialism. Postmodernism and educational philosophy refuse ready answers, as do existentialism and archetypal psychology. Educational philosophy, aesthetics, and archetypal psychology emphasize the centrality of the arts, images, and the aesthetic experience. There could be other leaves around our flower. What would you add?

E. THE POLLINATORS

PSYCHOLOGICAL PERSPECTIVES, PSYCHOLOGIES, AND PSYCHOTHERAPIES.

ExA is used in so many settings and for so many purposes that there are almost unlimited applications. Settings and clients run the gamut: counseling in a high school, bedside care in a maternity ward, prison and halfway houses after prison, shelters for domestic violence, executive coaching in boardrooms and team-building—the array is large, cradle-to-grave. Because the arts are a human, existential necessity, they are useful for any endeavor that requires a change or necessitates managing changes that are thrust upon us.

Think of psychological schools and approaches as pollinators: bees and butterflies that contribute something different but complementary to the ExA approach. These schools of thought have a different focus and thereby illuminate aspects of helping and healing that are helpful to ExA, and by their differences, serve as a strengthening and a resource. ExA doesn't require any of them, yet they all bring something useful. ExA stands on its own two feet as an individual field, but it reaches out its hand to others.

Psychology offers helpful theories in the areas, including the therapeutic relationship, group dynamics, and an understanding of treatment for serious mental illnesses. Many ExA practitioners work on a team with other professionals who are from the domains of medicine, psychiatry, and psychology. We bring something to the table that no one else brings; the aesthetic dimension.

Although our work is post-psychology, several branches of psychology or psychotherapy are compatible with our way of working, such as the archetypal psychology of James Hillman, positive psychology, and postmodern therapies such as solution-focused therapy and narrative therapy, as well as salutogenesis—an approach to health not focused on disease but on health building, articulated first by Aaron Antonovsky. These share with ExA the values of examining language, lived experience, and personal knowledge. They have an emphasis on the individual at the center of the work as the expert of their own lives. The other creative arts therapies, such as dance therapy, art therapy, drama therapy, and poetry therapy use the arts in some ways that are similar and in some ways that are different from our intermodal expressive arts therapy. Still, they can be allies. Social work, too, has a compatible philosophy of helping with an eye to larger systems, not limited to the individual.

We have our own shape. We stand in our own place. We have a powerful method of helping, and we work well with others. We can enter schools, psych hospitals, medical/surgical hospitals, government buildings, geriatric centers, and many other shelters to put forward our unique intermodal polyaesthetic way of working with the arts to create change.

CHAPTER FOUR

STUDIOS

INTRODUCTION TO THE STUDIOS

The term "studio" has a unique resonance. It originates from the early Italian word for a room dedicated to study. In Old French, it was used to describe a workroom. We go to the studio to work. While the arts involve play, they also involve the creation of "artwork." An artist's body of work is called an oeuvre, a term that entered English from the French (oeuvre), which ultimately derived from the Latin opera (the plural of opus, meaning "work" or "labor"). Because the word designates sustained effort, yet the creative process itself relies on exploratory play, the acts of work and play remain intrinsically intertwined in the arts.A studio is a space dedicated to creative pursuits of all kinds. While there may be some differences between them, all studios are special spaces for studying and practicing the various artistic disciplines, such as writing, dancing, painting, music, and theater arts. Studios can be found in various contexts, from radio shows and movies to the famous studios of Michelangelo and the Beatles. These spaces can be cluttered or spacious, large or small, messy or neat, and the artist's presence can be felt through the objects and materials within. Creative endeavors require a context, and a studio provides that space, whether it's outdoors or indoors, in a dedicated room or a corner of an agency.

The words "studio" and "workshop" evoke the spaces used by artists and craftspeople. Our task is to extend an invitation to the client or group to come in and experience what such a space has to offer.

As we move to the studio, let's recap our architecture of a session:

First Room: The Counselor's Chairs—First Conversation
Task: Greeting and Filling-In

Whether individual, small group, large group, or community, this is a moment to take stock of how people come into the room, emotionally, physically, mentally, or otherwise. This can be accomplished in many artful ways.

Second Room: The Studio—Artful Conversations
Task: Sensitize and Attune

The initial phase of the studio segment of the session involves engaging in activities that awaken the senses. Sensitizing allows the body and mind to become more attuned to the present moment, as well as to the chosen medium for the session.

Attunement or "tuning-in" refers to the resonance necessary for optimal outcomes. This means letting go of tricks or techniques, and being present with the client or clients. Embrace vulnerability, and be open, attentive, and activated. Allow yourself to genuinely care about the client(s) and cultivate an open-hearted curiosity about them and what you are about to do.

During this task, individuals can be encouraged to breathe, relax the diaphragm, and increase blood and oxygen flow. This process can be measured with tools such as an oximeter, which shows an increase in oxygen saturation after deep breathing or movement. Attention is also brought to the sensations of the body, such as warmth, balance, and proprioception.

Now there is an opportunity to fully engage in the present moment and set aside the distress of everyday life. This can lead to important insights and opportunities for change, such as noticing tension in the body, shallow breathing, or underlying fears.

Sensitizing is usually done in the medium that will be used in the session, such as movement or body awareness for a dance experience. For visual art, sensitize to the materials to be used, like color exploration or investigating the qualities of the paper to be used. Sound for music, action or play for theater. Using a different sense as a warm-up can also be effective, such as using body movement or drawing as a warm-up for writing. Bringing attention to the body is beneficial for any artistic activity, as all are bodily expressions.

Our work here facilitates the transition from ordinary reality to the imaginal realm, where the imagination can be fully engaged. This allows for the possibility of a deeper, more transformative experience, where the art created can become a container for emotions and experiences. Knill refers to this as the "alternative world" experience (2017, p. 59). He meant that, although we didn't go anywhere, the broom becomes a horse and the backyard the tundra; this glass of water is a magic potion and this tablecloth, the cape of invisibility. We created an alternative reality in this same room where we eat dinner and pay bills.

Sensitizing is a crucial step for a successful outcome in an expressive art therapy session, as it enlivens the senses, awakens the imagination, and allows for metaphoric materials to find form. In a process Paolo calls crystallization, an image emerges within the relationship between the client and the practitioner (Knill, 1994). It seems to hold the entire situation of concern, but externalized out of the client and into the room. This phase sets the stage for decentering, a distinguishing feature of the EGS model.

Task: Decenter

After the sensitizing phase, we move to decentering. This concept was first articulated by Knill and Eberhart, in *Solution Art* (2023), involving a shift of perspective. We want to leave the problem behind and begin doing and making. This emphasizes the use of the senses and the creative process to generate resources. The art disciplines serve as ways of knowing and expressing through color, line, movement, sound, action, and composition. Thus, the practitioner introduces an aesthetic experience tailored to the client's needs and abilities.

Eberhart recommends finding the "just-right" threshold: A task that is challenging, but not overly so. Not so easy that it seems demeaning or can be dismissed as child's play; teenagers are especially sensitive to this because they so recently left childhood. Not so difficult that it seems impossible. Take into account the possible difficulties related to age, disease, or other impairment. Not so many steps as to discourage anyone. It should foster exploration and play and be grounded in something authentic, something that comes from the client's life, not arbitrarily taken from a book or website. Several tasks and skills are needed for the studio, no matter what art discipline is being explored, regardless if the plan is for a play-oriented decentering or an image-related work, or even the creation of a ritual—each activity needs to have time for sensitizing and attunement.

Approach these activities with a sense of curiosity and adventure, allowing for exploration and experimentation. Provide an opportunity for the client to engage in a creative endeavor that can result in an aesthetic process or product—a process or product which offers new perspectives and resources for addressing their challenges. Allow opportunities for a person to be touched and moved by their own work. A chance for their helpful healing elixir to come from within, and point in the direction which holds the most promise.

We Create by Poiesis

I would like to be as clear as I can about a nuance: The knowing what to do next comes from within the client when a process of exploration has been undertaken, when there is something to respond to. That knowledge does not exist prior to art-making. Art-making itself is the process which creates the metaphor the client can respond to. These physical metaphors create the bridging between what is and what can be. This is not the same as saying, "I have all the answers already within me," but rather, "I create the resources and responses I need in the act of poiesis." We create our path by walking.

Curation as Validation: An Option

Paolo called curation a way to validate the work, to honor it and, by extension, the artist. It can be as simple as putting away the work tools and cleaning up the mess, then placing the work on the wall, where it can be seen and honored. The methods of doing this are dependent on the work itself. I give examples in the sections on the individual studios in this chapter. Curation usually fits in after the art-making is finished, but before the Aesthetic Analysis begins. For reasons specific to the situation, it could come after the Aesthetic Analysis. You decide.

Task: Aesthetic Analysis

When the making is complete, or the play time or ritual is concluded, there can be a time for aesthetic reflection on the process and any product. This is still in the studio setting. We use the acronym Knill gave us, SuPER, here. Let's recap:

Surface: What is easily seen or heard or experienced in the image or artwork? What basic elements of the discipline are on display?

Process: What was the process of making this image or artwork? What were the easy parts, where were the difficulties?

Experience: The experience of the process. What thoughts, memories, feelings, sensations during the making?

Reflection/Round-up: This most often is a title for the work, but can be other actions such as curation.

This will help you navigate by looking phenomenologically at the client's work. Remember, not all of these aspects will be equally important to every client in every case. You look for what is significant, not slavishly follow a formula. But the formula reminds you what could be important. There will be examples of SuPER in each studio.

Third Room: The Counselor's Chairs—Final Conversation
Task: Harvesting

Here you are back in a cognitive process, out of the art-making into reflection. Assisting people to find what changed for them. This will be different in each studio.

IMPROVISATION, EMBODIMENT, AND IMAGINATION

Three aspects of studio work are present in all the studios, regardless of the discipline or materials: improvisation, embodiment, and imagination. First, I will take a look at improv in general, then look at each studio with some examples of how improvisation works.

Improvisation in the Intermodal Studios

Each art discipline—dance, theater, music, visual art and poetry—has its unique improvisational tradition and tools, but for all expressive arts the attitude is playful and the method is improvisational. Stephen Levine reminds us not to impose our will upon the art materials or there can be no satisfying result and certainly no surprise! This is not about recreating an image we have in our minds. This attitude requires that we are fully present in the moment, not in our fantasies about what should happen. We observe what is happening. Right now. Improvisation can be considered an aspect of art-based research. By considering the art materials as the entrance to our imagination, we can surrender to the process. Shaun McNiff reminds us to "trust the process." Rarely do I see a person try too many options, instead they usually stop at the first satisfying one. An attitude of improvisation is necessary with art-making of any type. It invites chance and accident. This is a central method, because it is a way of thinking about art-making—beginner's mind. It requires playing with materials and allowing the materials themselves to have influence over what happens. Playing with materials to discover what they can do. In the arts, improv means something different. It is a method of working and playing with the materials of a specific art discipline. It is being in the moment and responding to the materials and the time, the ever-burning *now*. It has to do with using what is at hand, with being fully present to see, hear, and take advantage of what is coming. Improvisation is a deep and respected tradition in the arts. To be a good improviser takes practice and skill. The attitude of the improviser may be playful, but not reckless; relaxed, but not indifferent. It lets go of control and shapes as it goes.

Improvisation is a discipline of its own. Some artists like to improvise, some like to do it "as written." Artists who can most easily enter into a spirit of improv and play with their art materials develop those skills over time. They know the rules and elements of the art game enough to stretch and manipulate them. Being able to follow an impulse, to shape it, requires experience. There is a type of gentle fearlessness, self-trust, a willingness to fail and a wide-eyed look-out for things that are intriguing that inform the good improviser. It doesn't depend upon virtuosity. It does use knowledge of the basic elements of the art discipline one is considering. There is the way of the dancer and the way of the poet.

An important aspect of improvisation in the performative arts is the score, whether written or unsaid. Improvisation benefits from a score, a way to proceed, a map of a kind. Paolo calls the score our "agreements." We agree to this and that. We will start at this signal and stop at that one. The score is the frame, the limitations and set of givens. It can be a literal physical thing or not.

Improvisation offers us the liberty of failing, an opportunity for all creative beings. Artists of all disciplines are familiar with the discomfort of failing, yet when something doesn't work, we learn. In contemporary art, failure is a topic of great interest since it precedes success—if we continue, if we go on. This cycle of failing, falling, and getting up is part of the improvisational attitude. It brings strength to the human endeavor. As Chumba Wumba sang: "I get knocked down, but I get up again, 'cause you're never gonna keep me down." Let this be our theme song.

Improv in Music

Improvisation is used in many musical forms, both vocal and instrumental. In Western traditions, improv was a part of music in the Medieval, Baroque, Renaissance, and Classical periods. *Encyclopedia Britannica* defines it as "the extemporaneous composition or free performance of a musical passage, usually in a manner conforming to certain stylistic norms but unfettered by the prescriptive features of a specific musical text." So, often done within a given harmonic framework. It makes sense that something would have to be played before it could be written in any form.

Improvised polyphony was everywhere in the Renaissance; it was a basic skill practiced by every choir boy. Canguilhem (2011, p. 99) estimates that

> the vast majority of the polyphony heard in Philip II's chapel in sixteenth-century Spain was improvised. In earlier centuries the amount might have been even higher. The composed polyphony that comes down to us was a small fraction of the musical landscape. This realization transforms our sense of the past.

In the case of jazz, Barry Kernfeld notes that "the completely spontaneous creation of new forms by means of free improvisation, independent of an existing framework, is rarer in jazz than it might seem, not least because where two or more musicians play together, no matter how intimately they know one another's work, some agreed decisions about the progress of a piece are normally necessary" (Kernfeld, 2002, p. 315). Andy Hamilton (2000, p. 177) would agree, noting that sometimes improvisations are "fixed" in advance, even if they are not written down. Finally Alperson and Lee Brown point out that improvisers often work and perform against a musical context and tradition and that mastery of this tradition is thus necessary in order to improvise well in these cases (see Alperson, 1984, p. 22; Brown, 2000, p. 114). The frame in jazz is the musical score or the song they are "jamming on." They play the original tune, then they begin to improvise, to "riff" on it. Each instrument takes a solo. They manipulate parts of the basic melody, play with it, take it apart and put it together differently, maybe making the pace faster or slower, changing the key, repeating a certain section over and over on top of the rest of the ensemble that is holding the frame of the song, upon which the soloist can riff. These are methods to help the piece stay cohesive within the tradition of jazz, to hang together, to sound cool. This tradition can be expanded and changed over time, usually by an exceptional musician. It is not written in stone, but it does carry the musical manners, codes, options that the heritage of jazz has explored and built over its long history. Great improvisers know how to remain in those boundaries. What can I do within this frame, within this limit? How can I bend it?

Improv in Dance

Modern and contemporary dance improvisation has forms and traditions that allow an ensemble to create compositions in the moment. There is usually a score, and certain agreements set forth at the beginning of the improv. People who have created dances together for some time get to know the vocabulary and skills of their ensemble members. Dancers can play with the motif in agreed-upon ways, such as:

- repeat what you did

- repeat what another dancer did

- repeat something until it changes and mutates of its own accord

- do something backward or in reverse

- change levels

- take a gesture of the arms and do it with the legs

- follow each other, or do things in a sequence

- do things in absolute unison

- be still, pause

- manipulate the timing: do things in double time or half time, counterpoint, syncopate

- designate a place where the same action takes place; i.e., "In that corner we jump"

- have a specific place everyone goes, either one at a time, or all at once—a "hot spot"

- emergence—within an open structure, honor it when it comes, see what wants to happen; allow for the Third—a surprise, support it

- go back to the original motif.

Interview with Mary Peterson

Because I respect her as a dance artist and loved to watch her perform, I have had Mary Peterson teach the intermodal dance course and embodiment course at the Institute. I asked Mary to talk to me about dance improvisation. Her MFA in dance comes from UC Irvine. As a member of two long-lasting improv groups, Lower Left and LIVE, she performed for many years in many venues. She completed her Q-AGS (Qualifying - Advanced Graduate Studies) at the EGS after the three-year training program at the San Diego Institute. During our conversation, her little dachshund, Frankie, was playing with my feet, and the warm winds of summer tossed the palm fronds back and forth.

JGE: So, Mary, what do you have to say about dance improv and the notion of scoring?

MP: Most performances have some sort of score, even if it's only "after this, then that." Some scores are tighter than others. Sometimes props are involved, and that creates a shape. Remember, I practiced with LIVE every week for five years. In performing improv, we would consider what to score, how to score. We had different kinds of scores. Both Lower Left and LIVE performed Nina Martin's number score. A random sequence of numbers (e.g., 8, 2, 7, 1, 5, 3) indicating how many people would be on stage at a given time. Start with eight people on stage, then two, then seven, and so forth. The main question was "what does this moment need?" Lower Left and LIVE were considering how to compose in the moment.

JGE: So, a score using variants as a way to shape.

MP: Score as a way to begin. Begin with constraints, then break the constraints.

JGE: That works with experienced improvisers, not so much with beginners or non-dancers!

MP: They [experienced improvisers] have figured a few things out. A performance needs some kind of score. Maybe the lights change or the music. There does not have to be a theme; it can be abstract.

JGE: Yes, like working with just the basic elements of dance: time, space, motion, and the body. Exploring and manipulating one or the other.

MP: Yes, but not a free-for-all. It's awareness training, awareness of what is emerging in the moment. Composing in the moment.

JGE: I like that—awareness training. Composing in the moment—if people understand what composition looks like! Do, then reflect, do-reflect, again and again. That two-beat rhythm that we find in ExA. Happening simultaneously.

MP: Yes, and sometimes it is a score we know. For example, community art has particular constraints. People who haven't worked together before, people who have little or no experience.

JGE: Zero experience with dance or improv, coming from all over the world, many for the first time to the EGS. They are learning by doing.

MP: The less the experience of the people, the more constraints we need to have a good outcome. Lower Left and LIVE performers had studied with 10–15 improv artists, so they had a large vocabulary and years of experience.

JGE: And they had the artistic relationships that they had developed together. They had history and shared movement memories. So that is a rich resource. Thanks, Mary!

Many dance artists use improvisation in their work. Anna Halprin used scores for her large-scale dance/theater pieces. Within a predetermined theme, having certain mileposts, she has had 100 people dancing together. Each person is responsible for their open contribution to the dance, but within parameters that were set. We used her score for Planetary Dance at the Institute and performed it with members of the public. Contact Improv, created by Steve Paxton, can only be improvised, and yet, here too, basic moves and manipulations can be practiced.

After the death of his partner, choreographer Bill T. Jones used improv with participants from the public. They explored a theme of terminal illness for his production *Still/Here*. He used ordinary people in his workshops to gather movement gestures and themes. He then developed a dance piece, which he set on his professional dance company, the Bill T. Jones/Arnie Zane Dance Company. They won many awards for this work.

Improv in dance is a method for finding movement for a new work, but more importantly for us, it is a way to approach dance that allows everyone to do what they can.

Improv in Theater

The earliest well-documented use of improvisation in theater in Western history is found in the Atellan Farce [of Africa] in 391 BC. From The 16th to the 18th centuries commedia dell'arte performers improvised based on a broad outline in the streets in Italy.

WIKIPEDIA (2025)

Comedy, especially sketch comedy and theatrical clowning (as opposed to circus clowning), is almost always improvised. Here again, although actors themselves may not call it that, they have a set of tools, skills, and reference points with which they are familiar. They probably have a storyline to guide the action. These are the elements of a score. Sometimes in theater, these are referred to as "exercises." The legitimate stage also uses improvisation, particularly in rehearsal. At the Old Globe Theater and San Diego Repertory Theater I taught movement for actors to help them discover their physical resources. The development of characters was a focus, aimed at making the body flexible and strong so that the actor could change their physical appearance; postures, gait, gestures. These exercises were wide-ranging, from animal imagery (e.g., if the giraffe spirit lived inside your physical body, how would that body move?) to weather metaphors (e.g., if you were a typhoon starting to form, how would you move? A cloud full of snow? A rainbow?) and costume manipulation (e.g., put the petticoat on your head; put on something several sizes too big). Creating the character physically helped the actor gain grounding or rootedness in the development of the role.

Scene work also uses improv. Basic theater traditions like always saying "yes" to the offer of your partner, also referred to as accepting or taking the offer, are essential skills for the actor and help them release overly clutchy control and become more awake in the moment. Additionally, numerous named games and exercises are used as mini-scores.

I think of improv as trained spontaneity. The more you do it, the better you get at it.

Music, dance, and theater as performative arts may seem a comfortable place for the notion of improvisation, but visual arts also use an analog of the basic improv approach.

Improv in Painting

The painter and the materials (paint or paper, brushes or knife) are in a kind of dance of cooperation—each responding to the other. When painting, the paper (or other substrate) is the door to the imagination. As you make marks, you are knocking on that paper door. At some point, if you are lucky, something from the imaginal realm will appear in the doorway. Something will call to you. But there is no predetermined outcome.

In art history, this may be called process art, that school of art-making where the process is the art and is more important than a sketch of a desired outcome—there is no sketch. As prominent a sculptor as Richard Serra considered himself a process artist. How he could be anywhere near spontaneous with the metal tonnage he manipulates is beyond me, but that's what he said. From the 1940s to the 60s, action painting was a term used by painters who were more concerned with the action or physical act of applying the paint to the surface. This included painters like Willem de Kooning and Jackson Pollock.

Consider Wassily Kandinsky's work *Improvisation #30 Cannons*. Much like improvised music or dance, this artwork was created spontaneously, in the moment, without a predetermined plan or design. This lack of preconception contributes to the unique and unpredictable nature resulting in pieces that vividly capture the artist's immediate emotional and sensory responses. Composing in the moment, yes, but he already knew how to paint and he knew compositon elements.

Improv in Poetry

Elizabeth McKim, Poet Laureate for The European Graduate School, emphasizes what she calls serious play with words. She wants us to taste the sound of the word in our mouth and listen carefully, allowing the words themselves to guide our explorations. She encourages playfulness and simple associations to increase our fun with language. She does not distinguish between play and work—play is the work of the child and of creative endeavors. If we are too determined, too straight-lipped and tight-fisted, too afraid to make a mistake, we will only present frozen images or hackneyed clichéd offerings, whether in dance, painting, or poetry. Our poems will be stilted and dull. She has many games and fun frames to help us be surprised by our own writing. Because she works in the oral tradition, writing it down comes later, and the form is still fluid; it can be shaped and revised.

"Freestyle" is associated with spontaneous, on-the-spot creation that characterizes forms of performance poetry, like rap and spoken word. Freestyle, in this context, embodies the principles suggested by McKim—serious play with words, exploration, and creativity. This form of improvisation allows the artist to perform extemporaneously, creating rhymes and narratives without relying on a preconceived script or set of lyrics. The performer is guided by the words and the rhythm. This skill gets better over time with practice.

Embodiment in the Intermodal Studios
Embodiment Is Central to ExA
Although embodiment is a central concept in expressive arts, it's more implied than articulated. It's indisputable that the arts depend on the communication of the senses; they are expressions of the senses. It's the air and the ground of our work; omnipresent but difficult to be aware of. As our bodies and senses evolved so did our ability to work symbolically. But that is too simple—our consciousness and our sensuous abilities developed simultaneously. Our art-based approach to change is bespoke for humans and works for us because it fits us perfectly, having evolved with us. Human beings and the arts developed together; we are the expression of the aesthetic domain and reality, with all its manifestations. Art-making is a way of knowing for us, as natural as walking. Thus, the arts are the perfect medicine for what ails us—both to restore us and to provide a direction for growth.

Felt Sense and Interoception
In one way, embodiment is the ability to know what's happening within you while simultaneously attending to the world around you. Both. At once. As a complex and elusive concept, we must speak around it. It is difficult to speak of it directly; it must be felt and experienced, but perhaps not adequately expressed in words. Eugene Gendlin referred to this as the inner knowing as the "felt sense" of a thing or situation. With attention, the felt sense emerges. This can be learned. Eugene Gendlin's *Experiencing and the Creation of Meaning* (1997) drew attention to the notion that we have a way of knowing ourselves and the world that he called "experiencing." It

wasn't thinking; it was sensing. The "felt sense" (a term he coined), was about tuning into or noticing sensations in our gut and viscera, our "inner knowing," not our "inner thinking" or inner fantasies. This knowing from inside is referred to as interoception. In his most popular book, *Focusing*, Gendlin described steps to help people utilize their own deep knowing on any subject. This guidance helps steer a person's awareness toward subtle bodily sensations and imagery to support an authentic response to any given topic. For me, the failing of this approach was that the knowing remained a mental image. It never moved and was never realized in any other sensory way. With the technique of intermodal transfer, we can do better to amplify this information.

We know about ourselves through our senses, recognizing that consciousness is part of our fleshiness because our flesh, which includes our brain, is not something separate from us. We are it; we are consciousness. There is no other way. This is embodiment.

The Wits

At the time of William Shakespeare, the senses were sometimes called "the wits" or the "five wits," thus alluding to their role as forms of intelligence. The senses are intelligences that do not speak English or any other language, except the communication of their own domain—the languages of sight or sound, of movement, or tactile senses. These cannot be literally translated. We don't want to reify the images or their messages, but they can migrate from one form of expression to another—thus bringing new knowing. This is the basis of the intermodal transfer. Each new expression brings an opportunity to both have something new be revealed and simultaneously have something else covered, disguised, or hidden.

The senses are important to the ExA practitioner because they are our avenues of communicating with each other too. They are communication modalities or methods. A "mode," as the dictionary defines it, is "different ways (other than speech) that are used to send a message from one person to another." They are the methods or modes of trying to make ourselves understood. I make a sound and you hear it. I draw a line and you see it. When I move my posture and gestures communicate in a certain way. You can feel it a bit in your own body by way of mirror neurons. If you move the way I do, you might experience something similar to what I experienced. We communicate with each other through our senses.

A woman I know could do anything with her hands. She worked in fabric and needle arts but also making of all kinds: metal, wood, wool, ceramics. I saw her twist, pinch, pull, thread and weave, roll, and manipulate all kinds of materials. She gave new meaning to the term "handmade" because of her remarkable ability to be precise and beautiful in her handiwork. It was especially noticeable in her 3D images, but her paintings were also textured and wonderfully complex. Her hands themselves reached out and used all their remarkable knowings, as if tiny brains on her fingertips were working away at the project with eyes of their own and a whole mini-workshop of tiny tools to shape and prod the fabrication into order. By her example, she taught me the concept of the intelligent hand.

Kathrin Keune

Having a good student is every teacher's wish and dream. Someone who isn't on a paper chase to get the degree or the grade, but someone who wants to learn, who is seeking understanding. They ask questions to comprehend, not to stump the instructor or show off. Together the teacher and the student open up a greater appreciation or understanding of the topic they share a passion for. I am never a better teacher than when I have a great student.

The letters below were penned to Kathrin Keune over a period of several years. I have condensed and edited them for inclusion here. Kathrin graduated from the Institute in 2009. Later, the EGS conferred her MA in Expressive Arts, with a focus on coaching, consulting, and education. Initially my student, later I was her supervisor and, finally, a friend. Together, we have explored the philosophy and theories of intermodal polyaesthetic expressive arts, particularly as they relate to her consulting business, Arts-based Solutions. Her studio is in Burbach, Germany, situated in a beautifully restored farmhouse in the countryside. There, she offers workshops for the public. Among her corporate clients is the distinguished Max Planck Institute. Since I was originally a dancer/actor and she a singer/actor, many of our conversations revolved around the utmost importance of the corporeal experience in the ExA studios.

April 2010
San Diego, CA

Dearest KK,
We were in the studio tonight. The sky was dark, and the rising moon glowed through the wall of windows on the north side. I wished you were here. As the students lay on the maple floor, I asked them to pay attention to their breath without changing anything, but to notice how and where it entered the body, what changed as they breathed, and how it left. In a body scan, I named various parts and systems for them to visit in their mind's eye. This then led to a movement exploration based on those body systems. They explored the skeleton

by focusing on the bones as they pushed through muscle to feel the bones. Afterwards, they drew a skeleton and moved, letting the bones and the images and ideas about bones be the impetus, informed by the earlier work. Later, the breath was the focus. We imagined the pathway of the breath, in through the nostrils, noticing the expansion of the chest and belly, following oxygen-rich blood into the heart, through the organs and tissues, and then the outer reaches of our skin. We reflected on the connection we have with the atmosphere as public commons. The exercise moved from literal breath to imagination and dance. They moved with the breath as metaphor; as if the arms or legs were breathing, as if the breath could come in through the fontanel or the palms of the hands or soles of the feet. The movement that emerged from this was so lyrical, unusual, beautiful.

The atmosphere in the studio was calm, serene even, and with the moonlight shining through the windows, it had an other-worldly quality. I hope you, too, are dancing in the moonlight.

Love and moonbeams,
Greer

Self and Flesh

People can become comfortable with themselves as living anatomy. But it isn't always quick or easy. This is part of developing a realistic body image and self-image, important for all of us, not just those recovering from eating disorders or other diagnoses. It has to include both an accurate and positive assessment of one's corporeality. It is important to encounter our fleshy selves, as creatures, as animals. This is a foundation of identity and self. To appreciate our corporeal self is a powerful way to come to grips with our lives. Otherwise, you perceive your body as a thing, which it is not.

Professor Dr. Jürgen Kriz, the author of *Self-Actualization* and the professor who taught chaos theory as a model for change at the EGS, said: "You are more like the flame than the candle." Our lives are a process, a living sentient system, not an inanimate thing. He is a champion of process-oriented therapies, like ExA, because they embrace the complexity and uniqueness of each person. People need a therapy especially created for them and their situation, and one that includes the body.

Your Body Is Your Brain

We are not a body-mind or a mind-body. The mind and the body are not distinct and separate. In some real sense your body is your brain. Unfortunately, Descartes helped legitimize that concept of such a mind-body split in order to advance science. This notion persists and reinforces black-and-white thinking, or dualism. It perpetuates the terrible and costly belief that we are two things in one: a fleshy-bodied vessel and a lively immaterial mind; the master of the meat puppet. It denies us the rich rainbow of complex thoughts that can come when we allow ourselves to experience all that our senses can give to us. It leads to simplistic solutions to complex problems. And, most importantly, it is incorrect! It is discouraging how these old and inaccurate ideas cling on.

Folk wisdom is passed down, usually from family, and reinforced by popular culture, such as the body is a vessel or vehicle for the mind or some disembodied soul. This is analogous to the "ghost in the machine," as Gilbert Ryle referred to Descartes' assertion of the separation of the mind and the body. It is difficult to overcome and to study one's own inherited philosophy, but it is a necessary undertaking to become a fully qualified expressive arts practitioner. We need to think about our thinking and how we got to wherever we are. As much as possible, one must endeavor to come into the here and now of both art and science, to have opinions based on some exposure and knowledge regarding the current thinking in the field. The body is not a vehicle. The mind is material.

Do I Have a Body or Am I My Body?

This can be tricky. One experience that perpetuates the misunderstanding that I have a body is when I go to the doctor, we talk about my lungs or my feet as if they are just interchangeable parts I own. Our physical selves can be parsed and dissected; we can live without a certain amount of our flesh, a lung or a kidney, for example, or a leg or eyes, even part of the brain. Nevertheless, our physiology forms and informs our thoughts and beliefs. It cannot be otherwise. So much of our language derives from the fact of our physicality. As Lakoff and Johnson illuminate extensively in *The Metaphors We Live By*, our understanding of the world and the way we talk about it comes from the physical form of our consciousness—our flesh. Paraphrasing Lakoff, we say "on the one hand and on the other hand," which would make no sense if we were octopuses.

Although we share over 98% of our DNA with chimpanzees, small differences can make a big difference. Emerging from the cauldron of "life stuff," we became Homo sapiens. Our environment suits us exceptionally well, a harmony born from our evolution within it. This compatibility is the essence of biophilia, our intrinsic love for Earth. Optimal human well-being requires interaction with our natural habitat, making notions of Mars colonization seem out of touch with our biological realities. The hustle and bustle of life can create the illusion of tragic separateness. The question then arises: can we overcome this illusion?

May 2010
San Diego, CA, USA

Dear KK,

I just read the most exciting thing. A paper presented at a conference said that we have between 22 and 30 senses! I wondered if I had identified them all, since I have been researching this, in the way of the dilettante, for a few years. Sure enough, part of what has happened is that the senses that used to be thought of as a single dimension were subdivided. For example, "touch" is now divided into many aspects and called "haptics." We thought of touch as one thing, but the term haptics implies and includes 11 or so distinct ways of knowing about the environment from the hand. To our aural faculty, hearing, add echolocation. Yes, really! The bats and us. Maybe you've seen the videos of a blind man using tongue clicks and the resulting echolocation to make his way around his world. But we all do it to a certain extent. Walking in complete darkness, I listen to my footfalls as part of knowing where I am. Add to this list the senses necessary for movement, I ended up with about 15 or so. You know how important I think the senses are to our work. We need to feed and activate them. They overlap so intricately at some point it doesn't make any real sense to differentiate. And yet, it helps me to think about them, even if I put them back into the old "five senses" bucket at the end of the day.

See you soon, after the EGS.
Greer

Our Senses Are Tools

The delicate interface between our consciousness and the rest of the world is negotiated by our sensory organs. "Sense" comes from the Greek "organum," meaning "tool or instrument." Yes, with our senses we make our world. We sense colors, sounds, movement, texture, and taste, and at that juncture—of our skin and the environment—we perceive the world, whatever there is to be experienced. We take the world into ourselves. Our senses let the world into us, our ears and eyes, our hands and feet, are the interface between the world and our consciousness. The world enters us even as we act upon it; we are never out of contact. We cannot be, although we can lose the awareness of our connection. We are bound to and interpenetrated by the world; the intricacies of our life force, the earth and skies, seas, and all the animal and plant life. It's all connected. We inhale the oxygen that trees produce and they breathe in the CO_2 we exhale. It becomes like a vision or an opium dream. Well, I have no idea what an opium dream is like, but this is, as I would have said in my youth, "trippy."

Obviously, I am speaking not as a physician nor as a neuroscientist—which I am certainly not. I speak as an artist, an educator, an ExA practitioner. Like Whitman (1900), I find the body electric and fascinating. Knowing something about how it operates is inspiring to my work.

Muscles as Organs

Skeletal muscle could be considered an organ. An organ, when activated, sends signals in the form of chemical messages to the rest of the body. Likewise, when we move, our musculature sends signals to the rest of the body. It is one of our most ancient systems and has great resilience. Our muscles have a will to survive. Even with age-related muscle loss (sarcopenia) the muscles will respond when challenged, as in activity and exercise. Our bodies will adapt and have intelligence all on their own. We are more than meat. Feeling impulses from our flesh is subtle. Perhaps this is one of the reasons I value dance—it allows this most primal part of me to speak.

Time Is on My Side… or Is It?

When working with adults, allow sufficient time to leave the ordinary clock-driven world, *Chronos*, behind. We want to enter flow time, "time out of time," *Kairos*. Mihaly Csikszentmihalyi coined the term "flow" for the creative state of mind when you are so absorbed in something that time flies by and nothing else seems important. He investigated and described the balance of attention, control, and play that leads to the most productive and positive mental state for creation. This attitude of playful attention, of being in the "zone," is also needed for all the art disciplines. This is what we hope to achieve in decentering.

By drawing attention to what we are hearing, seeing, or sensing we make that transition over the threshold from the life-world to the timeless imaginal world, holding more possibility, or as Anne of Green Gables said, "More scope for the imagination!" Otherwise, we have almost no prospect of allowing something to actually emerge—we will take the time-pressured consciousness of everyday life and build a birdhouse, step-by-step. If we see the paint and the paper as partners, wait for and accept the emergent, the incongruous working beautifully together, then comes the happy accident. Surprise! Seduce the senses in the lovely way of the Muse—tempting touch with textures, enticing eyes with color and shape, and beguiling bodies through rhythm and pulse. Then the waking dream of the art-making time can be entered into fully and, hopefully, we can surrender to it.

July 2017
San Diego, CA

Dear KK,

Please forgive me for canceling our call and not writing. I buried my mother, Kathrin. Yes, she was almost 93. She said she loved her life and was ready to go. But I wasn't ready to let her go. I did have all the important conversations I needed to have with her; but I am greedy for time with people I love. Her breath stopped, she returns to the earth. Now I carry her in my heart and memories. This lovely woman—Helen. I can never fill her sling-backs.

 Clawing my way back to our conversations about imagination—think of the imagination as physical. Imagination is awakened and stimulated by inter-acting with the world as we experience it, through our senses. Imagination is not the same as daydreaming, all in the head and no action, fantasy. Rather, encountering the pile of wood and letting the hands explore as they say, "What could this be? What can I do with this," Or coming to the paper with all sorts of mark-making implements and saying, "What kind of mark does this make?" For this to work we have to already be in a receptive mood, allowing the imagination to fire up and guide. Thus, the ∃xA practitioner needs to have prompts, techniques, elements, approaches, frames—ways to get in, that guide and allow the clients to explore. Nothing is scarier to a beginner than "Do whatever you want." Or even, "What do you like to do?" When the client has no experience with the materials—this can be terrifying. That can shut a person down or lead to anxiety. As Paolo said, the threshold of risk and expertise for entering into the play with the materials must neither be too little nor too much. We could call this the "Goldilocks Principle"—the challenge must be "just right" for the clients.

Bye for now,
Greer

Feel Me, Touch Me

Touch is the first sense to develop in the womb. Touch, or the tactile sense, is made up of many different sensing cells with unique ways to distinguish what the hand or the skin encounters. Together these are called the haptic senses. Haptic sensing has two components: tactile and kinesthetic. The tactile component is the cutaneous sensations from the skin itself, with its numerous types of neural cells and intelligence; it tells us what type of surface we are encountering. The kinesthetic component is the proprioceptive sense of movement from the joints, muscles, and tendons. This includes the sensation of stretching the skin when the joints move. The hand is composed of various joints and tendons and is connected, obviously, to the wrist and arm. Usually the kinesthetic sensing of the hand works together with the purely tactile sensing. When we are using our hands, both types of knowledge are in force.

Unpacking the word, we find that "haptic" comes from the Greek words "to touch or grasp, to fasten and come into contact with." This etymology reminds me that "grasping" also means to understand. If we grasp it, we "get it," we know it. When something touches us it has an emotional impact. So, touching the world, as represented by the materials in the expressive arts therapy studio, can help us understand ourselves.

Touching can arouse our emotions, but attention must be paid. By touching we are touched. By grasping it, we learn. Remember E.T. stretching out his long, skinny finger to make contact? Our skin, especially on the hand, brings us into contact with the world in a way no other sense can do. The scope of knowing from the hand is small—just the surface of your hand or even a fingertip. Still, it can give us information about our environment that no other sense can. You can neither see nor hear the temperature of a thing, or its actual texture. Touch is the only perceptual system that can change the size of its perceptual field, from the pad of one finger to the sense available to both hands moving (Hatwell, 2003, p. 4). Or even the skin on the whole body. In my so-called research (meaning me poking around in the library, journals, online, having conversations, what-have-you), I have found the following aspects attributed to haptic sensing: Unique cells, not multipurpose "skin cells," conduct these senses. "At least four types have been identified and are classified on the basis of their adaptive properties (rapid or slow) and the characteristics of their receptive fields, small and highly localized or large, with indistinct borders" (Hatwell, 2003, p. 17). These specialized cells, such as Meissner corpuscles, Merkel disc receptors, Pacinian corpuscles, and Ruffini endings, help distinguish the multitude of sensations we encounter with the skin on our hands. Great names, eh? This is combined with the proprioceptive receptors situated in muscles, tendons, and joint capsules (Hatwell, 2003, pp. 17–18).

Using the senses at their fullest capacity both restores and develops the ability of the person to be in the world, to know it, and thus to know themselves since they are part of the world. It increases sensitivities and the intelligence available only by being aware with the body.

Sensuous Development

The senses can be "trained." The more you touch and manipulate things, the more refined and attuned your sense of touch becomes. The more you touch, the more you feel; the more you feel, the more you know about the world. Hands are intelligent and can learn how to manipulate the environment. Artists can touch papers and tell the weight differentiating filmy tracing paper, vellum, thick cold pressed watercolor paper; between paper that is smooth as Bristol or with gripping "tooth." I know a fiber artist who can tell the difference between weights and weaves of silk, by name, without touching them, just by sight, because she has handled them so much. Allow your fingertips to touch everything—corduroy, cotton, silk, leather, wool, brick, and stone. Even cotton with different finishes: polished cotton, percale, sateen, crepe, damask, canvas, dotted Swiss, and chenille. All with a distinct feel.

A person can manipulate an object: hammer a nail, touch a fuzzy leaf, snap a bean, weave yarn, knead bread dough, stir plaster: the actions and force of the hands adapt to the situation. All of this has implications for the studio.

Allowing time for the hands to awaken, to be nourished, will increase the efficacy of any tactile exploration. In my studio, I name the various actions that can be made with the tools and materials. Few people will undertake a complete or thorough exploration without such guidance. Most modern people do not have the opportunity to encounter the world in this way.

When working with clay, I remind people that it is, by itself, a type of earth. I encourage them to smell that raw earth scent. Then to do every type of manipulation the clay is capable of: roll it, pound it, stretch it, pinch it, twist it. Get to know the materials with your hands, name the actions that your hands perform.

While walking at the beach yesterday, my skin sensed the temperature of the air. I awakened to this fact and I had to have a minute of amazed appreciation—my skin itself was telling me about the warmth of the air. You already know this, we all do it, but I never before stopped to think about it. When my bedroom is two degrees warmer than I like, I can tell. This ability is called *thermoception*, that is, detecting the ambient temperature with the skin. We are walking thermometers.

To the sense of smell in general, add the particular smell of water. It's one of my favorite smells—petrichor, "the blood of the gods" in Greek. When it rains in San Diego, I get excited. In so sere a landscape as this, we revere this rare smell of rain on stone, soil, or even concrete. To this, add sensing relative humidity. When at the ocean, when in Saas Fee walking in the larch forest, or when in the Anza-Borrego Desert, I can perceive the relative humidity through my skin. Again, you know we can do this because we do it! We talk about the dry desert air and bring our chapstick and body lotion. But to give these knowings their names, to take a moment and become conscious of it, celebrates these abilities. Suddenly, my skin seems smart and I am more grateful for this, the largest organ of my body.

September 2017
San Diego, CA, USA

Dear KK,
Thank you for the questions about your older gentleman client. Let me say this: The hand changes over the lifespan. His inability to manipulate the paintbrush or pencils might require some accommodation. When one of my students was in a wheelchair, I taped a long handle to the regular handle of a paint brush so she could paint from her chair. Consider having fatter pencils and things, so the grip doesn't have to be so tight. They sell little rubber thingies that go on a pencil to make the grip easier, looser. Take into account the typical developmental skills of children as well as the possible decline of haptic sensing with older adults, including the results of arthritis, MS, tremors, and general loss of mobility and strength.

ExA overlaps with occupational therapy, particularly when focusing on the use of tactile stimulation and tools that are suitable for the patient's current hand abilities. This approach nourishes the hand by providing the right level of challenge and sensory experience.

Slow down so the object or project doesn't become the focus of the work. Let the process and the work itself become interesting. Stay with what is felt and what is happening. This requires a presence and attunement to the person and what they are doing. I know you pay attention. Working with elders in mind also helps develop our sensitivity. A poignant memory of my mom before she died: trying to pick up a grape from her plate. She had neither the flexibility nor steadiness needed. She couldn't grasp it, but she wouldn't take my help. Breaks my heart a little, just remembering her thin, stiff finger chasing that grape around the plate. Because all of our clients need respect and dignity, we must have a careful, loving observation of the hands. We may encounter touch-starved hands in younger clients, too. Any specific population may have special needs for their hands. When working primarily with writers, for example, I pay special attention to the stretching and care of the hands, arms, neck, and shoulders. However, writing is hard on the whole body! I hope this helps.

Love from my patio,
Greer

Do You Hear What I Hear?

Hearing is present in the developing human fetus at about 20 weeks. We know that fetuses in utero can hear the voices of those who speak to them. A newly pregnant woman I know is wearing a tiny bell that bumps along on her belly—music for her baby. Newborns hear pretty well, but hearing continues to develop over the first year. I have been told that hearing is also one of the last senses to go at life's end (along with touch). The Tibetan Book of the Dead mentions this—admonishing the newly deceased to listen for signals before going to the Bardo. How important it is that we contemplate the power of sound and silence on the human condition.

The shell-like opening of the outer ear is called the pinna or auricle. It allows sound waves to come in and it almost ushers the waves in with its amphitheater shape, guiding the waves into the canal. These sound waves percuss our tiny eardrum, called the tympanic membrane, a little skin membrane just like the skin on your djembe. Sound waves, coming from anything that vibrates, which is everything on Earth, oscillate the drum in our ear, the world's tiniest tympani. When sound waves pass the tympanic membrane, they move into the inner ear, the home of the tiniest bones—the hammer, anvil, and stirrup. Sweet, right? These little bones amplify the vibrations made by the drum. Then the sound wave passes into the labyrinth, or inner ear, with all its twists and turns. Within the labyrinth, the nautilus shell of the cochlea is filled with perilymph, a special fluid. The vibrations move through a double membrane with a tiny window that allows the fluid to move freely in the cochlea. Thousands of microscopic hairs inside the wall begin to move, to dance to the vibrations. Like a line of Rockettes, 24,000 of these tiny fibers are arranged in four long rows and they sway to the sound waves. It is here that a physical motion is transmitted into an electrical signal that then moves along the auditory nerve, taking the information to the back of the brain. We understand the message as a sound—of music, of a cricket, a distant train, or rain, of any of the vibrating things in the world within our hearing range.

Sound and Noise

Sound is not always pleasant. John Cage explored the boundary and relationship between sound, noise, and music. He experimented with making noise into something that we might perceive as music. I remember him with the top propped up on the grand piano putting things like washers and nails into the strings. This was his "prepared piano," so the sound of the strings would be altered when the mallet hit them. Or he would put giant Wollensak tape recorders around off-stage and have a literal loop of tape playing sounds, like random radio noise or traffic.

Noise pollution is a problem all over the globe and includes airplanes, traffic, trains, and other industrial endeavors. San Diego has a noise curfew (no loud noises after 10 pm) and will compensate homeowners who fall into a certain portion of the flight path. Saas Fee is a "silence village." We value an escape from the urban cacophony. I think one reason I love the desert so much is the Big Empty = quiet.

I encourage you to stimulate and support high sensitivity with a listening warm-up for any experiment in the music studio. Listening experiences can be satisfying, whether it is the ambient sound of the place or the chosen soundtracks. Chanting, singing, and toning instrumental music with a curated instrumentarium, postmodern soundscapes can be wonderfully sensitizing. Listen to breath sounds and sighs and non-language human sounds. Allow people to listen to breathing by placing an ear on the back of a neighbor—like a doctor, but without the stethoscope. Listen with a glass on the wall; listen by putting an ear to the floor. You can also explore the vibration that occurs in the body when you are making sound. By putting your hands on your chest, stomach, face, or skull, you will feel the vibration of your bones to your own voice.

It is usually a surprise that we can hear so much. Paolo would have us pair up and have one of the pair close their eyes (or did we use blindfolds?) and the other partner whispers the name of the blindfolded partner. In the plenum, with 100 people, half of them whispering, half of them listening blindfolded, the blindfolded partner needed to find the whispering partner, who was free to run around the plenum, avoiding the blindfolded one. But everyone always found their partner. Always.

Using the whole room as an idiophone, "play" the room with beaters of various types—from plain wood to fluffy beater heads to tightly wound heads and rubber heads of various densities. Chopsticks are the cheapest and deliver a satisfactory sound. Tap on the furniture, walls, run them along radiator grates and window panes. Play with body percussion. So fun.

When the elements of sound are explored, the listening can include listening for the various elements of music. Assign a small group to listen for the pulse or the timbre of the sounds. This will heighten their attention and therefore increase the vibrancy of their experience.

Safety

Like all the senses, hearing has a safety feature. Sounds that can alert us and help keep us safe include the sound of a car horn, fog horn, the tick-tick-tick of the gas stove igniting, the smoke alarm, the siren of fire engines or police vehicles, the whistle of a crossing guard, clang of train crossing, tone of the deep water buoys, a crying baby, the Doppler effect of a passing car, alarm clocks, bells of announcement on airplanes—so many sounds have one purpose—to alert us, to keep us safe. Now, in California, the street light crosswalks have a voice and an audible countdown to cross the street.

Our hearing range centers on the sounds and frequencies that offer the most important information, those occurring during human conversations. Can you hear me now?

Anyone at any age can have hearing changes, but it is a common part of aging. Older people can suffer changes in their hearing capacity from annoying to devastating, as well as conditions such as tinnitus, ringing in the ears. Being aware of these conditions can help us in our situational analysis to attend to the dimensions of sound that might shape the work. Again, using open-hearted curiosity, ask about hearing and sound experiences from your clients. A client with a hearing difficulty asked me to lower and modulate my voice so it wouldn't cause a roaring in his ears. I was happy to do so and glad he felt comfortable enough to ask.

Multiple Senses in Dance

How can the principle of embodiment inform the ExA practitioner using dance/movement? The senses primarily responsible for the movement experience are:

- **Kinesthetic sense:** The sense of motion of limbs and body; movement and changes in position, coming from detectors in the muscle bundles and the joint capsules.

- **Interoception:** The "gut" feeling or bodily sense, sensing the internal state of the body, including but not limited to heartbeat, respiration, hunger and satiety, any internal discomfort, need to eliminate, also a felt-sense of well-being. These work together and are interrelated.

- **Proprioception:** Awareness of the position of the body in space. Knowing where your hand is without looking at your hand. Feeling your body with your body, in muscles and joint capsules. Knowing how much force to use to move an object and, very importantly, sensing the surface you walk on with your feet.

- **Equilibrium or vestibular sense:** The Sense of balance or movement in space, coming from the inner ear.

All these senses work together to allow us to move, to dance, and to orient ourselves three-dimensionally in space.

Movement and Aging

The ability to fully move the body decreases with age. Let's be sensitive to movement and proprioception across the lifespan. Older persons may have sustained injuries. Elders may have lost capacity through lack of movement or illness or disease processes. They may have mistakenly believed "this is how it will be now that I am X years old." Medications can affect a person's ability to move. With some people, the deterioration can be ameliorated with use. The ExA practitioner must take into account the movement abilities of all her group members as they present themselves, now. Being sensitive to the aging body can also increase awareness of younger people with movement challenges. I have used dance/movement therapy with people in wheelchairs or regular chairs. The old saying, "If you can walk you can dance," needs to be updated. "Anyone who can move at all can dance."

> People want to move. Movement is our energizer. We are designed to move, to dance. If we are still for too long, our bodies do not do well. Our tendons stiffen, bones weaken, heart loses capacity. We can develop bed sores from being still. We connect with each other when we move together. Thus, the appeal of the dance club Dance Jam where I was DJ for 20 years. Having a place where people could move together without alcohol or smoke was one of the main reasons I started it. We need to move in rhythm with each other. Dancing uses the body differently than any other movement activity—it is expressive, not utilitarian movement, expressive not prescriptive.

Sensitizing

Without proper sensitizing, the whole endeavor, the entire expressive arts therapy session or class, may just drift into the ordinary task of pushing things around, cutting paper, or beating on a drum—without the right frame of mind needed for these endeavors to be deeply connected and touch the person and persons. It can become routinized, end-driven, obsessed with the outcome or product, what Paolo called "end-gaming." There will be no discovery.

All the studios must allow the person to arrive and become present and aware of themselves. This is the meaning of the check-in: not necessarily a report on the life outside the group or session, but a deepened awareness of their personhood, their sensations, emotions, of readiness to work, of energy and state of mind, of the accompanying images, the ghosts of mood. This is shared without comment, even if it is incomplete and fragmented. It stands unchallenged. No cross-talk.

When it is time to move into the studio portion of the work, the task becomes waking up, warming up the senses, and increasing the awareness of the self in relationship to the others and the room, expanding the sense of connection—to the space, and everything in it. This is delicate work.

To achieve this, you must be "tuned in." For me, this involves a simple ritual of sorts—a laying aside of my ordinary life and welcoming in my subtle awareness of the people I will be serving and the space we will occupy. It is an entire situational analysis but done inside myself—with my introspection and imagination. Yes, I also write down as many details as I can muster—but the final act is one of meditation. It is both pleasurable and demanding. I think through transitions many times, and still the reality surprises me. It comes with challenges and changes… but if I did not do this inner preparation, it would be a mess. I cannot anticipate what will happen, but I can have a vision in mind of the way we might go.

All art studios can take advantage of this critical opportunity by allowing plenty of time for sensitizing and warming-up—not merely to the material itself but also to the encounter with the material. Allowing the communication modalities to awaken, tune up, and become more acute.

August 2019
San Diego CA

Dear KK,
I just had my eyes checked, another new Rx for reading. Vision changing, movement abilities changing. I challenge what I can and accept what I cannot, like Marcus Aurelius suggested.

It takes special concentration and focus to turn our awareness from what we encounter on the outside of ourselves to what we might know from inside ourselves, and the boundary between ourselves and the world. This difficulty is magnified by the fact that many of our senses are developed for us to know the environment around us. We see the slightest movement in the trees or along the verge. We notice the color of the ripe berry versus the not-quite-ripe one. We see the edge of the log we are crossing the river on and recognize the faces of our loved ones. We can tell by the smell the meat is rotten or the apricots are ripe. We hear the rustle of leaves and the different sounds of water running, splashing, drizzling, plopping, and so forth. We walk on hot sand gingerly and quickly or on slippery ice so so carefully. We feel the temperature of our baby's forehead. We walk over sharp rocks and down slopes. In California, we tell the ripeness of the avocado by gentle pressure. You know how that is—today, it is hard as a rock; tomorrow, it is perfect, the next day it is garbage! All of these senses tell us about the world. They enrich our lives and help us make decisions about health, safety, beauty, and fun.

In order to use this intelligence for our own benefit, we must be aware of our own sensations, which are less discussed. They are there waiting for us to schematize them and put them into our minds and vocabularies so we can better grasp them. This is a widening ring of awareness.

Time for me to go to the studio. I'll see you there!
Greer

Imagination in the Studios

The vitality and energies of the imagination do not operate at will; they are fountains, not machinery.

D. G. JAMES, *SKEPTICISM AND POETRY*

Using Imagination for Change

Everyone's imagination is unique to them, like their body and their mind. We share much as human beings, but each has a distinct and original combination of genetics, physicality, culture, preferences, intelligences, era of living, life experiences, and so forth. No two people are the same, thus everyone's imagination is unique. It is enriched by all they have encountered in any and every way: what they read, and listened to, where they went, what they ate, who they knew, when and where they were born, under what circumstances, and on and on. The art materials we bring to our work serve as stimuli for the richness of imaginative play to emerge.

Restoring the imagination to its full, sparkling power is one of the primary aims of ExA. We honor imagination as a powerful human faculty. Paolo discusses imagination as having both positive and negative uses. Positive when it illuminates possible futures and resources; negative when it mires our minds in thoughts of potential disasters, anxiety and depression. He also points out that imagination is multimodal, having a "sensory aspect" (Knill, 1999, p. 40). It can provide us with visual, tactile, kinesthetic, auditory, gustatory, and olfactory images. It employs all communication modalities.

Physical Imagination

The word "imagination" originates from Latin, meaning "to picture oneself," indicating that it is a private faculty. The term "imago," or image, serves as its metaphor, reflecting something in water. Imagination and memory are waltzing together.

I like to say imagination is physical. Of course, it is a mental faculty, not a physical phenomenon. But I put it this way because, in my experience, engaging the imagination with the physical world yields far better results in all instances than merely thinking about something. Put something into the hands, give the body something to explore, give the ears a sound task. As Paolo says about dreams—a person can tell me about a dream, but we cannot work with it until we "bring it into the room." This means writing it, dancing parts of it, moving in its landscape, enacting it, or drawing an image from it.

Communication modalities stimulate the imagination and its images in the art disciplines. Dance and movement stimulate kinesthetic communication. Sound and music generate auditory communication. Tactile experiences encourage haptic communication, while smell and taste serve as examples of gustatory and olfactory communication.

Our senses are exalted in the arts through the use of imagination. We use the voice everyday, but the aria is something special coming forth from the audible/aural imagination. We move everyday, but the dance is something special. We see colors, but the painting, the tapestry... this represents the best we can do. Across time and around the world, human cultures develop through the imaginative and aesthetic use of the senses. We build on these things, showing and sharing our values and carrying the messages across the ages. What are we communicating in the arts? "This is what we thought was beautiful, this is what we thought was important. We saw the world this way." What it means to be human! Across the millennia artists still speak to us.

Imagination brings soulfulness, meaning the body is the conduit for soulfulness, since the bodily senses are how we create art. No one is big enough to hold soul, but we can participate in the *anima mundi*, the soulfulness of the world. While this may not be a fact, it is most definitely true. Imagination is recursive. Once is never enough. Again, this is not a fact, but a truth. We learn how to be human by throwing ourselves, again and again into the pool of imaginative play. The eyes learn to see—eventually finding objects within the simmering color—by looking and looking. Hands learn to recognize the thickness of paper by handling it. Ears learn to hear by listening. Bodies learn to move by moving. We know when working on a piece of writing, if you read what you wrote as the last thing at night before sleep, in the morning problems of a manuscript can be resolved or some movement can take place. The more you do this, the better it works. Imagination needs to be grounded in the present and allowed to move into a future, from what is, to what can be.

Imagination in the Studios

All the studios discussed below allow the imagination to come forward and play. Each studio evokes imagination in its own way, seducing us, putting a spell on us. The studios present us with ways to activate our hands and bodies, to open up our eyes and voices, to go through the door of imagination that the art materials present to us: down the rabbit hole, up the mountain, across the water, over the bridge, through the veil into the imaginary realm.

THE STUDIOS
Intermodal Dance Studio

> *There is a vitality, a life force, an energy, a quickening that is translated through you into action, and because there is only one of you in all time, this expression is unique. And if you block it, it will never exist through any other medium and will be lost.*
>
> MARTHA GRAHAM

STORY: The Hand Dance

In my Ray Street studio, during one of our weekend intensives, we danced. One of my students had fallen ill. It was a non-contagious malady. Some malfunction of her innards was prolonged, but not permanent. She needed to lie down during the class. This woman loved to dance, but didn't dare get up. So, she became the attendant witness, which seemed fine. We valued those who witnessed, and it seemed perfect that it was her. As we danced, I felt her longing. I went to her and offered her my hand, not to help her to sit up but in an undulating invitation to move with me. She could use her hands and arms without danger, as long as she remained supine. As she and I developed our dance and responded to one another, others came to dance with her as well. This wove her into the group ensemble. It brought a sense of pleasure to everyone. We dance because we can. It's a way of expressing our physical presence. We can dance about anything, or we can dance about everything. We don't have the anthropological record for dance because when you stop dancing, the dance disappears. But we can look at the development of an individual human being: babies dance.

Dance in Human Life

Dance movement is distinct from everyday, utilitarian movements, although accomplished dancers have made concerts, abstracting sports movements, and movements from ordinary activities. Any type of expressive movement can be pleasurable; just bobbing one's head to music is more pleasurable than standing stiffly still. The dance that emerges from our bodies can be as simple or complex as the person dancing. Try it—allow your body to move in response to a current issue, whether it's celebrating the full moon, an argument with your mom, your menses, becoming an aunt, or paying off your student loans. All of human life can be danced, and the moment we begin to dance we move away from ordinary or literal reality and move into the imaginal realm. I go from being Greer, a teacher and person putting away the groceries, to a dancer, moving from my inner world or in response to the outer world. It is an artful impulse that guides me and you. We are the dancers, but we are not the dance. The dance moves through us.

Dancing is part of our human history. In agrarian societies, people dance for planting times and harvest times. Some religious traditions call for dances or processions at various times in the church calendar. It is said the followers of Dionysus danced in the woods, to a frenzy. All tribal societies have dances to assert the identity of the tribe. The Plains tribes can be recognized for their headdress and style of dance, distinct from the Haida tribes of the Northwest. There are dances for men and other dances for women, which reinforce gender roles. This is found in nearly all folk dances, from the Balkans to the Pacific Island nations. There are dances to mark the seasons. In today's Western world, we still dance at weddings and at parties. Are mosh pits and raves today's mating dances? A great desire of mine is to restore the ability for all people to move for self-expression and to move with others. Like all the other arts, it is your birthright to dance your life. To dance is to be human.

STORY: From Mythology to Movement

At the beginning of my junior year at BYU (Brigham Young University), I was required to declare my major. Although I spent all my time in the dance studios and theater department, I thought English Lit would be my major. I loved myths, poetry, stories. I learned to read before I went to school. I had been journaling since I was 12. It just made sense. When I was ill, which was often, I stayed in bed and read. Coming from a literature class, I entered the dance studio. I felt the cool expanse of the clean space. It was early; I was alone. The high ceiling, the smooth wood floor, the long velvet drapes at the wings were comforting; they held a certain dignity—suggesting "studio as temple" or a place that demanded respect for its traditions and timelessness. Gazing all around, I saw the theater seating above the dressing rooms. It was a magnificent studio, unparalleled by any other I had ever seen at a university. The Mormons poured their resources into educational opportunities for their students. I had just come from my tiny desk in a lit class to this sanctuary of dance. I asked myself an astute question for a woman so young: Where can I be most me? Where will I develop more? Is there room for all of me here?

My heart pumped hard in my chest, and my eyes welled up. Which would be best, dance or English Lit? Not best for my future employment, not even what I was best at, but what would serve me best. I knew in my body it was dance. It might have been the first significant moment of consciously taking control of my life and following my own impulse. The decision felt momentous but also unsafe, selfish, and scary. Who did I think I was to choose the thing that I truly wanted without regard for the consequences? I thank that young woman all the time. How did she know? The knowledge of myself first through the body and movement, then the mind, then society, the discipline a dancer needs—these would benefit me forevermore. Dance gave me a window into the cultures of the world, since every culture dances. It gave me history, as we have always danced. It opened a door to national and global politics because the dance responded to the issues of the day. It would prove compelling. The corporeal connection to psyche and soul would be central and salient to my development; it was a rich path. Although not an easy one, I think it was one of the best decisions I ever made.

You Can Dance about Anything

You can dance about any theme. At the same time, you don't need any theme to dance. It's helpful to understand the building blocks, the basic elements and break them down, as dance can be challenging without some education regarding its principles. To facilitate an expressive arts dance studio, or to use dance in expressive arts practice, you'll be best served with knowledge on three levels.

First, know the body itself—the instrument. Understanding the skeleton and skeletal muscle groups will prove particularly useful. Any additional knowledge of human anatomy and physiology will also serve you well.

Second, understand movement—the materials of dance. Time, space, and motion/energy are the basic elements of dance. Understanding what they look like and how to achieve them is essential.

Third, you need to be able to prepare frames, studies, exercises, experiments, inquiries, and art challenges for your clients or students. These should pertain to them, be part of your course of study, be part of the group experience, or be part of a personal inquiry. These compositions or studies use the body instrument and the movement material to shape the elements of dance in a process of dance-making.

Much has been written by other authors about all of this, so I will be brief but provide an overview in "big stitches" so you know where you'll need to drill down to complete your education.

Human Anatomy: The Instrument

Know the names of the large bones and muscle groups. You need to be able to speak about the body. A simple book on human anatomy, like an anatomy coloring book or an artist's anatomy book, can serve as a good resource and inspiration. This vocabulary will be necessary if, during a dance or theater exercise, you ask people to raise their sternum or breastbone. Our bones are beautiful, with their bevels and curves. Possessing both the strength of stone and the delicacy of lace, knowing their names adds a lovely dimension to your aesthetic vocabulary. Knowing their names also reflects a form of respect, similar to knowing a person's name. Unless you decide to take an anatomy class, acquire this little helper and learn from your own body. Observe others as they move, focusing not only on specific body parts like feet and hips but also on the body as a whole. Note the size, shape, and vitality of the moving or dancing body. Pretend you can see the bones moving through the flesh and practice your X-ray vision to observe bones and muscles in motion.

Developing a rich and accurate vocabulary is essential, so knowing which part moved and how is the basis of this sharing. "I saw you round your upper spine, and then your scapula—shoulder blade—jutted out as you rotated your arm in the socket." Use anatomically correct terms to avoid confusion and to give the body, its parts, and its movements back to the client. This can indeed be a gift. I am on a mission to encourage women to use the term "vulva" for their external genitalia, rather than always referring to the vagina, which you can only see with a speculum.

During the warm-up phase, tune into the body itself. Most Western people, unless they are athletes or professional performers, don't pay much attention to their bodies during an ordinary day. Even if they exercise, using dance movement is much different from the prescriptive movement used in exercise. Bring conscious awareness to the body before moving on to other movement explorations. Stiff and uncomfortable body parts can be coaxed into participation with some blood, lymph, and fascia movement.

Body Awareness
Body Scan

A body scan is a mental tour of the body that can instantly increase awareness. The focus of a body scan can vary and can be performed as a meditation while lying down or sitting. I usually start from the feet and work my way up to the head, but you can do it differently. After a few moments of diaphragmatic breathing and allowing the muscles to relax, imagining sinking into the floor, I guide people to imagine their conscious awareness as a bright light. Then, I ask them to shine this imaginary light on their feet, greet them, and listen for a response. We take our time as we move upward: feet, ankles, shins, and calves; knees, thighs—covering all sides, front, back, inside, and outside; pelvis, torso; shoulders, arms, elbows, forearms, wrists, hands, and fingers. Finally, we return to the neck and head. Each part is given a moment of attention, and the pace is slow enough to maintain relaxed breathing. In some sessions, I include the organs, but not always. I encourage people to say "hello" to the various parts of their bodies as a way to befriend themselves. Our physical selves often endure criticism, and this practice aims to counteract that by bringing loving kindness to the body. The exercise can be adapted in various ways to suit your specific situation.

Breath

No breath, no life. Breathing is an ever-present partner in dance. To ensure that the lungs optimally deliver oxygen to the rest of the body, the spine, ribs, and diaphragm need to function well. Cultivating awareness of the breath will enhance all other activities.

I like to bring focus to the breath by making it both a subject of investigation and a metaphor for movement. Start by having students lie on the floor. Instruct them to observe the air as it enters the nostrils, travels down the trachea, and fills the bronchi and lungs. Have them notice the movements of their ribs, belly, and chest as the diaphragm and intercostal muscles between the ribs expand and contract. Use both the kinesthetic sense and visual observation for this. Allow ample time for participants to find their natural breathing rhythm, noticing the inhales and exhales, the rising and falling, filling and emptying.

Next, encourage dancers to imagine other parts of the body "breathing." How would an arm breathe? Legs? After some time experimenting, guide them to incorporate this form of breathing movement as they transition from lying to sitting, and then to standing, maintaining the rhythm and flow of the breath. How does the movement change the breath?

After exploring the rhythm and movement qualities of the breath, have students draw the shape of their breath as it enters and exits the body. I particularly like to do this without the outline of the body—just the breath. The results are often surprising and delightful. I like to suggest using blue and a soft, dry medium, like colored pencils or oil pastels, for this exercise. We borrow our breath from the shared atmosphere; it doesn't belong to us. It visits us, entering and then leaving. Our lungs are perpetually open to the world; delicate yet resilient. Breath both initiates and concludes our life. Have your group create a word bowl from this experience and construct a poem.

If the group is comfortable with one another, you can extend the exercise: Have participants place their hands on the backs of their neighbors to feel the breathing that occurs there. The lungs are, after all, located in the back of the body. Encourage them to place their hands under their own armpits and near the collarbone to feel how the rib cage moves with each breath.

The Bones

Ask students to push into their flesh in a kind of massage, to feel for their bones. They may do that in dyads if that is appropriate. Then draw the bones—from sensing and feeling. Finally, let the bones dance. Emphasize the wrist, for example, or the knee. Make a study about bones.

Joints

Continuing with an anatomical focus on joints is another way to heighten body-instrument awareness. Name the joints and give students some time to explore. Because everything is connected, isolating one joint can be challenging, but it can still serve as the focus of the work. How do you organize the body to concentrate on the wrist? Encourage students to examine a particular joint and arrange the rest of their body in a way that highlights it. Urge them to maintain this focus and move the joint in various relationships to the rest of their body—whether it's above the head, low to the ground, or behind them.

Body Parts

Another way to approach it is to see what each or any body part can do. What movement resources can this body part bring? Let's have a foot dance. This can be done with everyone moving, and then breaking into duets or other groupings.

Gravity

Another ever-present partner in dance is gravity. Begin experiencing gravity: Start on the floor and become aware of the body's weight. Feel where your body touches the floor and where it arcs away. Using as little energy as possible, lift your arms, head, and legs, one at a time, just a few inches off the floor. This awareness can lead to rolling on the floor or even replicating a baby's developmental movements—first rolling onto the tummy, then creeping with elbows and knees, and finally crawling on hands and knees. You can extend this exploration all the way to standing, always being conscious of gravity's pull.

All the above suggestions start inward—my breath, my bones, my movement; gentle and introspective. At times it is more appropriate to begin with high-energy, playful explorations. Go big, outward, exciting, and energetic. This depends on the group's composition, the available space, and other specific considerations. If your group has limited mobility or balance problems, then begin in a standing position with eyes open.

Personal Space
While keeping one foot stationary, students are encouraged to activate as much of the surrounding space as possible. This can be achieved by reaching above the head, down to the ground, in front of the body, behind it, and to each side. Students are also encouraged to use more than just their hands and arms; the head and feet can be incorporated as well as the pelvis. This exercise is both vigorous and enjoyable. Challenge the group to move throughout the room and maintain this expanded sense of personal space. A faster pace can be challenging and lead to amusing and unexpected outcomes.

Walk
Walking serves as an excellent starting point for a dance studio session. Encourage participants to allow their arms to swing freely and naturally as they walk. Guide them through the foot's transition from heel to ball, and then to toe-off. Initiate the session by coming to a "neutral" position—chin level with the floor, sternum lifted, and the body aligned with its center of gravity while breathing easily. This can serve as an exercise in itself or set the stage for further postural manipulations. Proper alignment enhances bodily function, benefiting students both in and outside of the studio by establishing a physically neutral state. Encourage your dancers to trust their feet and keep their eyes off the ground.

Run
Run, not to get anywhere, not to run from or toward anyone or anyplace. Run to enjoy the motion of the body, the sense of acceleration, and the freedom, like animals, like gazelles. This needn't be fast, but any pace that person can sustain. You can manipulate which people are running when and what their pattern is.

Stick Together
If group members are comfortable with each other, ask group members to get a partner. Find a way to attach their bodies: maybe joined at the hip, or perhaps the shoulder, the head. Then explore the space while conjoined: walk, run, and change levels.

Roll

Ask dancers to lie on the floor and begin to roll across the floor. Let them experiment with the numerous ways to roll. Take care of hands and noses. When they come to another body, how to negotiate rolling over someone? This takes patience and practice both for the roller and the person rolled on. Soft, slow movement wins the day.

Movement: The Material of the Dance

The basic elements of dance are time, space, and motion/energy. While these divisions are conceptual and cannot actually be separated, they are helpful to discuss what happened. Often, one element is more prominent than another.

The type of movement useful in ExA involves simple, easy actions that require low skill/high sensitivity. Orienting oneself to the body, engage in easy movements that anyone can perform. These movements can serve as a warm-up or as an exploration on their own.

When looking at dance, as any other art discipline, name the elements we see.

Space

How much space does this particular dance require? What kind of space is the dance performed in?

Does it stay in place and move around the axis of the body (axial movement)?

Does it travel through the space (locomotor movement), leaving a trace, like a path or floor pattern? Which directions does it use? It could go forward, backward, sideways, diagonal. It could go in multiple directions. It could meander. Does the dancer approach the audience or witnesses? Does she stay far away or does she move back and forth? Does she stand in the middle of the space or move diagonally across it? These uses of space are part of the floor pattern.

Space encompasses the use of high, medium, and low levels. For example, the dancer may be on her toes or on stilts. With the use of a prop, like a ribbon, the dancer can draw our eyes up to where the ribbon reaches. As a student, my class performed a dance/theater piece on stage scaffolding. We reached up to the ceiling—very dramatic indeed!

Alternatively, the dancer might be sitting or crouched at a medium level. She can also guide our focus with her eyes; where she looks, our eyes will follow. Conversely, she may spend time on the floor, the lowest level.

Could the dance be performed in any other room, or is it site-specific, requiring this exact location, with the space serving as a kind of partner or frame? I once performed outside behind a hedge to fulfill a score assignment called Neglected Spaces. Every student in the class chose a non-memorable place to perform.

A professor of dance at SDSU (San Diego State University), Liam Clancy, held an open dance event where he brought a portable wooden stage that was 4 feet by 4 feet. The event was called "Four by Four." Now that was a small space!

Experiments in space:

- The hallway, kitchen, under the tree, on the balcony, behind the hedge, by the pool, in the pool, over the pool, stairwells, under the table, abandoned buildings, and street crossings have all served as scenes for site-specific dances that I have either performed or facilitated. These dances are especially fun and exciting because they take place in non-traditional spaces for dance.

Time

The element of time manifests in various ways in dance. Initially, one might notice the actual duration of the dance—whether it's a one-minute solo or a 20-minute group improvisation. The time element is also about how time was utilized or manipulated. What was the pace or speed? Was it quick and lively, like a jig or jota? Or was it slow and sustained, like the bolero? Did the pace change throughout the piece? Tempo, pace, and speed refer to the overall rate at which the dance unfolds, while rhythm denotes the repeating patterns of beats that give certain dances their distinctive character, such as salsa or cha-cha.

A dance can be slow, stately, and dignified, like a pavane. It may feature sustained movement, where the action seems to hang in space momentarily—both ballet and Butoh employ this technique. Conversely, the dance can be quick and abrupt, like tap dancing, or even ballistic—resembling an explosion. Jazz and tap can be ballistic. Hip-hop is often characterized by explosive, sudden, strong, and direct movements. The dance may also incorporate a mix of these elements.

Experiments with time:

- Have dancers moving at different paces, some quick, some slow. Change.

- Have various rhythms going either at one time or one fades out while one fades in.

- Play with *sudden* and *still*.

- One dancer stays on stage the whole time, while other dancers come and go in different lengths of time.

- Use various rhythms; use polyrhythmic music.

- The one-minute solo is a standard in my studio. You can do these one at a time, or you can have a number of one-minute solos taking place at one time.

Motion/Action/Energy

Motion (also called action or energy) refers to how the movement was executed or the type or quality of the movement. For example: slash, punch, wring, wiggle, spring, press, bounce, bobble, glide, rebound, writhe, twist, turn, whirl, circle, rotate, float, fly, flee, leap, flick, dab, sway, and swing—these all describe types or qualities of movement. Locomotion is walking, running, galloping, sliding, skipping, hopping, jumping, rolling, creeping, or other words for how to get from place to place. Please know the difference between a hop, a leap, and a jump. This vocabulary refers to specific types of movement across the space. A sway is not a swing! Barbara Mettler's *Materials of the Dance* (1960) has a long list of words that describe movements, or words that encourage movement. I recommend it.

> I love to see how people walk. They amble, ramble, shamble, shuffle. They zoom and zig-zag. Marching or prancing, skipping, limping or dancing they go about their day.
>
> *(Personal journal entry, November 2022)*

Note repetition of movements or gestures, recurring shapes, or unusual postures. Note stillness. Similar to silence in music, stillness in dance is the contrast to motion and gives shape to the dance.

Start with the gesture in the hands and arms—that's easiest—then offer the challenge to bring these qualities into the feet and legs. Try the head, the pelvis. This is done in a light and easy manner. No one can do it "right," everyone can play. Find words that describe or evoke movement.

Experiments that emphasize the motion element:

- Have a single dancer or a group play with quick, bouncy, springy movements, while at the same time, another dancer or group explores slow, stretchy movements.

- Decide who the dance leaders will be and have them choose

movement qualities of their preference. Others in the ensemble then organically follow them, gradually taking on one of the leader's qualities to play with as long as they like. They have the choice of which dance leader to follow and when to change leaders or movement offerings.

- Play with direct and indirect movement across the floor. Go straight and directly across the floor to a target they have decided upon. Boom! Turn around and focus on another target. Go! Next, go indirectly, meander, like window shopping, or strolling at the shore, wandering. Students immediately feel the differences. I also like to vary the speeds: go slowly each way, at a medium pace, and then as quickly as you can. This is often hilarious, and good fodder for conversation and association. You can improvise and manipulate these forms to suit your situation.

Props: Use them! Props not only invite but require movement. For instance, a ribbon won't float unless you move it. Here are some items I use to encourage movement:

- colorful ribbons on sticks
- dowels for duets and quartets—holding these against the palms without grasping; start with duets, then a quartet
- stretchy body socks that a person can climb into
- a giant scrunchy that can envelop several people
- twirly skirts for turning, spinning, twirling
- balls of various sizes, including a massive one, which a person can drape themselves over, and small soft ones that don't hurt if you are bopped in the face
- a lengthy piece of stretchy fabric that resembles a long ribbon, in bright red; this prop, which is approximately 50 feet long and 18 inches wide, was left over from a concert I did and has been featured in many improvisations
- a parachute, specifically an army surplus cargo parachute that is at least 25-feet wide; this item has served various purposes, from acting as a shroud to becoming a wedding dress
- a large, heavy rope net
- pool noodles
- hula hoops and other large pieces of PVC
- scarves of various kinds, sizes, and fabrics

Outsized props engage the physical imagination of adults. I am partial to this type of charismatic prop; it brings something to the relationship, and it challenges us. I have been collecting these items for many years. If well cared for, they can last for decades. Starting with what you have is perfectly fine. I've also had good results with inexpensive, readily available items like crepe paper rolls, newspapers, sticks, and stones. Placing something in the hands of a novice dancer often helps liberate them from self-consciousness. One of my favorite techniques is to get a group moving with a prop and then take it away, asking them to reproduce the movement. The results are usually lovely and surprising for everyone involved.

Music: Music is an automatic motivator in dance. But beware! It can also be a driver so the dancers dance to the music and when that music is gone they cannot move. I prefer live music whenever possible, because then it is a dialogue, but it is not always possible or convenient. Musical taste is so individual, you need to use what you know and like. Pre-recorded music for dance exploration needs to be wordless or in a language no one knows, unless there is a very specific reason. Look at the beats per minute—and compare that to what you want to achieve: something soothing and slow for a meditative activity; something midrange, like a heartbeat; or something driving and high energy. I like to look at the instrumentation. Bass instruments are more somber (alto flute or cello), whereas soprano saxophone is enlivening. I am also fond of world music, like gamelan, because the polyrhythms allow for variation in a large group; not everyone is on the same rhythmic pattern, which is lovely. Know the music well. Do not use music you have not listened to all the way through several times. This is delightful homework, though, right?

Movement themes for groups and communities: In addition to the props and exploration of dance elements as mentioned above, consider using various themes that resonate with the life of the group. These themes might include:

- greeting dance
- goodbye dance
- walking dance
- rising and falling
- animal images—be specific
- insect images: this is one of Paolo's scores and is always entertaining and amusing; be specific—are you the fly or the bee?
- birds—of the region or during migration; be specific—birds do not all move alike.

Environments: At the EGS, we have created scores inspired by the trees, the river, the wildflowers, the Alps, and the retreating glacier. We're not imitating these elements but drawing inspiration from their shape and form or movements and translating that into our physical expression.

Curation as Validation: Often, the movement is playful and is an end in itself, the low skill/high sensitivity way. Sometimes it is dance-making and a dance image emerges and is brought to life, given shape. If that occurs, then I like to take it all the way to curation.

For dance, curation means showing and sharing the dance images that emerged. For a frame, nothing beats the frame of time. Try the frame of a one-minute solo as mentioned above. That can take place in the middle of a circle of witnesses, or it can be in a more formal proscenium space. Taping off the area can add to the specialness of the dedicated stage space. "Over here is the performance space. Over there is for witnesses." Lighting is critical for dance validation. It helps us see what is being offered and "brings it to light." It elevates the dance. Try simple aluminum outdoor lights to bring in this aspect of theater and performance. I have put flashlights to good use, as well as twinkle lights and candles.

Paolo's concept of superimposition (Knill *et al.*, 1996) is especially helpful when curating dance. Besides the space designation and the lighting, adding the elements of costume or music can help a dance piece. Be careful not to let the music lead and push, unless you are using music as the primary organizing element. In that case, dramatic music is useful for long-form improv. Best of all is to have the dancers make their own music. But again be sensitive to the situational analysis—who is this, what is the purpose of the group, why are you gathered, what themes are emergent, and how can you support the entire dancerly effort? Most lovely if there could be witnesses. Try one half of a group as witnesses while the other half moves. Or divide the class into trios or other divisions. Being the witness is an important way to learn, so don't hesitate to enroll people that way.

The Architecture of a Session for Dance

The order and tasks of the dance studio are precisely the same as any other studio:

First Room: Counselor's Chairs—First Conversation
Task: Filling-In

With an individual I might get the filling-in verbally, or I might ask them to "show me with their body" how they are today. Or both.

With a medium-sized group (let's say 8–15), where each individual cannot speak, you can use movement check-ins:

- Show me with your body how you are today.

- Find a place in the room that corresponds to how you are feeling now. Check in from there with one word or phrase.

- Choose an animal from this pile of images and check in as that animal.

Depending on the size of the group, people can add a few sentences (headlines and highlights) or even one word about what they bring in. Or they can share with a partner or small group. Or they can write a sentence in their journal about their current reality.

As I mentioned above, with a very large group, they may not report their filling-in to me. I ask the students at the EGS to check in with themselves. I don't know what they are bringing, but, at the end, I ask them to check back to see what, if anything, has changed.

Second Room: Studio–Artistic Conversation
Task: Sensitize/Attune

In the dance studio, we need to warm up the body, blood, bones, muscles, and joints, as well as the social aspect and the imagination. Use the suggestions above from the body focus, the materials of dance focus, or a theme or image that is related to the life of the group. I always ask people to be responsible for their own physical safety. Or ask people to lie down and connect with their breath. I use all the examples above.

Task: Decenter

Any of the above themes could lead to a full exploration. You can give scores from the elements of dance, use images, props, music, take movement cues from a painting or other visual art pieces, from poetry—anything can be the basis of a score for dance. Add feedback and multiple "takes" for adjustments and refinement. Change roles (those who were witnesses and giving feedback can now change places with the dancers).

Optional Task: Curation as Validation

Each dance composition will be unique and therefore need its own approach to the elements of curation. See notes on curation above.

Task: Aesthetic Analysis
Use the SuPER formula:

> Surface: Use the vocabulary of the body as an instrument, the movement material, and the elements of composition to describe the dance. What was seen in terms of the body (or bodies) as a whole? What aspects of time were prominent? Which aspects of space were observed? What types and qualities of motion were present? As much as possible, use the language of dance. What images or emotions were evoked?

> Process: What happened for individuals? What happened for the ensemble; for witnesses? How were difficulties managed?

> Experience: What was present for the individuals?

> Reflection/Round-up: Does this experience get a title?

Third Room: Counselor's Chairs—Final Conversation
Task: Harvest
Each dancer can share what she has experienced about her development or situation. What has changed? This can be shared with a partner or in small groups. It can also be written privately in a journal. After giving time for people to feel their response, I ask if anyone would like to share. This also permits a range of outcomes. Usually people want to share.

Intermodal Music Studio

> *You can't copy anybody and end with anything. If you copy, it means you're working without any real feeling. No two people on earth are alike, and it's got to be that way in music or it isn't music.*
>
> BILLIE HOLIDAY

Music in Our Lives
Music is our companion. Research shows music has multiple important roles in our lives, but you know this. When I am teaching intermodal music I put up a huge piece of paper and ask people to write how they use music in their lives on a graffiti wall. The following uses show up: Motivate a workout or housework. Focus during study (I have Malte Marten handpan in my headphones right now). We celebrate with the songs or chants that go with the occasion, like the birthday song or holiday songs. Events like

football games have fight songs for the team. Serenade your sweetheart, remember "our" song with your lover, and create a mood for lovemaking. Create calm and relaxation, like a lullaby to soothe a child or meditation music before bedtime. To dance. To celebrate national identity like the hula or the haka, as well as all national anthems. Increase *esprit de corps* with marches. Reinforce membership in various groups or clubs like the Whiffenpoof of Yale or the Girl Scout Anthem. We worship with hymns, chants, or other music deemed sacred by tradition. Some hymns accompany the end of a life, and requiems to celebrate it. Road trips need a playlist. We live with music. What can you add to the list?

Musical Development in Human History

Many instruments have claimed to be the first! The voice seems the obvious choice, but the idiophone has made such a claim, and so has the drum, which is ubiquitous across time and cultures. The bullroarer of Australia is 20,000 years old. A flute, 60,000 years old, was discovered in the Divje Babe cave in Slovenia. It was made by Neanderthal people from the thigh bone of a young cave bear; well-made and beautiful. Our ancient instruments moved with us over time and place. They developed into the magnificent array of instruments we have today. Each tribe modified and enhanced the basic music-making design, according to their preference and what was available.

There are roughly seven types of instruments, categorized according to which part of the instrument vibrates and therefore makes the sound. These are: Idiophone, where the body of the instrument vibrates when either struck (like xylophones, cymbals, or rattles) or plucked (like the mbira or thumb piano). Membranophone, where a membrane vibrates when it is struck (like a drum) or blown (like a kazoo). Chordophone, where it is the strings that vibrate, like in simple zithers or composite instruments like lutes, harps, and guitars. Aerophones, where it is the air that vibrates is free, as in the organ, harmonica, or accordion. Instruments like flutes, oboes, saxophones, and euphoniums are considered non-free aerophones ("free" means the air vibrates outside the instrument; "non-free" means the air vibrates within an enclosed tube). Electrophones, where the sound is produced by electronic action or amplification. These inventions led us to where we are today. We are still inventing.

Every cell in your body is circadian, a rhythmic response to the cycles of light and dark. The heart is a drum, the lungs a bellows that fills and empties, and every organ has an internal clock that tells it when to wake and when to sleep. Our walking gait is rhythmic, our speech is musical; some say we started with singing. We are music.

Music in Healing

Music's transformative power can be profound and deeply healing. Oliver Sacks, best-selling author and professor of neurology at NYU School of Medicine, once observed:

> Music can lift us out of depression or move us to tears—it is a remedy, a tonic, orange juice for the ear. But for many of my neurological patients, music is even more—it can provide access, even when no medication can, to movement, to speech, to life. For them, music is not a luxury, but a necessity. (Sacks, 2007)

Similarly, Debasish Mridha (2015) reflected on music's capacity to reach areas where medicine sometimes cannot, asserting: "Music can heal the wounds which medicine cannot touch."

Making Music

The benefits of listening to music are well-researched and documented. However, in intermodal ExA it is important to make our own music. We call forth and reinstate the musician in each of us. This brings additional benefits above and beyond listening—which already can be so helpful. The Vermont podcast, Timeline, by James Stewart (2020), reports that making music together benefits us emotionally, socially, and physically. "Actively participating in making music, actually making the sounds either by yourself or with a group, has been found to boost executive brain function, strengthen speech processing, improve memory and promote empathy." The *British Journal of Psychiatry* published an article in 2015, reporting a study that found singing together is "a useful intervention to maintain and enhance the mental health of older people" (Coulton *et al.*, 2015). The Music Industries Association of the UK makes a list of ten benefits of making music, mostly for children, but their list includes impressive things, like increasing executive functioning, strengthening the ability to process and retain information, promoting empathy, fostering math and science ability, improving motor skills, and sharpening self-esteem. An experiment conducted by Kraus demonstrated that two years of musical training significantly enhanced children's ability to process speech syllables (as cited in Calderone, 2015). This suggests a promising pathway to bolster literacy skills.

ExA values all the aspects of the musical experience: listening with individuals and groups; singing together; creating music with individuals and groups, as well as communities; building instruments; and finding instruments. In addition to all the benefits and values from research, music touches us and moves us. Why do we weep? Why do we cheer? Music arouses, calms, and helps us celebrate and mourn. Music makes what I feel inside audible.

The Basic Elements of Music

Music consists of sound and silence. The main sense used is the auditory sense, although the vibration of music can be felt, as Evelyn Glennie, a deaf percussionist, masterfully demonstrates in "Touch the Sound" (Riedelsheimer, 2004). The kinesthetic sense of the body also plays a significant role in the act of playing an instrument. For sighted individuals, the visual imagery of the instruments and the performers contribute to the overall musical experience. The basic elements of music, listed below, further facilitate a comprehensive understanding and appreciation of this art discipline.

These are the elements to listen for, both to manipulate as you are composing and also to remember as you do an Aesthetic Analysis:

- **Pulse (or Tempo):** The ongoing speed or underlying beat of the piece.

- **Rhythm:** A pattern of beats, some emphasized, others not. For instance, the cha-cha and waltz are both rhythms. It involves counting out the recurring beats, which may be regular or irregular.

- **Dynamics:** Denotes how loud or soft the music is at any given time and may change within the piece.

- **Timbre:** The voice or quality of sound of the various instruments used. If a bell and a guitar string are playing the same note, the perceived difference between them is the timbre. The timbre is what helps you recognize whether an instrument is an oboe or a piccolo.

- **Melody:** Refers to the main musical line of a song or piece, the part we usually sing.

- **Harmony:** The relationship between the notes that are played simultaneously. It adds depth to the melody by creating a fuller sound.

- **Pitch:** Refers to how high or low the sound of an instrument is.

- **Texture:** Involves the various timbres included in the composition, creating a rich or sparse auditory landscape.

- **Form:** The overall structural organization of a piece of music, its style. Examples include a lullaby, a cowboy song, a rock song, an aria, and a ballad. Make your own list.

Architecture of a Session for Music

First Room: Counselor's Chairs–First Conversation
Task: Fill-In

For example: Participants choose an instrument from a pre-selected array. They use the instrument to "check in," creating a sound and commenting on its relationship to them. Ensure a wide variety of timbres are available.

Second Room: Studio–Artistic Conversations
Task: Sensitize/Attune

Sensitizing in the musical studio can begin with listening to the ambient sounds, specific recordings, live instruments, or music with diverse qualities. The more you listen the more you hear. It can begin with people playing instruments in non-ordinary ways, interacting with each other. This could follow from the check-in example above.

Sensitizing can begin with the voice. Start with humming. This is good for the delicate larynx (the vocal folds). Progress to vowel sounds. A favorite exploration for beginners is the sonic environment. Have people lie down in a circle, face up, head-to-head. Then instruct them to listen and respond to what emerges. Sounds, but no words. Or, call and response: one person makes a rhythmic phrase, which the other person or persons repeat back.

Attuning and warming up with instruments: Play and experiment with simple instruments—choose instruments that someone with zero experience can have a satisfactory experience with. Even low skill doesn't mean no skill, so giving a minimal orientation to how the sounds are made can be helpful. These might include claves, rattles of all sizes and timbres, rain sticks, simple drums, bells, and tuned blocks.

Play with "kitchen instruments." In my studio I had "tuned" flower pots and a variety of both bells and gongs from pot lids and metal tableware from the thrift store, chosen for their sound. Take your beater, go listen, and get some! The advantage of these is there's nothing precious to break or ruin (I can tell stories). The humble appearance invites play. Can't you just see the baby on the kitchen floor, with the cupboards all open, banging away with a wooden spoon? Yet the quality of the sound can be enchanting.

Play with natural objects: rocks, leaves, water. Elizabeth McKim has students clap stones together, especially when outdoors, to create a rhythmic background. Pouring water from heights into buckets of various materials. Leaves can be crushed or rattled. Sticks can make claves or beaters.

Everything vibrates and vibration is the basis of sound and sound is the basis of music. See what you can find.

Pass one instrument around a circle to see what sounds each person can make with it.

Explore similarly all the instruments that will be used in the music making.

Task: Decenter
Play and experiment:

Use simple instruments accessible for beginners.

Introduce "kitchen instruments," natural objects, or found sound-makers.

Create an oeuvre, a score that you can repeat, allowing for improvisational variations.

Utilize the BRAS acronym (Beat, Rhythm, Accent, Solo) for structured music making.

BRAS is a formula for creating music with non-musicians. This will give you a nearly fail-safe way to create music that has a shape—whether participants have ever done it or not. It comes from Jonathan Glasier—the founder of the Interval Foundation and publisher of *Interval Magazine*. He was a student of Harry Partch, the maker of magnificent handmade instruments and a microtonalist of renown. Jonathan and I shared a studio for many years and developed a sound and movement company (Organic Sound and Movement) interested in microtonal music and improvisational performance.

B for Beat—the Motherbeat, the basic pulse and tempo of the piece. There is one motherbeat. Good to have an experienced person do this because it requires holding the pulse for the whole time. I like the walking beat, but a heartbeat is sometimes good.

R for Rhythm—recurring figures of beats, both loud and soft. There can be more than one rhythm. They can overlap.

A for Accent. Think about the sounds that are already going on. The accent might be a dry wooden sound or clack, or it might be a wet ring or metal sound. There can be more than one accent.

S for Solo. When the group can stay together and hold its shape, a solo instrument can be introduced, and that solo part can move around the circle. The solo can be a voice.

Remind people to start in silence and stillness, to listen. Then establish the motherbeat. If the group is new, you may need to hold the motherbeat—either a heartbeat (ta TUM, ta TUM) or a walking beat (ta ta ta ta). It is critical to the outcome that the motherbeat is steady and constant. Have the players come in one-by-one, around the circle, play together, then go out one at a time. Take two if needed. Add the accents. Take two if needed. When the group can hold this form for a few minutes, add the solos, one at a time. Part of the success is the curation of the instruments. An orchestra of all metal (which can be lovely, ringing, wet with slow decay) has a different feel from the orchestra with all wooden sounds (dry, fast decay). Choose the instruments carefully for their role—and if it doesn't work, change it. For example, a bell is a great accent instrument, but not as good for a solo.

Third Task: Aesthetic Analysis (SuPER)

Surface: Describe the sound qualities. Describe exactly what you heard—describe the qualities of the sound, and how it behaved.

Process: Discuss individual experiences. Each person can say what it was like for them to play and also to listen. This can be done in small groups and reported back.

Experience: Share the collective experience. What did the experience of making music together bring to the individuals?

Reflection/Round-up: Consider naming the piece or adding lyrics.

Optional Task: Curation as Validation
Listening to the music you create is a form of curation. Record the session or divide into groups for playback and reflection. You can divide a large group into sections and take turns listening to each other.

Third Room: Counselor's Chairs—Final Conversation

Task: Harvest
How did this experience affect the participants? What shifted? What opened? What disappeared? What changed?

Intermodal Visual Art Studio

I found I could say things with color and shapes that I couldn't say any other way—things I had no words for.

GEORGIA O'KEEFE

Studio Processes

Knowing studio processes can bring richness to your ExA practice. Bringing the languages of the studio, of the workshop, and of the arts can enrich the experience for you and your clients. Beyond that, the senses of the hand and the eye need stimulation to begin to speak to us. The hand can know and do so much, the eye can see so much! Using a variety of processes can afford a much richer experience than always relying on paint or oil pastels, as good as those are and as varied as those applications can be.

Here are some basic processes if you are not a native of the visual art studio. These can bring necessary variety to you and your clients. You can add to the list.

- **Printmaking:** Printmaking is a process in which color, paint, ink, or another substance is applied to the surface of an object, which is then pressed onto paper, cloth, or even a cave wall. Famous examples include Japanese fish prints and woodblock prints, which are some of the most beautiful images ever created. Remember making potato prints in kindergarten? Vegetable prints offer an easy, inexpensive way to explore convex and concave forms. They also teach you how much pressure to apply for a good print and what tools to use to shape the image. Almost anything can be used to create a print, but styrofoam is especially receptive to pressure from a ballpoint pen and holds its shape nicely.

- **Stamping:** Stamping involves printing with a handheld, often rubber, incised matrix. Ink or another medium is applied to the stamp and then forcefully pressed onto the desired surface, such as paper or cloth.

- **Stenciling:** In stenciling, a cut-out pattern or object is placed on a surface, and ink, paint, or another substance is applied into the cut-out design, leaving the pattern on the surface. The term "pouncing" is used to describe this method of bouncing the brush or tapping it onto the surface. Special brushes are available for pouncing.

- **Resist techniques:** Resist techniques involve masking a portion of an image to preserve the original surface. Wax or other substances can be used as masks to keep areas free of added colors and textures. Tie-dye is a form of resist, where twists and rubber bands act as the "mask." Masking itself is also a process, involving either physical means like masking tape or chemical means such as masking fluid.

- **Bas-relief sculpting:** Bas-relief is a technique involving shallow carving, usually on a wall. You can do this using cardboard, or soap.

- **Chiaroscuro painting:** Chiaroscuro in painting focuses on the crucial role of light and shadow, exemplified by artists like Rembrandt and Caravaggio.

- **Impasto painting:** Impasto refers to the thick application of paint, almost like shallow sculpting, commonly applied with a palette knife. Think of van Gogh.

- **Encaustic painting:** Encaustic involves adding wax and oils to paint, creating thin, translucent layers that give the artwork depth and luminosity.

- **Marbling:** Marbling involves laying colors onto water or a substance called "size" and then transferring the pattern onto paper or fabric.

The high-sensitivity approach of expressive arts therapy emphasizes the awakening of the senses as a way to warm up, sensitize, and tune in. We can explore the processes and experiences that emerge just from investigating these techniques. They serve as frames in themselves and often lead to full decentering in the image-making process.

Sculptures/3D

- **Bricolage:** Bricolage is creating a sculpture from materials at hand, especially from discarded or once-used parts. This method of creation holds great appeal for some clients. The prospect of using tools such as a hammer, a saw, clamps, and measuring instruments, not to mention power tools or soldering can be exciting.

- **Assemblage:** Assemblage, similar to bricolage, also includes the concept of gathering or collecting, often involving dissimilar objects.

- **Carving:** Soapstone lends itself well to carving, but surprisingly, soap can be an even better medium. Use large bars of laundry soap.

- **Molding and Modeling:** For molding and modeling, materials such as clay and soft white bread loaves can be used. You might also consider using Plasticine.

- **Dioramas:** Dioramas can be miniature or a full-scale model of a scene. They can be created from an array of materials, even recycled. Whole cities have been crafted out of cleaned recycling materials, including office supplies. Buildings can be made from paper scraps, such as cardboard, cereal boxes, packing boxes, and their padding. Transparencies or tissue paper can serve as windows. From beverage bottles and coffee cans to plastic bags, all these items can have a place in this creative process.

- **Installations:** Usually large scale, often multimedia. Sometimes site-specific. Placing objects in some particular way.

Colors and Materials

Color is a physical thing: It's not just a surface… It's that sort of interplay between the 'stuffness' of color and its illusory, somewhat evasive, 'other' qualities that much of the work is about.

BRITISH ARTIST ANISH KAPOOR IN A BBC INTERVIEW

Evidence of early humans using natural materials to create colors is abundant. One compelling example is a prehistoric assemblage from around 100,000 years ago, discovered in Blombos Cave, South Africa. This "paint processing kit," as described by Dissanayake (2018), included abalone shells with yellow ochre residues, pieces of charcoal, and seal bones from which oil may have been extracted and mixed with the ochre powder as a binder. Was this shell the first palette? Also found were umber, sienna burnt and raw, kaolin soft white, and black charcoal mixed with fat or spit. Iron gave a rusty/red color, the same as our blood. It was a transition from vegetable sources of color to more enduring mineral sources. First, cave people decorated themselves; later, they made cave paintings.

Start an exploration of color with the color wheel. Note there are several versions of a color wheel. One notable resource is Pantone, a company that selects "color of the year" that influences design and fashion trends. Their website provides valuable insights into color choices and trends. Countering the commercial feel of Pantone is *Werner's Nomenclature of Colors* (Syme, 2018), a classic and delightful reference to colors derived only from the natural world. This resource offers a wide range of color descriptions and classifications. Additionally, the Golden Paint Company offers a brochure featuring actual swatches of their colors across different formulae they produce, providing a tangible and comprehensive understanding of their color offerings.

The act of mixing colors with a mortar and pestle relates to the concept of artistic autonomy and personal expression. Through this process, artists can create unique and personalized shades, granting them the freedom to explore their individual style and vision. The tactile and muscular engagement of grinding the colors establishes a deep connection with the materials, fostering an intimate and immersive experience in the creative process. This hands-on approach encourages experimentation and empowers artists to take full control over the colors they use, thereby enhancing their ability to effectively convey specific moods, feelings, or concepts through their artwork.

Art Timeline of Styles and Influences

My students create a timeline of art styles and influences that starts with master artists and the canon. To this we add artists that reflect who we are and our cultural interests. Since we are largely a female community, we emphasize and search for female artists and add materials that are often thought of as typical for women or associated with women's endeavors such as fiber arts: needlework, weaving, soft sculpture, and quilting. Our explorations have included the identities of the participants, such as BIPOC and LGBTQIA+, and represented our diverse nationalities and other specific interests or affiliations. We have investigated and included artists with disabilities, both physical and mental, and artists of a specific religion or age group.

Having some knowledge of art history and including lesser-represented artists enriches the studio experience. Since expressive arts therapy is mostly associated with modern, expressionistic, and contemporary styles, we begin at the start of the modern period, about 1890.

Architecture of a Session in Visual Art
First Room: Counselor's Chairs—First Conversation
Task: Fill-In
Filling-in with visual art can be as simple as having each person pick a color from an arranged array and relate it to their situation, observing that no color inherently means anything specific, since meaning is both culturally

and individually determined. The choices could be papers or pencils or chalks, anything where the color is the main factor. Or it could be a small piece of clay the size of a golf ball that they manipulate for one minute and then share what they made. Ask, "when is the last time" the people did the thing they are about to do. Paint, or work with clay, or weave. It can be offering various images in an array and having people choose one and relate it to their situation.

Second Room: Studio—Artistic Conversations
Task: Sensitize/Attune

Visual art includes everything from a pencil scribble to a giant installation made of recycled things; from land art, to tapestries, weavings, doll making, book making, videos, and more. In visual art, we are using the eyes and the hands, so these are the senses that need to be sensitized. First, let's feed the hungry eye.

The eye has distinct organs for detecting color, so allowing a person to experience color as purely as possible has many benefits. If we have a capability and let it lay fallow, undeveloped, that automatically brings a kind of wounding. If you have legs and can walk, but never do... doesn't that sound like a loss? A diminishment? If it concerns your aesthetic ability, it is an aesthetic wound.

Color: Using a color warm-up for any project that involves color in a central role can be done in several ways. One is to gather some of the paint chips from a home improvement store. These are so useful. I encourage you to get these for several activities in your studios. Allow the clients to see which color chooses them. Play with colored scarves, with no intention except to see what they can do, see the bright colors, and have fun. Bright overhead lighting helps with this, or sunshine. People also love dribbling watercolors with no directive except to experience the various colors. Do this with chalk, which also can be vivid, especially on black paper, or tar paper. Acrylic, which is a bit messier and requires more setup, is also good for color play. Quality colored pencils or good markers also allow playing with color. Let the ground (the primed support or surface beneath the paint) suit the pigmented materials.

Paper: If you are doing something on paper, it is a wonderful and simple warm-up to have the client touch the paper, lift it, feel its weight, look closely at it, and smell it even. Use newsprint and see the little pieces of wood pulp in it. It does have a certain "woody" smell. It is lightweight and especially nice to use with vine charcoal. Introduce the concept of "tooth" in the paper that will be used for drawing—so people understand how the paper grabs the color that is moved across it. Make the paper a partner in the art-making. It is fun to offer things like newspaper, acetate, tissue, construction paper, roofing paper, cardboard, wrapping paper—see what is on hand. See what kind of mark-makers work on these various surfaces.

Large Paper: When working with a large, six-foot paper I ask them to touch the borders of the paper: Is the edge smooth or deckle? Use their arms to feel its size. We have also dragged or flown the paper around the room, if space permits. These activities develop a relationship to the paper. After exploring it, I ask students to touch the paper with their dry paint brushes as I call out various emotions. "Use your whole body to touch the paper with authority, strongly. Caress it delicately. Tickle it. Touch it with reverence." They see how the body gets involved and how emotion can change the way the brush is used and how that will change the look of the brush strokes on the paper.

Watercolor: When working with watercolor, especially if my artist/client is not familiar, I cut several smallish papers for several simple experiments. Wet the paper and then use a wet brush to dab and drip pigment onto the paper. See how vivid the paint can be. Then on another small paper, make some pools of color and drop isopropyl alcohol onto it. See how the color moves away from the alcohol. Or, using a straw, blow the pigment around on the paper. Hold it up so the paint drips, then change directions. Or, into a pool of pigment, drop or sprinkle some salt. When it dries, brush it off and see the shapes the resist gave. Finally, after the small papers have dried, go in with a sharp black permanent marker, find a little creature, trace around it, and give it eyes. Or find a landscape.

Collage: Years of having people cut or tear images out of magazines taught me something... magazines have interesting articles! People get caught by the words or the recipe. Now I rip out the pages. I do not have to edit, and the whole page can come. The advantage is worth it to me. I put these into large plastic containers in categories of "people, animals, places, and things." Spread images out on tables, and allow people to move through the array of choices. This warms up the eye and the hand can reach out to take what it is attracted to. Or put it back. Or take it and not use it. Spread out various colors of backgrounds. I vary the size of the backgrounds.

Task: Decenter

After sensitizing comes the decision to either play in the art materials or work toward an image or oeuvre. This decision might be made depending on the entire situational analysis: Do you haul your materials to the location to meet your clients? Do they come to your studio where many options are at the ready? Are you teaching a unit in a college? Everything always depends on everything. Playing with art materials can easily turn into an image.

You can give a theme or let playing with the materials determine what might emerge.

Task: Aesthetic Analysis

This is a reflective understanding that involves contemplation of the artwork. It's not about using a pre-existing framework to interpret the art, but rather allowing the artwork to reveal its significance in a phenomenological way. This is direct experience and observation of the work as it presents itself, without preconceptions or imposed interpretations. Stepping back to reflect on what was made, and how, is a crucial part of the process. This Aesthetic Analysis isn't about imposing meaning onto the artwork but rather allowing the artwork to reveal its metaphoric message to its creator. This approach respects the uniqueness of each individual's creative expression. The last thing to do before you leave the studio space/time is honor the work, the effort, and the artifact by doing Aesthetic Analysis. Each studio does this in a slightly different way. The Aesthetic Analysis begins with a careful consideration of what is—what has emerged, the art-baby. It has never existed before in the world, so it is not possible to know immediately what messages it brings. Maintain patience and open-hearted curiosity. Encounter the image itself, the new little one.

The SuPER analysis:

Surface: Look at the work, just look. Allow your eyes to go where they want to go. What is most interesting? What calls? Follow the lead of your eyes with consciousness, with awareness; look and really see. Take in the whole art piece. Allow your hand to travel over the whole surface as you look, if that helps you stay focused, or use a slender pointer, like a stick. Then look at compositional elements. Have you ever seen people count the toes of a new baby? You will be counting the "toes" of the painting or other visual work as well. It is necessary to keep your eye on the surface of the image. Keep your eye on the thing you want to see. When you look away you are having a memory of the thing, but are not seeing the thing itself. Remember, the more you look, the more you see.

The client is also looking. You look together. Then engage in a conversation about what is there. The client speaks first, leading the conversation about what they see. But as you are also looking, you can contribute to the observations. This can enhance their experience and engagement with the artwork. Here are possible things you might see:

- Observe the overall facture of the piece: How is it made? What is the surface or ground of the work? Is it paper, cardboard, or wood panel? If it is a sculpture, of what materials? Is something taken away as with soap carving? Or is it an additive process, such as bricolage or construction? Is it a diorama, installation, or site-specific piece? Discuss this aspect.

- Consider the size or scale: Is it as tiny as a postage stamp, an ATC (artist trading card), or a playing card? Or is it as big as a person, a wall, or the side of a building? Something in-between? The size communicates to the eyes and the rest of you. Compare a large Rothko painting with an Indian Miniature.
- Examine the materials of mark-making: Is it pencil, cray-pas, oil pastel, chalk, or paint? What kind of paint; watercolor, oil? Investigate. Are there other elements? Collage of papers, sewing material? Objects like buttons? Mixed media? Rediscover this with your client.
- Assess the overall shape: Is it flat or does it have elements that bend? Or have holes in it? Or protrusions? Perhaps it is 3D. Is it rectangular or round?
- Analyze the style: Is it delicate or chunky? Refined or primal? Full of little details or grand swipes? Does it remind you of any other artwork, artist, school of art, or time period?
- Look at the colors used: Note the saturation, hue, value intensity, shade, or tint. If color is absent and the piece is made of neutrals, note that. If color is sparsely used, note where it appears or where it is absent. This is where your color vocabulary will be essential. Many hues are named "yellow." Be familiar with the color wheel and how the colors relate to one another.
- Examine the lines. Paul Klee said: "Take a line for a walk." Are they straight, curved, thick, thin, intersecting, or not? A line can lead the eye around the painting. It can be continuous or broken. See what is there.
- Notice the application: Is it lightly on the surface, or has the artist made thick impressions and indentations into the surface; impasto? Imagine how it was made. What did the artist do to make those marks? How were they moving?
- Look at the texture: Does anything on the surface create actual texture or resemble some kind of texture? Maybe it is a wash of delicate thin watercolor, leaving barely a hint of a tint.
- Consider the use of space in the piece: Is there negative space or areas that are blank? Is it on the top only, or all over the surface, or squeezed down into one corner?
- Evaluate the values, the light and shadow: Like Rembrandt's chiaroscuro, the dramatic juxtaposition of light and dark gives the

impression of a 3D object on the 2D surface, if that is present. Does light seem to be coming from some direction? Are there shadows here or not? What impression of light is there? Is there some type of perspective and depth that lends a type of realism? Is the surface treated flat so as not to create dimension, but focusing on the surface only? Think Jackson Pollock.

- Look for other types of contrast in addition to light and dark.
- Search for the element of rhythm or repetition of elements: Do lines repeat like fence posts, in even measurements? Or are they randomly placed?
- Look for the overall balance: Is the balance symmetrical or asymmetrical? Or intentionally out of balance?
- Search for patterns, repetitions.
- Look for a central subject: How is it arranged? If there is a focal point or some emphasis—what is the proportion?
- Search for distinct geometric shapes: Do they graduate in size from large to small? This is gradation. Think the polka dots of Yayoi Kusama.
- Look for distinct images or icons, or other figurative objects: Or is it abstract (looks sort of like a thing, but highly distorted) or non-representational (no real subject at all). Picasso is abstract; Rothko is non-representational.
- Is there a sense of movement? Maybe a river or a line that leads your eye around the piece. Think *Nude Descending a Staircase, #2*, by Marcel Duchamp, 1912.
- Assess the variety: Are there a lot of different things, or few?

Allow the image to reveal all the compositional elements as they spontaneously appear. Not every art piece has all these elements. It is up to the client to decide what is trivial and what is significant, but in this step, we take an inventory of what is present with us in the work.

Process: After examining the surface, inquire about the process of making this artwork. How was it made, step-by-step? Was there difficulty at the beginning? Where were the challenges? Was the material cooperative or not? Were there surprises? How did the artist meet the challenges? What strategy did they employ? Although making art can be relaxing and pleasant, we don't want to gloss over the struggles. Giving failures their opportunity to be acknowledged will help make the harvesting much richer.

Since I was there, I witnessed the client making the thing. I can add my observations. "This part seemed tough. That didn't work, so you did something else." This recognition often allows the client to admit and remember the trouble or difficulty and make it part of the experience.

Experience: Inquire about the client's experience: the thoughts, emotions, sensations, and memories that came while engaged in this making. I make room for her to explore what she feels internally but has never spoken. This translation from deep gut to language is a long journey! I breathe and attend. This is like a birth. It takes time. Be careful to notice and remark upon the changes in the voice or face of the client. Gently and with open-hearted curiosity I ask: "When you said this your eyes watered." Or: "When you told me that your voice changed. I am curious about that. Did you notice? What was that?" Gently set your observations in front of the client.

Reflection/Round-up: Now, I consider my emotional response. How am I feeling as I look? Again, it is the client who must consider her feelings, but I am there, I have a heart, I can feel, and my emotional response to the artwork may be a resource for my client. Am I puzzled, curious, leery, relaxed? Does it frighten me? Make me smile? If this seems like it might be helpful to the client, I transparently share these thoughts and feelings.

When people are eager to tell me what is going on and what each thing means as they create it, I call this the "first story." And it can be helpful, even though it often recapitulates what the person already knew when they came in. I encourage a more thorough phenomenological look. We want to see if there are resources beyond what the person already knew if there is a surprise or an "aha!" or a new perspective.

An image can be "both/and." It can be both the story they were telling themselves when they were making it, and at the same time be the new story we discover as we take the aesthetic tour. Often the trouble that brought them into my studio and the resources for the solution are there in the same painting, dance, or poem. Which is why we want plenty of time to explore what occurred.

Before we move back to the Counselor's Chairs, we need to place the work somewhere—honor it. This is Curation as Validation. Here are some ideas for the validation of the works of individual clients and groups in the visual art studio:

Optional Task: Curation as Validation

STORY: The Golden Door

For ten years, Francine Hoffman and I offered a week of expressive arts at an exclusive high-end spa, the Golden Door. We called it Creative Renewal. At the end of our week, we gathered all the art the women had made. The large Japanese-inspired dining room turned into our gallery where we displayed the work. That night, we used lots of quick, easy ideas for showcasing the small works. We put contrasting colored paper under watercolor pieces; all on black tablecloths. Small light colored clay pieces were placed on contrasting dark ceramic tiles. The life-sized self-portraits, painted in the bamboo grove, were hung on one wall. Votive candles were dotted around as well as small blossoms. The result was magical. When the participants came into the room, the exhibit was a surprise. I could see the pride and excitement they felt as they asked for photos to be taken with Francine and me. They brought friends over and shared what they had made. Women who had not participated in the expressive arts week also showed interest and enthusiasm. It was a gratifying night for us. It was made special by the careful curating of the art.

Here are some items that help elevate the artwork. None of this is necessary and I'm sure you will have more ideas, but this will get you started:

Black Cloth: Table size is good and black velvet is best. It is a lustrous background for many things! Diamond jewelry is set upon black velvet for a reason. It is a wonderful frame. Placing an object or painting on the black velvet brings it to life, helping various aspects leap forward. The velvet alone says, "This is special."

Easels: Both tabletop and standing easels. These allow the piece to be placed vertically, rather than horizontally on the tabletop, and thus be seen from another perspective. An easel is an artist's tool, part of the studio equipment, so it brings the tradition of the studio to the moment.

Light: All galleries have lights! Shining a light on it, whether on the wall or the table, will elevate the object. Likewise, putting a votive candle in or near the work will bring another dimension to the viewing. The candle often brings a feeling of reverence, which is perfect for things like reliquaries, totems, or talismans.

Paper Frames: Find a color of paper that brings contrast or complement to the piece and place it so that there is a border of the paper showing around the piece. This works well with pieces too small or fragile to be on an easel. Or you may have too many pieces for each to have an easel if you are curating a group exhibit. We've done poetry pages, small clay pieces, small watercolors, pencil drawings, and abstracts this way. Stunning.

Tiles or Stones: Clay pieces look great when placed on tiles of contrasting colors or pieces of stone or pieces of rough wood or bark gathered from the environment.

Clothesline: Visual work on paper can be hung on a "clothesline." Whether free-standing or close to a wall, this is a simple and fresh way to display works. We have displayed our Random Valentines this way as well as the *100 Paintings in Ten Minutes* exhibit in the gallery on Ray Street and many other things using the clothesline.

Tablecloth: Writing also calls to be honored or shared, especially when there is a visual aspect, such as a handmade cover or handmade paper. Putting journals wherein poetry has been written grouped on a cloth or table arranged in a grid or organic shape sets them apart, and makes them look special. The particular page the poet wants to share can be secured in the open position and the rest of the journal securely kept private by using large clips or wire or string to wrap the other pages shut.

Large Leaves: Put small objects like papier-mâché dolls, tin foil animals, other small sculptural pieces, and even small books on great large leaves. This gives a fresh organic feel to the display.

Make small books or embellished pages to write poems on. Some poetic forms have the advantage of already being appealing visually. Displaying them as a quilt on the wall allows them to be appreciated in their visual aspect.

"Blackout" or "erasure" poems, where most of the text is obliterated from a found text to leave only the words that comprise the poem, look wonderful displayed on a background.

Hang fabric pieces on dowels as tapestries or flags.

Put sculptures in lucite boxes.

Use a grid. A grid is the curator's best friend, especially for group work. Anomalous things look organized, and the eye can see them better on a grid. This is especially true if the object shares some other aspect: rubber band dolls, plaster and tape figures, plaster of Paris animals, and embroidered leaves.

Having placed the objects in an honoring position, the artistic process is complete.

This Aesthetic Analysis/Curation as Validation is the end of the art-making section for the session. The application to the life-world comes after the artwork has spoken! The next step is to go back to the Counselor's Chairs and see what the harvest will bring.

Third Room: Counselor's Chairs—Final Conversation
Task: Harvest

Like all the other studios, we come back to the Counselor's Chairs, that metaphoric seat, and reflect upon the journey from the beginning of the filling-in, into the studio, the working through, the curation (if done), and now ask what strengths, resources, new perspectives, or other shifts have occurred. What happened in the art-making studio that might have relevance in the life-world? What changed, how did it change and what can be applied to the dire-straits situation? Remember, there is no one special thing. Every session and every person is different. People can discover themselves in many different aspects of the art-making. You are not looking for the right one, any one will do. Be patient and allow the client to do the work of building the metaphoric bridge from the art to her life. This requires great sensitivity, but no fancy method. How does the art echo the life? Keep looking at the art and trust the process.

Intermodal Drama/Theater Studio

All the world's a stage and all the men and women merely players. They have their exits and their entrances; and one man in his time plays many parts.
WILLIAM SHAKESPEARE, *AS YOU LIKE IT*, ACT II SCENE 7

The essence of theater is storytelling; a story enacted by actors—people who show us what happened—action. There is a dramatic arc to the story, which is called the play or the script. It has a beginning, a middle, and an end. The dramatic arc provides the basic structure or path the story takes. The main characters are introduced in a scene where they are developed and the basic premise of the play is introduced—what is going to happen, where, and by whom? Where is the treasure, who is the killer? These elements, the actor or character, the story, and its development in scenes, plus the body and the voice for theater, are the parts of drama that make a good transition to ExA. I also believe that technical theater—lighting, costume, and set design—also have an important place in our work.

Character: The most essential element for theater is the actor. Someone is doing something. The actor plays a role: Portia, Captain Janeway, Minnie Mouse. The role is the character.

Paolo said the expressive arts therapy does not have a personality theory *per se* because as an arts-based process we are more character-based. Personality is composed of thoughts, feelings, and behaviors that are consistent over time. But we change over time, especially if we are looking to do so. This is a more fluid and infinite matrix, placing each of us in our own spot. When we discussed this, I resonated with it, knowing how much I had already changed in my life; some changes I sought and fought for, others came to me, both positive and negative. Although some factors of our lives may be carried forward, this way of thinking about human beings is more open, hopeful, and positive than many psychological theories. No matter how enticing, personality theories inevitably come down to the 12 types or the four kinds or the eight categories. The number of possible combinations of our DNA alleles is in the trillions—more than all the humans who have ever lived; then, think about the environmental influences, the influence of culture, of the times (meaning the 1950s or the 1300s). In other words, every single human being is unique. Billions of human possibilities, each unique.

James Hillman writes about people as being characters, not as a self. Robert Landy developed role theory, to allow the notion that we are multitudes, as defined by the roles we play over time. He created a protocol for finding and developing the roles we each have. These are arts-based ways of approaching the issue. Roberto Assagioli developed his theory about each of us having many sub-personalities. We could consider Jung's archetypes to be in that vein—numerous images/myths that we enact (although we don't think the number is limited and we don't think the path is defined). The art discipline that most easily lends itself to this exploration is theater. Characters or roles allow for nearly infinite possibilities of change.

Plot or Storyline: There are a limited number of plots or storylines. The absolute number varies from about six to about 36, according to which expert you consult. They are recycled and reinvented endlessly. How many movies, novels, and even songs do you know with these themes: human against nature, human against human, rags to riches, riches to rags, true love found, betrayal, repentance, the voyage and return, the quest, rebirth, comedy, or tragedy? These basic themes also play out in our lives. We can use these as inspiration for scene work and story development.

Dionysus, God of Theater: Dionysus is the god of many things: wine, revelry, and theater. In the Western tradition of drama and theater, he is recognized as the progenitor. Tragedy was the main form of his theater, and comedy emerged as a response. The theatrical traditions of Greece included rituals, pageants, parades, and the use of masks and the chorus. These elements are easily used in our theater studio.

Dionysus brings wild, unpredictable energy to our work. This is another thing that distinguishes our way of working from more traditional arts therapies: we take some risks in the art-making. Not Apollonian step-by-careful-step, but Dionysian emotion, passion, and a certain amount of risk-taking. One reason that the setting of the frame and the agreements are so important—it is this boundary, the outer wall, that protects us from getting burned by the fire of creativity. We need both the Apollonian frame, agreements, and traditions as well as the Dionysian impulse, passion, and experiment. Frame and fire.

As in all the arts, look to theater for a source for inspiration. The possibilities are many:

Consider classical Japanese Noh theater, or Kabuki, and after World War II, Butoh. What aspects lend themselves to your situation? All cultures developed their distinct form of theatrical storytelling. This includes dance dramas in Bali, puppets, pageantry, mask work, clowning, mime, passion plays, and more. From China come shadow puppets and circuses with acrobatics. Could these inform something you are working on? Think about the American vaudeville or cabaret.

This rich and varied well of art traditions and forms can be called upon when working with people from around the world or in your own backyard. I assume that careful research and appreciation, in the safe and sacred space of art-making, precludes appropriation, which is more likely to occur when you forget to honor the art itself, or pretend to be someone you are not, or you ridicule another's heritage. I studied Butoh to learn it, yes, but also to understand the soil from which it grew. The traditions of the arts come from the great ancestral legacy of our species, so respectful blending and sharing is a time-honored practice. Especially in the ritual space of the arts.

Modern Drama Therapies

Psychodrama was developed in the 1930s by Jacob L. Moreno, a psychiatrist from Vienna. A man before his time, he was the first to use the term group therapy. Several of his ideas and techniques can work beautifully in an ExA setting. It is often a single person working with a personal issue. The group provides additional essential roles, like auxiliary egos and the double. To be certified in psychodrama takes 780 hours of training as well as supervision.

Playback Theater, developed by Jonathan Fox, works with an individual in a group setting, similar to psychodrama. The backbone of this approach is the playback troupe, a group of people who learn the various techniques and forms of playing back the story. They also develop spontaneity within given playback structures. It begins with the leader, called the Conductor, interviewing a person from the audience (called the Teller) who shares a story. The playback troupe then re-enacts, via a format chosen by the Conductor, a part of the story. These forms are not intermodal expressive arts but are compatible.

Uses in ExA: While both dance and drama are strongly based in the body, drama therapies focus on the social aspects of our lives.

Drama therapy and its variations are based on group work. Although some work on role or personae can be done by an individual, and the empty chair can be used with one person, the endeavor is best when done in a group setting. This is partly because the work is best with witnesses, and because many roles and actions require others to participate. Drama therapy is based on sociometry, our place in the human family. Family of origin, yes, but also for any group we find ourselves in: family of creation, work, or team. And these characters need not be living to have a role in our inner play.

A key direction in any theater work is to "accept the offer" of the other. Say "yes" to all suggestions made on the stage. Or put via negative—don't block the action, as this will prevent the scene or story from unfolding. Let yourself get in trouble—it's pretend.

Architecture of a Session for Drama
First Room: Counselor's Chairs–
First ConversationTask: Fill-In
An example: Have a pack of cards with characters on them and let people choose a card that they resonate with, speaking from the voice of the card character when they check in. You can make your own cards by finding characters in magazines or writing a list onto cards.

Task: Sensitize/Attune
The indispensable thing about theater is the action of someone. The voice, body, and imagination all need to be warmed up. The actor goes into action and does something, so the body needs to be warmed up. The voice, in case he says something, also needs warm-up, and without the imagination, we got nothin' since the theater is a place for "what if" and "let's pretend." But let's start with the body.

Body: Physical warm-ups, as in the dance studio, are also good for the actor: Range of motion work, working through a list of natural movements, various kinds of locomotion, and partner work all help the actor get ready for action. When I taught movement to actors at the San Diego Repertory Theater's Conservatory and at the Old Globe Theater, the objective was to help the actor get both strength and flexibility as a foundation for her instrument so it could adapt for the character.

Body Leads: From a neutral stance, walk and sit with emphasis on various postures: Let the chin lead, or the chest, or pelvis. This can easily lead to character development. Exaggerate until it is huge, like street theater or clowning, then reduce the size of the gesture/posture to something subtle. Between each "take" allow the actor to shake and stretch to come to a neutral posture.

Walk on imagined surfaces: hot sand, deep leaf loam, sticky molasses, ice, shallow water; make some up. Keep going until the entire body is used and clichés are discarded. Divide a large room into zones: Over here is the slippery ice, over there is the warm ankle-deep water. Or change the whole room at once after a few minutes.

Voice

A voice studio serves as a dedicated space for individuals to engage in therapeutic vocal practices. Traditional vocal warm-up exercises, such as humming, sirens, tongue twisters, and projection exercises, are integral to this process. These warm-ups are not only aimed at preparing the vocal apparatus but also serve as tools for self-expression, exploration, and healing.

Humming exercises, for instance, can create a soothing effect, allowing individuals to connect with their breath and find a centered state. In a group, people can mingle until they find a hummer whose hum is similar. Sirens, with their smooth transitions between vocal registers, encourage individuals to explore the full range of their voices, fostering a sense of liberation and self-discovery. Sirens, loud and soft, evoke a different feel. Tongue twisters help improve articulation and speech patterns, promoting self-expression and communication skills. Plus, they are usually accompanied by laughter because these are difficult to do and at the same time funny to observe. Projection exercises, focusing on vocal power and presence, allow individuals to channel their emotions and intentions into their voice, facilitating personal growth and empowerment. This is particularly important for soft-spoken people, and in my practice for all women. I go to the back of the room and hold a hand to my ear as if to say "Let me hear you."

Preverbal Language Cocktail Party: The scene is a fancy-schmancy cocktail party. It's best if everyone is already costumed, but even in ordinary clothing, this can work. Guests mingle and chit-chat, but no one is speaking any known language. Best if everyone has a role that they have either been assigned or given themselves, to give a point of view: I'm a lazy doctor, I'm the fantastic chef. This emphasizes spontaneity and accepting offers from others.

Poet from Another Planet: The scene is a convention, gathered to honor an esteemed poet from another planet. The hostess introduces the honored guest poet, reminding people of her accolades, many publications, and remarkable accomplishments. The Poet enters and begins to speak in sounds and utterances that cannot be understood. But the hostess translates! To allow for greater participation if the class or group is large, the hostess and translator can be different people. The hostess/translator and the poet continue, finding a rhythm where the poet can proclaim, and the translator host can reveal the words. Hilarity ensues. End when the poem is finished and the poet takes a bow.

Charismatic Props: These are objects that have some appeal to your imagination and your senses. Some such props that I have used include a bright yellow plastic bucket; a large metal mesh sieve; a length of green garden hose, clean and flexible; a length of red stretchy cloth; a blue hula hoop; a thick wooden dowel; a double-sized newspaper page; and a large odd-shaped piece of plastic that was part of some packing material. Go look in your garage! Pass these around a circle, one at a time, allowing each person to turn this object into something else, demonstrating its use without words. Then pass it along to the next person.

Costumes: A box of costume pieces is a great stimulator for the imagination. Build a collection over time. Have pieces that are out of the ordinary either by construction or color. Curate your collection. By limiting the palette you have something that looks coherent when people work together. My costume boxes include a box of all black and a box of all white, plus rainbow pieces, and neutrals.

Hats: Hats are easy since you don't have to be too careful about sizing, but good ones, unique ones can be expensive. Collect them over time. Hats and glasses can make an entire character. Scarves are even easier and generally not as pricey. Gloves also are a good transformer.

Interactions, Scene Work, Ensemble Building
What Are You Doing?

One actor goes on stage and begins pantomiming a recognizable action, like milking a cow. Another actor enters and asks, "What are you doing?"

The first names an action that he is *not* doing, like washing dishes. The second actor begins doing the thing that was said (washing dishes, not milking a cow). The first actor exits. Now the third actor comes on and asks, "What are you doing?" The second actor responds with an action that he is clearly not doing. And so on.

Animals

I have a large box full of animal portraits taken from the covers of the San Diego Zoo News. They are a wonderful resource. Have the actor choose an animal portrait and slowly develop the movement pattern of this animal: first use only the eyes, mouth, head, and neck; then add the shoulders, arms, and the upper torso; then the pelvis; then the legs and feet. From axial movement, add locomotion. Think of how the body you have would move if the spirit of the animal inhabited it.

What I Could Not Tell You

Write a letter to a person, living or dead, telling them what you need to say. Then in a designated area, read the letter aloud, from page to stage.

Magic Telephone
Similar to above, the phone rings and someone in the circle answers it. It is a call from anyone, living or dead, someone the actor knows personally or not. The caller has a message for the actor.

Scene Work–As It Was; As I Want It to Be
Ask someone to describe a scene from their life that is vexing or troublesome. Let them choose actors to play the required parts, including someone to play themselves. The person should give dialogue to the actors or phrases that are important to the scene. They should suggest blocking—where the actors stand or sit, as well as when and where they should move. After the actors perform the scene, the person can ask for adjustments. When this is done, allow for responses and feedback. Then the "as I want it to be" version can be portrayed, after which discussion and analysis can be done. The person whose scene this is may or may not take a role. Be sure to de-role the participants. Ask everyone in the room how the scene related to them.

Sculptures
Have a group member shape the bodies of other group members to depict relationships of interest to them. This is often the family, or some part of it, but needn't be; it can be some other important relationship. After the person sculpts the group members, she can step back and see if that is accurate. Adjustments can be made. All the players can be debriefed with their responses to the role they were called upon to play. Be sure to include any witnesses in this discussion as well.

Entrances and Exits
Using music as the score and context, setting the mood. Walk into a scene as the music cues you to do so: as the angry parent, the lonely friend, the suspicious detective, the creepy drug dealer, or the sexy secretary.

Card Sort: Role Hunger/Role Nausea
Using the list of roles from Robert Landy or one you created yourself, make small cards with a role on each one. Have people divide the cards into two piles: "Roles I am hungry to have" and "Roles I am sick of having." I have people pick their top two or three in each category and take them to the stage, to show us these characters.

Book of Characters
Put collections of photos or paintings of people doing various things. The characters can be old and young, dancing, plowing, singing, cooking,

doctoring, teaching, painting, reading, and sleeping; anything. A person either chooses a card or draws one blindly and then develops this character and delivers a monologue.

Mask Work

Can be done in collaboration with a mask-making session. Masks are historically a performance/ritual object, so they should be performed. A word in general: The mask is considered its own character. If the mask has an open mouth, then tradition says it can speak. I have concealed eye holes in several of my plaster masks because I want the character to be sleeping, but I need to see a bit for safety's sake, so I poke small holes so I can see out just a little.

Plaster bandage masks are laid on the face when wet. They are time-consuming. It takes several hours to dry and then it needs to be embellished. But it is a form based on a person's actual face. Paper masks can be created with recycled paintings or bits and bobs. A paper plate can also be the matrix for masks. Preformed masks of several types (cardboard, plastic) are also available.

Second Room: The Studio
Task: Decenter

Any of the above exercises could be an entire group. Allow group members to take turns in the different roles. Be sure to de-role the witnesses each time and ask for their responses. The resources I have listed also offer many ways in.

Optional Task: Curation as Validation

Curation in drama involves taking it to the stage, having witnesses, and using as much superimposition stagecraft as is necessary to realize the vision. This might include lights, costumes, a score or script. It could include song, music, text. It might consist of ensemble work, dialogue, soliloquy, chorus.

Third Room: Counselor's Chairs—Final Conversation
Task: Harvest

After an evening of theater making, when we come back together, we talk about what happened and how it affected us, talking about shifts in body, mind, emotions, and relationships to past and present people and events. What morsel can we take? Then we leave the shining room and go back to our caves.

Final Curtain Regarding Theater Studio

Our lives are like theater. We play many roles throughout our lifetime, and on any given day. The action in our lives is rising or falling. Supporting characters move in and out, some over decades, some for one season only. The student develops into a friend, the neighbor develops into a problem. We suffer losses, we achieve successes. Characters enter and exit. First, we know what we're doing, then, we haven't a clue. The scene changes—I'm in southern California now, I was in the Swiss Alps before, soon I'll be at the edge of the Atlantic Ocean in Maine. I sit at the deathbed of my mother, the dutiful daughter. A newborn is put into my lap, I'm a grandmother. My role as a mother was paramount then, and my role as a writer is taking shape now. I dance in the moonlight, I witness the sunrise; I hide from the noon sun, and sing in the rain.

Intermodal Language Arts Studio

> *Poetry is the lens we use to interrogate the history we stand on and the future we stand for. It's no coincidence that at the base of the Statue of Liberty there is a poem.*

AMANDA GORMAN

Interview with Elizabeth Gordon McKim

Elizabeth Gordon McKim is the Poet Laureate of the European Graduate School. For over 20 years, she has held lunch-hour poetry seminars she called Poetry Salon-Saloon, under the view of the disappearing Allalin Glacier. There, at the Red Table in the courtyard of the family inn, she listens to the poetry of her students and gives ways to enter into the theme of the day with sound and movement, story and song. There in the garden, crowded with students eager to be with her, she speaks on the importance of the poetic voice in our work and our lives. Elizabeth asks us to make long vowel sounds and play with preverbal language. In the oral tradition, the voice is the place the poem is born. So we babble and coo, sing it out, chant it out, rap it out, and put words forth from our hearts and minds.

An annual event at the EGS was a performance with Eliz and Paolo. They enjoyed a long relationship of performance and friendship that has taken them all over the world. They performed together every year at the EGS, until his death in 2021.

McKim's latest publication, *elizab—Eth—eridge* is the poetic memoir of her ten years with celebrated and respected Black American poet Etheridge Knight. He first started writing poems in prison. It is a memoir, a compendium of photos, letters, drawings, and prose. This, her seventh book of poetry, is preceded by: *Lovers in the Freefall, Body India, Boat of the Dream, Burning Through, Family Salt,* and *The Red Thread.*

With her long-time friend Judith Steinbergh, McKim also published *Beyond Words: Writing Poetry with Children,* which was, in part, based on her many years as a poet in the public schools of Massachusetts. Lesley University sent her and other artist-teachers all over the United States as part of the Creative Arts in Education program, teaching teachers how to add poetry to their curriculum.

In 2022, she was awarded the First Inaugural New England Poetry Club's Sam Cornish Poetry Award along with Askia Toure, one of the founders of the Black Arts Movement. McKim is a community builder, a local and international poet of the oral tradition. We watch her grow into her old age as she begins again… again.

STORY: I Meet My Womentor

I met Elizabeth McKim the first year I was a teacher at The European Graduate School. We were rooming in the same house, Everest, in the faculty apartment, where we met for meetings, dinners, drinks, and convivial gatherings. One afternoon, she and I took a walk. While we were walking under the larch trees, we started to head upward toward the glacier and the poet began to recite her poem "House, Earth, Water, Sky." When she came to the line "the green goes over and over" I got that catch in my throat; my face got sad. I began to weep. We kept walking. She kept reciting, I kept weeping. We moved along, in a measured way. Her poem brought to me the image of the grass growing over my brother's grave and the graves of all those I had buried. And then all the world's dead, and some premonition of my own death. Her voice was strong and gentle; my tears flowed like the glacier milk that ran down the face of the mountain. We walked until the poem was done, and the tears, too. Then we walked in silence. I hardly knew her, but I already loved her. That was the beginning of our friendship based on truth, loss, love, and poetry. Now, I meet with her at her place in Maine, on the edge of the Atlantic, for our annual writer's retreat. Here we both work on whatever writing project we may have cooking. I commemorate this retreat in an essay titled "Poet's Know Things" (Essex with McKim, 2022). She has been a guest teacher at the Institute for the poetry intensive for years. When Eliz is around, everything is poetry. She is the voice of the living poet, and I am delighted to call her my womentor.

Below is part of an interview I did with her regarding the oral tradition, the place from which she creates her poetry.

Oral Tradition: Song, Story, Poem

JGE: Eliz, tell us about the oral tradition. What is it? What do you mean when you say oral tradition?

EMK: I mean the things you heard out loud, before things were written down: songs, stories, poems, prayers, lullabies, riddles, and babbling nursery rhymes. All those communications that occurred before you could read or that didn't need to be written. Out loud. Also connected to the image and visual-verbal understanding, as Bob Holman said, the oral tradition you find in films. The oral tradition is very wide. I first learned about the oral tradition from Jerome Rothenberg, who wrote "Shaking the Pumpkin" and "American Prophecy." I am interested in poetries from around the world. These are the things that really inform and enlighten me. As well as beginning with the child, the infant—very local and familiar and evolving but is also connected to the history of the development of human culture. Every culture has its oral traditions of legends, myths, and jokes. Love songs and odes, praise poems, curses, and harangues. They all harken back to the voice. As I was growing up, jump rope songs and counting songs, and the stories of my family were very deep. The African and African-American early stories of animals are stories told by ancestors to the mothers and fathers. Each one of us has this oral tradition from our families. The things that were told to the children from these early teachings, from your mentors, these become part of our own oral tradition.

JGE: I see. I remember sitting on my mother's lap while she read to me. Those nursery rhymes and fairy tales were the beginning of my love of literature and words. Eliz, what are the building blocks of language? The foundations from a poet's point of view?

EMK: I think the building blocks are nouns and verbs. Persons, places, and things—as entities. Verbs link up the nouns. We experience these in the body, the motion and commotion; the ongoing and circling, and the verb to be: presence. I am, you are, you will be. It has to do with presence. You can't have a language without nouns and verbs. Going back to the early childhood learning of language, we start with "mama, dada, uppie, bye-bye." Words that add a consonant to a vowel sound. Sylvia Ashton-Warner was a teacher/poet/writer who wrote *Teacher*—part diary and part description of her inspired teaching methods with Maori children in New Zealand. Most of her young students had trouble reading and writing. Their texts were from England and not connected to their lives. No connection. So she had the children bring her words that were understandable to them, such as hole, fire, mother, blood, meat. She called this "organic language." Paolo Friere [Brazilian educator and author of *Pedagogy of the Oppressed*] said to teach the *companjeros*, it has to be coming out of what they know. That's how reading and writing can grow. Etheridge Knight was a jailhouse scribe, writing letters for those inmates who could not write. There was an intimacy and an urgent need in these letters that developed his sensitivity to language.

JGE: You play with consonants and vowels—leading to various kinds of soundings, rhythms, and rhymes.

EMK: Here, in New England Anglo culture there is often a repressive shaming about sounds; "babyish." Except if you are playing music, or playing around with snippets of song.

I love babbling sounds and movement. It is another way for me to enter dreamtime improvisation in the jazz zone. Somewhere early in my life, I discovered the enjoyment of sounding, dancing, and moving in rhythm.

My deep connection to the work of movement therapist Norma Canner and musician teacher Paolo Knill has sustained me as an artist and a teacher over the years. I am now 85. I continue to be grateful that I was at the right place at the right time to meet them and to join creative forces in the ways we did.

As I started in the pioneering program at Lesley under the direction of Shaun McNiff, I was also enrolled in the MA program, Sound, Movement and Language, at Goddard College. Norma Canner was my field faculty. It was life-changing. I followed her around for two years and took the courses she offered. At Perkins School for the Blind, I worked with other students with drawings; the movement, sounds, and poetry under Norma's direction.

JGE: Tell us what you mean by preverbal language.

EMK: I do not use the word gibberish, meaning nonsense. No. We babble and make sounds—like babies. The babbling a child does has meaning. Think of this as recovering lost language. I call this preverbal language. It's all part of this oral tradition.

I have realized that the language of sounds can also be very healing to people. In the early days when I was starting out, I had experiences with those who did not have language, who only had sounds, or who spoke a different language. To be able to have sound was a deep mode of communication. I can remember in the very beginning working with a beautiful woman from Vietnam who was ashamed of her non-verbal condition. We played like children with sound. I've found in many different areas sound is a profound way to communicate.

Paolo helped me understand that I had music in me, performing together as we did for so long, him making music and me poetizing. Now I work weekly with musicians at the Walnut Cafe. They say "We want you to be here with us." It is important to hear poems out loud—like blues ballads. You can sing your poem. The chorus can give your work a dimension. I didn't realize it could be so powerful. Don't keep it inside, let the voice come out. How liberating it is to bring the voice out, trying to find the form and shape.

JGE: You share a chant whenever you teach. What's that about?

EMK: Repetition is important. Keep repeating. Do it and it changes. Movement does this and it is the same way with sound. It is a body experience. I was so lucky to get back to the body. Repetition is an important aspect of the oral tradition. The Greeks used to call them formulas. Chants and spells and prayers are to be repeated. Do it over and over. Part of a sacred tradition. How could a chant start? The chants rise up and come back to the silence. Chants are based on the in and the out of the breath, heartbeat, and pulse. The chant that I created, the Poetry Bus, uses the rhythms of breath, pulse, and heartbeat. Exhale and inhale. Because it has gestures, it is a way to get the body involved when writing poetry.

Ta da, Ta da, Ta da da, Ta da
This is the way the poem begins
It's you and me, and you, you and me
And us and us as we ride that poetry bus.

We push, we pull
We push, push and pull
We push, we pull
And we gather that wool.
We dig, we dig
We dig in the dirt now
And it won't hurt now
We reach, we reach
We reach for the sky now
Don't ask me why now.

'Cause it's you and me
You, you and me

And us and us
And we ride that poetry bus.

This little chant suggests that we are in it together, on the poetry bus. Gathering the wool suggests finding your material, the words that you want or that want you. Pushing and pulling refers to the struggle of editing, leaving things out and adding things in. Digging in the dirt reminds us to go into the dark places as a source while reaching for the sky reminds us to find the light also.

JGE: Thank you, Elizabeth. We are so lucky to have your voice, your wisdom, and your humor. Merely being with you improves my writing!

Expressive Writing

The building blocks of poetry are words. Seems obvious—no words, no poetry.

Words are composed of sounds, an even smaller piece of poetry. Finding sounds and words to play with is a way to warm up to poetry and writing. Listening to poetry awakens the poetic mind and voice of the poet within.

We need words that are concrete and specific. Use the specific words for the time of day (dawn, dusk, twilight, high noon) and the lights in the sky. San Diego is known for its sunny climate, but I think of the sun as piercing or blistering. Cool, distant starlight is favored by the Elves in Lord of the Rings and they speak of it with reverence and respect. The undulating green curtain of the aurora borealis mesmerizes the Arctic. The night sky is filled with moonbeams, candlelight, and flashlights. The city brings us stoplights, neon, and the flashing and blinking of police cars, fire trucks, and ambulances. The quality of light could be bright, dim, golden, glowing, piercing, pale, or twinkling. The garden path has wayfinding lights. The disco had its sparkling mirrored ball. Go inside and find firelight, and lamplight, candlelight, and a nightlight. Doesn't this make a difference in the light you see in your imagination?

Carefully notice the special qualities of the weather. It can be wet, yes, but also foggy, drizzling, sprinkling, pounding, or a gentle shower. For wind, we could have a breeze, a gale, a gust. Many locales have special names for winds. In San Diego, we have a breeze coming from sea to shore, which we call the onshore wind. Our weather report includes the surf conditions, "choppy swell from the south." In the fall we get the Santa Ana winds, hot dry winds from the desert to the coast. These winds bring with them fires and migraines, baking and blistering. When I lived in Germany we dreaded the dry, warm Föehn for much the same reasons. In Hawaii, I loved the prevailing trade winds, so moist, soft, and caressing. The Mediterranean has its famous sirocco, and France its mistral. Specific naming brings place, texture, and aliveness to our writing, poetry included. Sounds more captivating than just "wind," right?

Places have specific names with historic significance. Using them adds dimension. Naming the mountains and rivers, the kinds of soil, the trees and minerals, and specific features adds to the sense of place in our poetry. Not just "desert," but the Mojave or the Anza-Borrego. Not just a mountain but San Jacinto or Mt. Miguel. Usually the more specific you get with names and words, the better. Not always, but usually.

Poetry and its play with and respect for words can lead to metaphors. Yes, our work is metaphoric—so even though we do use language for literal everyday conversations, poetry and expressive writing can bridge us over into the imagination and its world of images and metaphors.

There are a few pitfalls to avoid:

Cliché: The first pitfall is cliché, a phrase that is overused and unoriginal: "Hot as hell, gentle as a lamb, innocent as a child." You get the picture. Although once they may have been fresh, time and overuse have made them stale. They have lost their savor. If you are facilitating a group using poetry, help your students avoid cliché. I simply say something like the above and then let it go. If people do use cliché, I do not make a big deal of it or chide them. We learn to move into the poetic dimension by hearing poetry, reading poetry, and making poems. It takes time.

Forced Rhyme: Although rap has made good use of this, most poems that speak to us now avoid forced end-rhymes. Poems from a time past can use this convention and it works because it is embedded in the style of that era. Of course, it depends on the poem.

Abstraction versus Specificity: Reading great poets brings us down to earth and to a specific place. "This grasshopper, I mean," says Mary Oliver. Concepts like love, peace, and freedom must be described by their conditions, not just dropped into the middle of a poem. That is deadly.

Beginning poets need inspiration. I have several tried and true poetic forms for beginners that have little or nothing to do with soul-revealing, cloying stuff and these can lead to great results:

- **Blackout Poetry/Erasure Poetry:** Find a text-rich page from a magazine, newspaper, or old book. As you read it, circle or otherwise mark the words that stand out to you, the ones that grab your eyes. Read these until you find a poetic message, then black out the rest of the words on the page. (Google Blackout poetry for many examples.)

- **Found Poetry:** Start with a compilation of words and phrases from various sources, including headlines in magazines or newspapers, fortunes, bits of paper found on the ground, or labels that you then organize and order into a poem.

- **Object Poems:** Write on objects like paper plates, mask shapes, boxes, or even chairs. Let the object inform your poem.

- **Group Poetry:** Have each person write a line or lines on a given topic. Restrict in any way that serves the project. Then have the group arrange the lines into something they like.

- **Word Bowls and Word Hordes:** A collection of words related to the class or activity you are doing. Go on a nature walk and collect nouns and verbs that speak to you on the walk. Those are then written down and put into the word bowl. This is a resource that people can pull from and use in making a poem, either adding or subtracting words as they want.

- **Poems of Address:** Write to persons or things that you have something to say to. I've written poems to my dead relatives and friends. My poems of address seem to feature people that I can no longer speak to for whatever reason, but it could be a stranger, it could be a place.

- **Listening In:** As you go about your day, say over lunch, listen into conversations that you overhear. Use those phrases or words as your source materials. This can range from hilarious to touching.

- **Poems as the Voice of Paintings:** In a museum or gallery, have students write dialogue for the figures in the paintings. This is obvious for figurative paintings, but works also with abstracts.

- **Personae Poems:** Write a poem in the voice of someone or something. Let your imagination be your guide and look around: it could be the broom waiting in the corner, the high heel you wore last night. Elizabeth brings a collection of stones and has students write from the voice of the stone. I like to draw my stone first to get to look at it deeply and get to know it: "I am the smooth green stone, waiting since paleozoic time for someone to touch me. Once I was water."

- **Haiku:** Elizabeth calls the haiku the "little muscle of poetry" because it is so concentrated. It consists of three lines with 17 syllables total in this arrangement: 5, 7, 5. She conducts Haiku Hunts and Haiku Hollars. We frequently go to the Japanese Friendship Garden in San Diego for the Haiki Hunt and then share them in the Hollar while under the screened veranda.

Poetry and Storytelling

Spoken word and performance poetry benefit from a microphone. This is not an inexpensive tool, and its use takes a bit of instruction. However, it ensures that all performers can be easily heard at the back of the room, especially if the room is large and filled. Taking recordings or photos speaks to documentation but also to the importance of an artifact of an event, something for the portfolio, which overcomes the decay of time.

Stage a reading. Giving the reading is part of the oral tradition. The size of the audience is not what makes it special, it is the aesthetic response that does it.

Create a chapbook. Usually a small handmade book of a few poems on a certain topic. May be printed or handwritten from a single author or a group.

The Journal in Expressive Arts
My First Journal

When I was 12, I received a red fake leather diary with a small gold lock and key for Christmas. This began a relationship that continues to this day. Right now in fact. The word *journal* comes from the French word for day, *jour*, like soup du jour. It brings to mind a diary, what happened that day. Journaling is not merely the record of the day's activities. For an exhaustive example of a journal like that see Samuel Pepys' diary, a famous and exhaustive recording of his entire day's activities that went on for years. Anis Nin's journals inspired women for generations.

Numerous studies show journaling helps ameliorate both depression and anxiety. Journal therapy has research and professional publications dedicated to its proliferation and understanding.

My journal has been my companion for decades. It is a portable, accessible way to gain self-understanding. Reflecting on what has happened, yes, but also to record dreams, hopes, and aspirations for where you want to go. It is useful in areas such as self-development, health, relationships, scholastic endeavors, employment concerns, and homemaking. Even your garden and kitchen endeavors will benefit from a journal entry.

I know no other method that is as self-contained and more useful than a journal. My journals have evolved over my lifetime. Looking back through them at winter solstice/New Year's and on my birthday (roughly six months later) is a way to keep track of myself, see themes, enjoy small moments, and have a sense of the direction of my inner self. It's a treat. I have journaled about my challenging health issues and my medical treatments, and certainly about my relationships: friends, lovers, and family. My travels and poetic noticings are in the journal. I draw, paint, collage, and collect ephemera. Some pages have hours devoted to them, some are rough or unfinished.

The Illuminated Journal is a class that helps people who think they cannot write or who enjoy the company of others on the journal journey. I have now amassed a huge number of prompts both for writing and for visual journaling. I will give you a sample of these and encourage you to create your own.

Simple prompts: The seasons, the weather, the phases of the moon—I always pay attention to what's happening in the sky and where we are on the wheel of the year. Look for signs that the season is changing. Observe the Solstices and Equinoxes. Celebrate the return of light or turning leaves.

We look outside and then inside: I is anything returning for us? What is blooming for us? What wants to wake up, what needs to go into hibernation? Have people sketch or make abstract marks on this theme: What are the colors of spring where you are? What is budding? What are the sounds, smells, and quality of light where you are on the equinox? In the Illuminated Journal, I ask people to paint, draw, sew, collage, print, paste, and tape, and otherwise make the pages colorful and memorable. Our experiences are remembered by the ear, the eye, and the body. I want the journal to capture that. Nature will give you endless inspiration for your journal.

Character Study

You can write about your mother, your significant other, your children, your teacher, your neighbor—we all find ourselves in dozens of relationships! A couple of exercises are particularly good for exploring these; one is a character study. Place your chosen person, your character, in a setting where we might find them, especially a place that they have created. What are they doing that is characteristic? What are they wearing that reveals something about them? Be specific and use the rich language of the senses.

Dialogue: Choose a person, living or dead, with whom you would like to have a conversation. Begin with a question, then listen for a response. Let the conversation flow with at least two responses from each party, though more often yields better results. You can have a dialogue with anything. Your painting, a plant, or a stone. Alternatively, you could simply allow the object to "speak," without engaging in a dialogue; just listen to it. A soliloquy. Draw the object you are conversing with, creating a memorable journal page.

Having conversations with your body is an important way to take care of yourself. When parts or systems of my body are challenged I both draw it and dialogue with it.

Architecture of a Session for Language Arts
First Room: Counselor's Chairs—First Conversation
Task: Fill-In
Examples:

Share three nouns and three verbs about how you come in.

Share one word for your body, one for your mind, one for your spirit, one for your environment.

Make a word bowl together, then pull words for a short poetic statement.

Make a simple drawing of your situation and write around and on it.

Tell the story of how you got here, in two minutes.

Second Room: Studio—Artistic Conversations
Task: Sensitize/Attune
Examples:

Use the "Poetry Bus" chant.

Listen to a poem. Take the words you like from it and rewrite in a new poetic form.

Do a word hunt in the room: write the nouns and verbs.

Listen to the environment and write about what you hear, see, and sense.

Task: Decenter

When you stimulate the poetic mind, everything can be fodder for the poetic voice.

Send people on a Haiku Hike.

Take your students to a marketplace or special garden to look and listen for inspiration.

Give a theme.

Use magnetic poetry boxes.

Share a small image or a letter. People make one line from the impulse.

Remember that writing takes time, so set the time.

Task: Aesthetic Analysis Using SuPER:

Surface: Listening to the poem in the mouth of the poet is the best way to attend to the surface of the poem. In poetry studio editing is the job of the poet or group.

Process: Allowing the people to tell each other in small groups what they did to find the poem. What was difficult. How did they overcome the difficulty?

Experience: Allowing people to share how it felt, what thoughts, feelings, sensations, memories, or dreams came forward for them as they wrote or recited their poems.

Reflection/Round-up: A title. The ending or summation. What needs to be done so we can be done?

Optional Task: Curation as ValidationExample:

Have a reading. Let people stand up before one another and share out loud what they have written. Invite friends.

Find ways to make the poetry visible. Hang papers on the wall, or place them on a table.

If people have written in a journal, you can clip or rubber band the pages open to the poem.

Make a group chapbook.

Third Room: Counselor's Chairs—Final Conversation
Task: Harvesting
With poetry ask: "How did things change for you? Did the poems address your situation? What inspiration did you receive?" I can sometimes be more filled and healed by someone else's poem, so be sure to include that as part of the Harvest. What touched you most might not be your own work.

Intermodal Nature Studio

Those who contemplate the beauty of the earth find reserves of strength that will endure as long as life lasts. There is something infinitely healing in the repeated refrains of nature—the assurance that dawn comes after night, and spring after winter.

RACHAEL CARSON, AUTHOR OF *SILENT SPRING*

STORY: The Ants Go Marching One by One

I must have been about seven. Is that the age when girls play jacks? I was practicing by myself on my front porch. From onesies to tensies, around the world, and pigs in the pen. I could do them all, and it was fun to play and perfect my technique. Then, something caught my eye. I saw a long line of ants, marching along the edge between the walkway and the lawn. One of them seemed to be carrying something, maybe a leaf, high above his head. I got real close to see. It looked like a wing. It was a wing. What? Another guy seemed to be carrying a big piece of an insect leg, much bigger than himself! Grasshopper leg. Eew. I followed the line backward and sure enough. They were dismembering a big grasshopper, piece by piece. It was kinda gruesome, but, at the same time, fascinating. I watched until they hauled all of Mr. Grasshopper's pieces away. Looking at things closely was a habit I cultivated. Following my curiosity and observing without interfering. This inclination would serve me well as I moved into adulthood and ExA. It laid a foundation for observing Mother Nature and her cycles, rhythms, and justice; her forms and patterns.

There is now a resurgence of interest in reestablishing our relationship to the natural world. People are longing for a sense of place.

Land Art

Evidence of land-based art from ancient people includes such figures as the Uffington White Horse from the Iron Age, carved into the chalk hillside in England. The Blythe Intaglios, near Blythe, California, were dated to 1000 BC. The largest human figure there is 171 feet long. In Peru, we see Nazca Lines from the Nazca people over 2,000 years ago. Mysteries. These are some examples of geoglyphs, ancient ground drawing, low relief mounds, or other geometric or effigy work that was formed by humans out of earth or stone. We don't know their significance to the people who made them, but they touch us with their beauty today.

Land art, a phrase coined by American artist Robert Smithson, was an influential trend starting in the 1960s, especially in the United States and England. It includes such landmark projects as Robert Smithson's *Spiral Jetty*, 1970, Maya Lin's *Storm King Wavefield*, 2009, and Walter De Maria's *The Lightning Field* (1977). These are worth googling if you don't know them. It will give you a sense of scale. Andy Goldsworthy has so many eye-popping works, it's hard to pick just one. He creates works made of leaves and ice, wood, and powder. Using nothing artificial. Watching his documentary, *Rivers and Tides*, is an evening well spent. Similarly, be inspired by the works of the light and space artist James Terrell such as the vast Roden Crater in the Arizona Painted Desert, or the much smaller, even intimate, Skyspace in Pomona, California, where the sky is framed to highlight the changing color of the sky and passing clouds.

Our eco-poiesis course takes place outdoors usually in the springtime when the bloom of wildflowers is prominent. Locations vary. Torrey Pines State Beach features tall multicolored cliffs and wide sandy beaches with lots of stones for stacking. Dolphin pods swim by. At Mission Trails Regional Park we wade in the San Diego River, explore the grinding holes from the ancestors of the indigenous Kumeyaay people, climb the old oaks, and watch the birds and the wildflowers. Students come with a packed lunch, their journal, and their art kit. This gives us a chance to rebuild our relationship with our home locale by playing and working in her spaces. Reigniting our sense of place.

Danica Arimany, a student from Guatemala, said in her reflection paper after eco-poiesis:

In his lecture, "What Kind of Society Nurtures the Soul," James Hillman speaks about the aesthetic oppression we endure while living out our sensorial lives within the confines of our modern architecture. Maybe, he implies, the existential rage we feel is not about what our father said or did twelve years ago... maybe it is connected to your experience zooming across a crowded city in a metal box, and parking in a concrete lot devoid of greenery, and walking into a building without windows where we sit and stare at a screen all day. Maybe we aren't designed to live our daily lives like this. Maybe rage or depression is a normative response to an abnormal circumstance. Maybe, if we paid attention, we would advocate for more aesthetic and peaceful environments and lifestyles. Maybe we would choose against destroying the green spaces around us, and against enduring lives that end in nervous breakdowns and dissatisfaction. Maybe.

Architecture of a Session for Nature Studio
First Room: Counselor's Chairs—First Conversation
Task: Fill-In
For the filling-in, have people look into the landscape and find something that corresponds to their current reality. Or remember a time when they were outdoors in a contemplative way. Remember, you don't have to know what they are thinking or feeling, as long as they have a chance to check in with themselves. Typically, just holding class outside brings a shift in awareness.

Second Room: The Studio—Artistic Conversations
Task: Sensitize/Attune
Sensitizing involves slowing down the breath, being on the actual ground, taking off shoes, looking slowly, listening to the ambient sound. Observe with all the senses.

Task: Decenter
Send people off on their own or in dyads to investigate various assignments:

Create a solar print,—using sunshine to "photograph" an arrangement. Use solar sensitive cyanotype paper to arrange elements on (like leaves and stones).

Make blind contour drawings of leaves or elements in the landscape.

Create a pre-cut frame that can be thrown down upon the ground and brings random composition into focus, which can then be drawn or photographed.

Write and sketch outdoors. Lie on the earth and breathe. Watch clouds.

Develop an eco-dance using the sounds, motion, and elements of the environment to create sound and movement pieces.

At some point, the class gathers to make something as a group, using the resources of the environment. Classes have created huge sand sculptures, such as a crowning goddess, a dancing woman, and a dragon.

Optional Task: Curation as Validation

In the open air studio, we might have the curation, the celebration of the images and experiences before any Aesthetic Analysis. We can visit individual creations.

Photos and video are good media to capture some of the experiences. Be sure it comes at a point in the process that does not interrupt the flow.

Then, there is a time for reflection; poems from individuals or the group.

Third Room: Counselor's Chairs—Final Conversation
Task: Harvest

Harvesting is a summary of the activities of the day and the personal reflection. As above, this can be shared in the group, or in smaller divisions of the group, or written in a journal.

If holding sessions outdoors is not possible, bring natural materials into the studio to augment any of the other studios: Try dancing with a long and bendy branch or reed. Make a headpiece of flowers or grasses. Use stones as a rhythm instrument, or a piece of grass or reed as a whistle. For drama, make a mask from natural materials such as leaves and grasses. These can be woven as they come or attached to a mask form, either half mask or full face. For visual art, palm frond masks are a favorite to paint, since these smooth and shiny leaves are shed regularly by the palms and have great shapes. Rock painting is a meditative project using paints especially designed for that purpose. Paint dot designs or write words. Use vegetable matter as dye such as onion skins. Try hammer and flower printing. Or printing with potatoes, broccoli, or whatever you have.

A SUMMATION OF A KIND

Expressive arts therapy is part of an aesthetic revolution, turning away from an emphasis on "getting and spending." It turns us away from pounding the human soul into a tiny square. It asks us to embrace the inner and outer world, and create a more soulful life. It is "both/and." Cultural creatives make time for what else matters: family, friendships, cultivation of interests other than work. We have the phenomenon of quiet quitting, where employees are exerting only the effort required to fulfill their job description, no overtime, and no taking on additional tasks. The definition of success has changed with young people. Gen Z is willing to leave jobs that don't align with their personal values. The thought wouldn't have even crossed my mind until I was much older. People are valuing relationships and experiences over things. More people are growing some of their own food. Perhaps the proliferation of expressive arts offerings is part of this movement. When I opened the Expressive Arts Institute in San Diego in 1998', it was the only one in the United States with that name. There were two other institutes connected to the EGS, but they were not called expressive arts institutes. Now about 50 places, from universities to private studios, call themselves expressive arts and offer courses. The Network of International Expressive Arts Training Institutes has 26 members as of this writing. All are connected to the EGS and each from that model.

ExA activates imagination with the senses as we interact with the world. With the images and objects we create we also create ourselves. We create community. We create a kind of life worth living.

Paolo J. Knill is the strongest voice for elucidating ExA theory, moving from the bird's eye view to the worm's eye view: He could see the overall and also the details. He created structures and theories that help articulate and illuminate the practices of ExA. Into the mix of glorious stories of recovery, amazement that working with art materials actually helped people, and knowing we couldn't squeeze the art into a small box left over by Freud, Paolo reminded us that art-making is our birthright—"a human existential" he often said. Art exists because we exist. It is our companion and can be our guide. Paolo showed us principles that guide the use of this humble healer, art, images, and aesthetics, to be used by all of us, for the sake of all of us.

I don't know if he would agree with all I have written herein. Perhaps we would have had heated discussions, and disagreed about some things. It would be done in the spirit of conviviality. I rarely won those discussions, but I never lost his friendship.

STORY: The Lucky Dinner

After the final goodbyes have been said to the mountains, to the cows, and that last student is on the bus down the mountain, the faculty breathes a collective sigh; of relief, yes, but also of longing. It is over; will it begin again? We each put ourselves out for the students. The courses are taught from 9:00 am to 10:00 pm with a long lunch break, and a short dinner break. The walk to campus is a 10-degree grade; three times a day, up and down, and up and down, and up again and down again. Since the students (and the teachers) come from around the globe, their English is at different levels of fluency, leading to both difficult and tender translations. People get sick, emergency medicine is needed. We are on a first name basis with the pharmacist who can translate our prescriptions into the European equivalent. Weary and wrung out we meet for dinner. The ones I recall best were hosted by Steve and Ellen Levine in their summer chalet. In the tradition of the region, its name, "Lucky," was painted on its side. Ellen would assign us to bring salad, side, dessert, or wine. And here we came, trudging up the hill again, laden with the food for the feast. We settled in. Ellen would bring some lovely steaming dish to the table that we all embellished with our offerings. We drank the wine of the region, Haida or Dole, and ice wine, from vines that froze, with dessert. We told the stories of the worst and the best. We congratulated each other on triumphs; what are people working on, the clown show, the classes, the student performances, the book. We consoled each other for the tragedies, who had a tough class or a medical situation. We laughed, made fun of ourselves, confessed. A faculty unlike any other I have been a part of. We made a promise that we will see each other again, next year, on the mountain. Until we don't.

This is how we do it
The world is burning.
We are the tender tinder. We all are suffering,
Someone is lost in the woods,
Someone is stuck or pinned down
Something is broken
Something is missing.
Someone is spinning
Out of control and miserable
Crying into the wilderness.
Someone is alone, looking into the abyss.
The rainbow is broken.
We all know this.

Somehow we arrive.
Come to the doorway, the opening, the aperture.
Come in through the bathroom window.
Come in a wagon, a litter, a sponge.
Come from the bottom of a well, from hell.
From the dark box, nailed to the floor.

We cross over the door jamb, the lintel, the threshold.
Come into the place that is prepared to receive us.
Our pockets are heavy with debris, old tickets and tissues
For the fire, or the cauldron.

Clocks stop.
This is time out.
This is time out of time
Dogs guide the door
The curtains are drawn.

Here the deep ear, the open heart
Begin to work, to resonate, to vibrate
Large things get small.
Small things look much bigger.
We can look inside with eyes like X-rays:
The magnetic resonance of strange attractors.

Together we peer into the dark.
We are spelunkers,
We dive into deep waters.
We hear the unspeakable
And translate it into the language of the foot and the hand
Which we understand.

In dreamtime
The shamans come
Bang the drum
Start to hum
Make a mark
Scratch a spark
Eat the pain
Which is a lost art.

Wear the Fool's Cap.
Plant the philosopher's stone
Like an acorn.

Strangers, we enter mystery.
We are safe in the hut, the barn,
The little house that art built.

We know a world is ending.

We become tuning forks.
Soon we are ringing
Bells of peace.

Sad hearts begin to sing.
Into the silence, into the stillness,
The scary place, the sacred space.

The minstrel of soul hears sound in silence.
The dancer feels movement in still feet.
The architect finds shelter in crumpled paper.
No effort is too small.

An angel comes down
Or maybe a clown.
In any case, an emissary from the other place
Carrying a message for the effort
Of seeing and hearing,
Of staying and playing.

It is simple:
We are here
For the sake of each other.

It is a pea of comfort in a sea of pain.
We take it as nourishment, a talisman
A gift.

Sometimes the present is a surprise.
A key,
Which turns in the lock,
Which opens a box,
Or cuts through the knot
Or not.

We say goodbye. We cry.
We embrace.
We take our treasure and leave this place.

The clocks wind up
A world is ending
And so it begins again.

Glossary of Useful Definitions

What is expressive arts therapy today? We've been asking for 60 years. The model of ExA, as I practice it, has some important differences from other models. This "at a glance" listing will help you get oriented to some underlying assumptions. Every therapeutic model has guiding philosophies and principles as well as methodologies and techniques. These are some of the "leading ideas" that either arise from or resonate with my approach. As this is about how the arts can facilitate change, be it coaching, psychotherapy, or education, it can easily be integrated with other philosophies and practices without losing its potency. The arts have always been with us, before psychology, and they belong to all of us as a birthright.

Action-oriented: ExA wants us to do things, make things, take actions. It shares this preference for action with drama therapies, other creative arts therapies, gestalt, and other action-oriented psychotherapies. The client is active in the session, not only in the dialogue, but doing things, making and experimenting.

Aesthetic Analysis: A process of sensitive and aesthetic evaluation of the artwork, emphasizing its artistic rather than psychological elements. A phenomenological way of examining the work.

Archetypal psychology: A psychological approach that deals with universal symbols and themes, pioneered by James Hillman; a post-Jungian approach, emphasizing images and soulfulness. In contrast to a purely literal way of looking at human life.

Chaos theory/Cha-Org/systems theory: Our metaphor for change. Systems move from organization to chaos and back again. We use the perturbation of the strange situation (the art-making) to help introduce new perspectives and new organization.

Confidentiality: An essential ethical principle in therapy that ensures that all personal information is kept private, except in specific, predefined situations. Usually guarded by both laws and ethical standards. Some educational settings also are covered by confidentiality.

Decenter: In ExA therapy, the process of moving away from one's immediate problematic situation, leaping away, to gain a broader perspective. Entering a studio or aesthetic experience. We leave the problem in order to find solutions.

Dionysian and Apollonian: Borrowed from Greek mythology, these brothers were diametrically opposed: Apollo for order and Dionysus for wildness. ExA used these terms to discuss the wildness of unfettered creative endeavor, which also needs the structure of frames. Taken from Nietzsche.

Eco-poesis: Art-making with the earth in mind—either by being outdoors or by using natural materials. Not merely plain air, but interacting with the the natural environment. We retain our biophilia, our love of nature, and are nourished by being in and using natural materials.

Embodied consciousness: The notion that we are conscious because our flesh is intelligent. Our minds and bodies are not separate so our fleshy knowings contribute to our cognition, behavior, and emotions. Knowing through the arts is always knowing with the body.

Ethical boundaries: Ensuring the students' narratives are respected, not overshadowed by the facilitator's interpretations. Refers to boundaries of relationship, and fact of treatment, among other covered facets of practice. Usually described by professional organizations, such as IEATA's (International Expressive Arts Therapy Association) Code of Ethics.

Existential philosophy: Deals with human existence, freedom, and the search for meaning.

Expressive arts therapy (ExA): The polyaesthetic and intermodal use of the arts to effect change.

Harvesting: Post-art-making reflection to connect the resources discovered during the decentering or studio phase of the session with the difficulties discussed in the filling-in. Can the art-making point to resources within the client's capability to help create the change in the life-world the client desires?

Image abuse: The pitfalls of relying solely on predefined symbolic interpretations.

Imagination: Imagination is multimodal (Knill *et al.*, 1996). To revive the imagination to its full and sparkling facility is one of the primary aims of ExA. Not limited to cognition, it is the main facility with which we begin to make change. We stimulate the imagination by playing in the arts and the senses; what I call physical imagination.

Improvisation: Spontaneous creation or performance, composing in the moment, usually with some score or frame. A main methodology in all the art disciplines. We play with art materials and allow things to emerge from that play. We do not try to recreate some mental image.

Intermodality: Moving between one communication modality and another, thus, changing the art discipline. The heart of the intermodal process is this communication through our senses. The arts are deeply rooted in the body and thus our senses, and they describe the way or path to move from one mode of communication to another. This movement is not arbitrary. It is not on intuition or whim, or even intellect, but follows the pathway of the senses and imagination, which can be different for each individual. Intermodality is distinct from interdisciplinary and polyaesthetics. Intermodal transfer is not an additive approach—piling on various unrelated activities, moving from one thing to another willy-nilly. It is an integrated approach (using the logic of the senses and imagination). A transition from one to another, following a thread—often the thread of an image or impulse.

Oeuvre: artwork-oriented or work-oriented: ExA honors and recognizes both process and product as important. I encourage people to play with the art materials without any push or need to have a product, but sometimes an image emerges.

Phenomenological approach: A descriptive approach to the artifact focusing on the direct experiences of the viewer without imposing predefined meanings. Describing what is.

Philosophy: All approaches to human health and wellness have a philosophical bias, whether articulated or not. At the EGS the work is rooted and steeped in specific philosophical traditions that help define it. Aesthetics, existentialism, phenomenology, and postmodernism are main underpinnings. My view is also supported by feminism and embodiment. In addition, this approach is also centered on and resides within the province of the arts themselves and the philosophy of aesthetics which articulates the value and meaning of the arts in human life. This is significantly different from approaches that use the arts, but understand and interpret what is happening through a psychological lens. Knill's theories keep the art-making products that emerge in the domain of the arts themselves.

Poiesis: Poiesis comes from ancient Greek, meaning "to make," or knowing by doing, in the arts. It refers to the notion of making something in response to our experiences in the world. This was championed by Stephen Levine.

Polyaesthetics: How art disciplines coexist and interact and are implied in each other. Separation can be useful but artificial.

Post-psychological: Theories and therapies that move beyond psychological perspectives. These approaches treat each person as unique. A new therapy needs to be created for each one. ExA is one such therapy, which depends on the human connection and the process of relationship.

Process-oriented: This refers to the ongoing therapeutic relationship between the client or group members and the EXA practitioner in the "here and now." I am not referring to the process of art-making. We are less interested in the past and more interested in what is happening now. In that sense, we are closer to existential or humanistic counseling and related to depth approaches such as those of Jung and Hillman, which advance the notion of *archai* and images as being central to human existence.

Rituals: Set activities or practices in therapy that have symbolic meaning; something everyone in the community can do, regardless of age or ability, using simple movements, actions, or songs used to mark or celebrate an important event in the life of the person or the community.

Safe container: Refers to creating a space (physical, emotional, and psychological) where clients feel secure, respected, and able to express themselves without judgment.

Situational analysis: A method used to understand the context in which the therapeutic session will occur.

Socio-grams: A game used to explore the relationships and interactions within a group. Usually done in a circle or clusters.

Solution oriented: Knill and Eberhardt (2023) make it clear we do not want to pay so much attention to the problem that we become "problem-tranced." It is necessary to know exactly how the problem appears in the person's life, to know their lived experience and language, but it is solutions we are interested in. This is why ExA is so well suited to coaching and educational applications; it is not restricted to counseling or psychotherapeutic settings, nor tied to the medical model.

Spectrograms: A game or activity used to categorize or understand a certain feature or characteristic within a group. Usually done in a line, e.g., "line up from youngest to oldest."

Strength-based: Influenced by salutogenesis and the notion of building health, not only treating disease. A person is never reduced to the label. Even greatly challenged people have wonderful gifts. ExA searches for these. Sometimes they are obvious but have not been named before.

Studios: Refers to the therapeutic space where art is created.

SuPER (Knill's acronym): A way to conduct an Aesthetic Analysis of any art form.

- Surface: Phenomenological description of the artwork, the basic elements of the art discipline and composition.
- Process: The sequential experience of creating, where the problems arise, what was easy, what was difficult, and how difficulties were resolved.
- Experience: Feelings, sensations, thoughts, and memories during creation.
- Reflection/Round-up: Summarizing the entire art-making experience, often a title.

The Third—image itself: The image itself is given special status as a third "personae" in the room. We do not think of every image as a self-portrait revealing only the interiority of the person whose image it is and pertaining exclusively to them. Also, it is in using the arts as the investigatory process that we expand awareness and help support and make changes. The notion of the Third assists us in making the artwork a partner, with volition and voice. Coming from that point of view allows a valuable change of personal perspective.

Transformative experience: The profound impact of combining expressive arts with deep reflection and intercultural understanding.

Bibliography

Alperson, P. A. (1984). On musical improvisation. *The Journal of Aesthetics and Art Criticism*, *43*(1), 17–29. https://doi.org/10.2307/430189

American Psychiatric Association. (2021). *Diagnostic and statistical manual of mental disorders* (5th ed., Text Rev.). https://doi.org/10.1176/appi.books.9780890425787

Anderson, H., & Goolishian, H. A. (1992). The client is the expert: A not-knowing approach to therapy. In S. McNamee & K. J. Gergen (Eds.), *Therapy as social construction* (pp. 25–39). Sage Publications.

Antonovsky, A. (1979). *Health, stress, and coping: New perspectives on mental and physical well-being*. Jossey-Bass.

Atkins, S., & Eberhart, H. (2014). *Presence and process in expressive arts work: At the edge of wonder*. Jessica Kingsley Publishers.

Barry, L. (2008). *What it is*. Drawn and Quarterly.

Beauvoir, S. de. (1949). *The second sex* (H. M. Parshley, Trans.). Alfred A. Knopf. (Original work published as "Le Deuxième Sexe").

Berg, I. K. (1994). *Family-based services: A solution-focused approach*. Norton & Company.

Berg, I. K., & Steiner, T. (2003). *Children's solution work*. Norton.

Bollas, C. (1987). *The shadow of the object: Psychoanalysis of the unthought known*. Columbia University Press.

Brown, L. S. (1994). *Subversive dialogues: Theory in feminist therapy*. Basic Books.

Brown, L. S. (2000). Feeling my way: Jazz improvisation and its vicissitudes—A plea for imperfection. *The Journal of Aesthetics and Art Criticism*, *58*(2), 113–124.

Butler, J. (1990). *Gender trouble: Feminism and the subversion of identity*. Routledge.

Butler, J. (1993). *Bodies that matter: On the discursive limits of sex*. Routledge.

Calderone, P. (Director). (2015). *Embodied listening* [Film]. Independent production.

Canguilhem, P. (2011). *Singing upon the book according to Vicente Lusitano* (A. Stalarow, Trans.). *Early Music History*, *30*, 55–103.

Coulton, S., Clift, S., Skingley, A., & Rodriguez, J. (2015). Effectiveness and cost-effectiveness of community singing on mental health-related quality of life of older people: Randomised controlled trial. *The British Journal of Psychiatry: The Journal of Mental Science*, *207*(3), 250–255. https://doi.org/10.1192/bjp.bp.113.129908

Dissanayake, E. (1988). *What is art for?* University of Washington Press.

Dissanayake, E. (2001). *Homo aestheticus: Where art comes from and why*. University of Washington Press.

Dissanayake, E. (2018). Ancestral minds and the spectrum of symbol. In *Early rock art of the American West: The geometric enigma* (pp. 91–129). University of Washington Press.

Eisenhower, D. D. (1953, 16 April). Chance for Peace speech, American Society of Newspaper Editors, Washington, DC.

Eisley, L. (1996). How flowers changed the world. In *The Earth Speaks*. Random House.

Essex, J. G., with McKim, E. G. (2022). Poets know things: Encountering (an)other in writing and retreat. *Poiesis: A Journal of Arts and Communication*, *19*, 14–31.

Filipovic, J. (2012, December 1). Justice Ginsburg's distant dream of an all-female Supreme Court. *The Guardian*. www.theguardian.com/commentisfree/2012/nov/30/justice-ginsburg-all-female-supreme-court

Friedan, B. (1963). *The feminine mystique*. W. W. Norton & Company.

Fuentes, A. (2017). *The creative spark: How imagination made humans exceptional*. Penguin.

Gendlin, E. T. (1969). Focusing. *Psychotherapy: Theory, Research & Practice, 6*(1), 4.

Gendlin, E. T. (1997). *Experiencing and the creation of meaning: A philosophical and psychological approach to the subjective*. Northwestern University Press.

Gleick, J. (2008). *Chaos: Making a new science*. Penguin.

Goldsworthy, A. (1990). *A collaboration with nature*. Harry N. Abrams.

Goldsworthy, A. (2001). *Time*. Harry N. Abrams.

Hamilton, A. (2000). The art of improvisation and the aesthetics of imperfection. *British Journal of Aesthetics, 40*(1), 168–185. https://doi.org/10.1093/bjaesthetics/40.1.168

Hatwell, Y. (2003). Manual exploratory procedures in children and adults. In Y. Hatwell, A. Streri, & E. Gentaz (Eds.), *Touching for knowing: Cognitive psychology of haptic manual perception* (pp. 67–82). John Benjamins Publishing Company.

Hillman, J. (1973). *Suicide and the soul*. Harper & Row.

Hillman, J. (1995). A psyche the size of the Earth: A psychological foreword. In T. Roszak, M. E. Gomes, & A. D. Kanner (Eds.), *Ecopsychology: Restoring the Earth, healing the mind* (pp. xvii–xxiii). Sierra Club Books.

hooks, b. (1981). *Ain't I a woman: Black women and feminism*. South End Press.

Howard, P. J. (2000). *The owner's manual for the brain: Everyday applications from mind-brain research*. Bard Press.

Huberman, A. (Host). (2022, March 14). The science of creativity & how to enhance it. [Podcast episode]. *Huberman Lab*. https://hubermanlab.com

Hyde, L. (1983). *The gift: Imagination and the erotic life of property*. Vintage Books.

Johnson, M. (2007). *The meaning of the body: Aesthetics of human understanding*. University of Chicago Press.

Johnson, M. (2013). *The body in the mind: The bodily basis of meaning, imagination, and reason*. University of Chicago Press.

Kazmaslanka, L. (n.d.). Polyaesthetic experience: An introduction. http://kazmaslanka.com/polyaesthetic/Polyaesthetic_Introduction.htm

Kernfeld, B. (2002). Improvisation. In B. Kernfeld (Ed.), *The New Grove dictionary of jazz* (2nd ed., pp. 313–323). Grove's Dictionaries.

Knill, P. J. (1994). Multiplicity as a tradition: Theories for interdisciplinary arts therapies—An overview. *The Arts in Psychotherapy, 21*(5), 319–328.

Knill, P. J. (1999). Soul nourishment, or the intermodal language of imagination. In E. G. Levine & S. K. Levine (Eds.), *Foundations of expressive arts therapy: Theoretical and clinical perspectives* (pp. 37–52). Jessica Kingsley Publishers.

Knill, P. J. (2005). Community art: Communal art-making to build up a sense of coherence. *Poiesis: A Journal of the Arts and Communication, 7*(1), 126–144.

Knill, P. J. (2017). The essence in a therapeutic process, an alternative experience of worlding? In E. G. Levine & S. K. Levine (Eds.), *New developments in expressive arts therapy: The play of poiesis* (pp. 31–46). Jessica Kingsley Publishers.

Knill, P. J., & Eberhart, H. (2023). *Solution Art: A textbook of art and resource-oriented work*. Jessica Kingsley Publishers.

Knill, P. J., Barba, H. N., & Fuchs, M. N. (1996). *Minstrels of soul: Intermodal expressive therapy*. the EGS Press.

Knill, P. J., Levine, E. G., & Levine, S. K. (2005). *Principles and practice of expressive arts therapy: Toward a therapeutic aesthetics*. Jessica Kingsley Publishers.

Kopytin, A. (2017). Environmental and ecological expressive therapies. In A. Kopytin & M. Rugh (Eds.), *Environmental expressive therapies: Nature-assisted theory and practice* (pp. 23–47). Taylor & Francis.

Kriz, J. (2006). *Self-actualization*. Herstellung und Verlag.

Kriz, J. (2018). *Self-actualization: Person-centered approach and Systems Theory*. Routledge.

Lakoff, G., & Johnson, M. (1999). *Philosophy in the flesh: The embodied mind and its challenge to Western thought*. Basic Books.

Lakoff, G., & Johnson, M. (2008). *Metaphors we live by*. University of Chicago Press.

Langer, S. K. (1942). *Philosophy in a new key: A study in the symbolism of reason, rite, and art*. Harvard University Press.

Langer, S. K. (1953). *Feeling and form: A theory of art*. Charles Scribner.

Lehrer, J. (2007). *Proust was a neuroscientist*. Houghton Mifflin.

Levine, E. G. (2004). *Tending the fire: Studies in art, therapy & creativity*. the EGS Press.

Levine, E. G., & Levine, S. K. (2009). *Principles and practices of expressive arts therapy: Toward a therapeutic aesthetics*. Jessica Kingsley Publishers.

Levine, E. G., & Levine, S. K. (2011). *Art in action: Expressive arts therapy and social change*. Jessica Kingsley Publishers.

Levine, S. K. (1988). Image abuse and the dialectic of interpretation. *Canadian Art Therapy Association Journal, 3*(2), 18–26. https://doi.org/10.1080/08322473.1988.11432173

Levine, S. K. (1997). *Poiesis: The language of psychology and the speech of the soul*. Jessica Kingsley Publishers.

Levine, S. K. (2005). The philosophy of expressive arts therapy: Poiesis as a response to the world. In P. J. Knill, E. G. Levine, & S. K. Levine (Eds.), *Principles and practice of expressive arts therapy: Toward a therapeutic aesthetics* (pp. 15–73). Jessica Kingsley Publishers.

Levine, S. K. (2010). *Philosophy of expressive arts therapy: Poiesis and the therapeutic imagination*. Jessica Kingsley Publishers.

Levine, S. K. (2012). Nature as a work of art: Toward a poetic ecology. *Poiesis: A Journal of the Arts and Communication, 14*, 186–193.

Levine, S. K. (2017). Longing for beauty and the work: An interview with Paolo Knill. In S. K. Levine & E. G. Levine (Eds.), *New developments in expressive arts therapy: The play of poiesis* (pp. 48–65). Jessica Kingsley Publishers.

Lommel, A. (1967). *Shamanism: The beginnings of art*. McGraw Hill.

McNiff, S. (1992). *Art as medicine: Creating a therapy of the imagination*. Shambhala.

McNiff, S. (2008). Art-based research. In J. G. Knowles & A. L. Cole (Eds.), *Handbook of the arts in qualitative research* (pp. 29–40). Sage.

Merleau-Ponty, M. (2012). *Phenomenology of perception*. Routledge.

Mettler, B. (1947). The relation of dance to the visual arts. *The Journal of Aesthetics and Art Criticism, 5*(3), 195–203.

Mettler, B. (1952). New directions in dance and music. *Journal of the American Association for Health, Physical Education, and Recreation, 23*(2), 7–34.

Mettler, B. (1960). *Materials of dance: As a creative art activity*. Mettler Studios.

Mettler, B. (1990). Creative dance—Art or therapy? *American Journal of Dance Therapy, 12*(2), 95–100.

Moon, C. H., & Lachman-Chapin, M. (2001). *Studio art therapy: Cultivating the artist identity in the art therapist*. Jessica Kingsley Publishers.

Mridha, D. (2015). *Verses of happiness: The only book you need to be happy!!!* Epitome Publishing.

Noë, A. (2009a). *Out of our heads: Why you are not your brain, and other lessons from the biology of consciousness*. Macmillan.

Noë, A. (2009b). *You are not your brain: A new model of neuroscience*. Hill and Wang.

Noë, A. (2015). *Strange tools: Art and human nature*. Hill and Wang.

POIESIS. (2005). *POIESIS: A Journal of the Arts & Communication, 7*, 140.

Riedelsheimer, T. (Director). (2004). *Touch the sound* [Film]. Piffl Medien GmbH.

Rimell, V. (2016). *Shamanism and the beginnings of art*. Cambridge University Press.

Roeder, T. (Director). (2001). *Rivers and tides: Andy Goldsworthy working with time* [Film]. Skyline Productions.

Ryle, G. (2009) The concept of Mind: 60th Anniversary Edition Gilbert Ryle. London u.a.: Routledge.

Sacks, O. (2007). *Musicophilia: Tales of music and the brain*. Alfred A. Knopf.

Sagan, C. (1994). *Pale blue dot: A vision of the human future in space*. Random House.

Stewart, J. (Host). (2020, November 13). In tune – The neuroscience of group music-making. [Podcast episode]. *Timeline*. Vermont Public Radio podcast.

Syme, P. (2018). *Werner's nomenclature of colours: Adapted to zoology, botany, chemistry, mineralogy, anatomy, and the arts.* Smithsonian Institution.

van der Kolk, B. A. (2014). *The body keeps the score: Brain, mind, and body in the healing of trauma.* Penguin Books.

Vonnegut, K. (1963). *Cat's cradle.* Holt, Rinehart and Winston.

White, M. (1995). *Re-authoring lives: Interviews and essays.* Dulwich Centre Publications.

Whitman, W. (1900). I sing the body electric. In *Leaves of Grass.* D. McKay.

Wikipedia. (2025). Improvisational theatre. https://en.wikipedia.org/wiki/Improvisational_theatre

Woodruff, P. (2001). *Reverence: Renewing a forgotten virtue* (2nd ed.). Oxford University Press.

Yalom, I. D. (1995). *The theory and practice of group psychotherapy* (5th ed.). Basic Books.

Subject Index

Author Index

RAISING READERS
Books Build Bright Futures

Dear Reader,

We'd love your attention for one more page to tell you about the crisis in children's reading, and what we can all do.

Studies have shown that reading for fun is the **single biggest predictor of a child's future life chances** – more than family circumstance, parents' educational background or income. It improves academic results, mental health, wealth, communication skills, ambition and happiness.[1]

The number of children reading for fun is in rapid decline. Young people have a lot of competition for their time. In 2024, 1 in 10 children and young people in the UK aged 5 to 18 did not own a single book at home.[2]

Hachette works extensively with schools, libraries and literacy charities, but here are some ways we can all raise more readers:

- Reading to children for just 10 minutes a day makes a difference
- Don't give up if children aren't regular readers – there will be books for them!
- Visit bookshops and libraries to get recommendations
- Encourage them to listen to audiobooks
- Support school libraries
- Give books as gifts

There's a lot more information about how to encourage children to read on our website: **www.RaisingReaders.co.uk**

Thank you for reading.

hachette
UK

1   OECD, '21st-Century Readers: Developing Literacy Skills in a Digital World', 2021, https://www.oecd.org/en/publications/21st-century-readers_a83d84cb-en.html
2   National Literacy Trust, 'Book Ownership in 2024', November 2024, https://literacytrust.org.uk/research-services/research-reports/book-ownership-in-2024

Jessica Kingsley
Publishers

JKP is a leading specialist global publisher at the forefront of social change. We aim to promote positive change in society and encourage social justice by making information and knowledge available in an accessible way.

Our specialist areas span autism and neurodiversity, health, social care, mental health, education, disability, gender, sexuality and complementary health and bodywork.

We're committed to publishing books that promote diversity and inclusion, including representation of diverse race and heritage, disability, neurodiversity, gender, sexual orientation, age, socio-economic status, religion and culture.

If you have an idea which you think would fit JKP's publishing, you can tell us about it directly by completing a proposal form at

www.jkp.com